The Second Colonial Occupation

The Second Colonial Occupation

Development Planning, Agriculture, and the Legacies of British Rule in Nigeria

Bekeh Utietiang Ukelina

LEXINGTON BOOKS
Lanham • Boulder • New York • London

Published by Lexington Books

An imprint of The Rowman & Littlefield Publishing Group, Inc.
4501 Forbes Boulevard, Suite 200, Lanham, Maryland 20706
www.rowman.com

Unit A, Whitacre Mews, 26-34 Stannary Street, London SE11 4AB

British Library Cataloguing in Publication Information Available

Library of Congress Cataloging-in-Publication Data

Names: Ukelina, Bekeh Utietiang, author.
Title: The second colonial occupation : development planning and the legacies of British colonial rule in Nigeria / Bekeh Utietiang Ukelina.
Description: Lanham : Lexington Books, 2017. | Includes bibliographical references and index.
Identifiers: LCCN 2017027726 (print) | LCCN 2017028560 (ebook) | ISBN 9781498529259 (Electronic) | ISBN 9781498529242 (cloth : alk. paper)
Subjects: LCSH: Economic development--Nigeria--History. | Nigeria--Colonial influence. | Nigeria--Economic conditions. | Nigeria--Social conditions.
Classification: LCC HC1055 (ebook) | LCC HC1055 .U44 2017 (print) | DDC 338.9667--dc23
LC record available at https://lccn.loc.gov/2017027726

Printed in the United States of America

For Mum & Dad
Dorothy Ukege Agba & Celsus Ukelina Utietiang
On your 50th Wedding Anniversary
(December 3, 2016)

Contents

List of Abbreviations ix

Acknowledgments xi

Preface xiii

Introduction xv

1 Joseph Chamberlain: Constructive Imperialism and Colonial Development 1

2 Negotiating Development: Nigeria's 1945 Development Plan 25

3 The Agrarian Bias: Mackiean Policy of Agricultural Development in Nigeria 69

4 Late Colonial Agricultural Development: The Mokwa Scheme 121

5 The Legacies of British Rule in Nigeria 157

Conclusion 177

Bibliography 187

Index 199

About the Author 207

List of Abbreviations

CDC	Colonial Development Corporation
CD&W	Colonial Development and Welfare
CEAC	Colonial Economic Advisory Committee
CIS	Center for International Studies
CO	Colonial Office
CSG	Chief Secretary to the Government
DFP	Director of Food Production
HMSO	Her Majesty Stationery Office
IBRD	International Bank for Reconstruction and Development
IMF	International Monetary Fund
JPC	Joint Planning Committee
MIT	Massachusetts Institute of Technology
NAP	Niger Agricultural Development Project, Mokwa
NCG	Nigerian Central Government
NEC	National Executive Council
NRG	Northern Regional Government
OFC	Overseas Food Corporation
SAP	Structural Adjustment Program
S of S	Secretary of State for the Colonies
U.S.	United States

Acknowledgments

In the fall of 2009, I took a seminar on "New British Imperial History" with Dr. Joseph Morgan Hodge at West Virginia University, Morgantown. As part of the seminar, I reviewed his book, "Triumph of the Expert: Agrarian Doctrines of Development and the Legacies of British Colonialism." This book and my subsequent discussions with him sparked my interest in development history. When in 2010, I witnessed the crisis of development in the old neighborhood I grew up, I knew who to talk with. My numerous conversations with Joseph Hodge and a long list of readings on development history he gave me, opened to me a new field of historical research. Dr. Robert Maxon, the Co-Chair of my dissertation committee is a scholarly father to me. He will always be *Mwalimu* to me. He painstakingly read the initial drafts of this work, offered suggestions on sharpening the analysis, most especially in the economic perspective. I will always be grateful to Hodge and Maxon.

Research for this book was done in archives in the United States, Britain, and Nigeria. I am grateful to all the tireless staff of these archives who helped me. This research was made possible through fellowships and grants from West Virginia University's history department and the Eberly School of Arts and Sciences. My thanks to Elizabeth Fones-Wolf, the former department chair for all the support I received for this research.

The ideas and suggestions of other scholars have helped shaped my work. John Lonsdale's works on the British empire and the concept of the "second colonial occupation" he coined with D.A. Low provoked me to think of late colonial development in a new light. Funso Afolayan did a thorough review of this book and provided feedback that helped improve the central argument in the book. My special thanks to T. Omega Arthur for reading the first draft of this book and offering insightful suggestions and to Dan Weimer for his encouragements throughout the revision process.

I am grateful to my editors at Lexington Books: Kathryn Tafelski, Madhumitha Koduvalli, and Emily Roderick. Special thanks go to my copyeditor, Sarah Chalmers. I wish to also thank Prince Cletus Ekanem who worked with my brother, Unimke, to design the cover art for this book.

My final thanks go to my family and friends. I owe you a great deal for your love and support throughout this process. Thank you for being there for me!

Preface

In the summer of 2010 I visited the old neighborhood where I grew up. It is located in a little town called Obudu in the southern part of Nigeria. After graduating high school in 1995, I moved away to attend college. Around the same time, my parents relocated to the countryside to take care of my grandmother whose health was failing in her advanced age. As years went by, I heard from family members that our old neighborhood in Obudu was undergoing rapid changes. During my childhood, the neighborhood had been primarily composed of educated middle-class families. We had two elementary schools and two secondary schools only a few blocks from each other. These were by all accounts excellent public schools, and I believe that I received a very good education. The imageries perpetuated in Western media, of Africa as poor, hungry, backward, and without public infrastructure/ utilities was not what I experienced growing up. We had running water, constant electricity, landline phones, paved roads, televisions and radios, etc. Many families, including mine, owned a car and were never hungry. The children I studied with in grade school were clean, intelligent, and well nourished.

During a visit to Nigeria in 2010 from the United States, I decided to return to this formative place. What I encountered was a different reality from what I had known. The changes I had been told about did not prepare me for what I encountered. The whole area had undergone dilapidation. The schools had deteriorated and were now failing, there was no running water, electricity was at best erratic, and unplanned houses were squeezed into every available space. It now looked like a slum. What I also discovered was that this problem was not unique or confined to my old neighborhood. With a few exceptions, it was now a national problem. While I wept for my old neighborhood, I was left with the question: What happened? How did we get here? How can history help us understand what happened to Nigeria's development? These questions evoked my "historical turn," the point at which I decided to look back and find out how "development" came about in the first place, and its roots in the specific case of Nigeria. History became a tool for looking at the past to find answers to the present development crisis in Nigeria.

Introduction

Nigeria has undergone several phases of development, both in the precolonial and colonial period. In the early years of European encounters with the people of Nigeria, their interactions were restricted to the "water edge."[1] What pushed these encounters beyond the water edge and enabled the exploration of the interior were the technological advances that had taken place in Europe as a result of the Industrial Revolution. These developments in Europe became a catalyst for Europeans seeking to exercise dominance over vast regions of Africa, expressions of control that would metamorphose from the economic arena to political control as well. European nations now bestowed upon themselves the power to control and determine the future of African nations in both the economic and political spheres.

NIGERIA'S ECONOMY: BEFORE AND DURING COLONIAL RULE

Prior to colonial rule, Nigeria was linked to the world market through slavery and agricultural production. After slavery ended, agricultural products became the major export from Nigeria. The four main exports were palm oil, cocoa, cotton, and groundnuts. In 1806, West Africa (which includes present-day Nigeria) provided 150 tons of palm oil to Liverpool annually. By 1839, Britain was receiving 13,000 tons of palm oil annually, with the main supply from the Niger Delta Protectorate. Palm oil supply reached a peak of about 30,000 tons in 1855 and remained an important export commodity thereafter.[2] Michael Crowder notes that "[i]n 1908, exports were valued at £3,094,175 as compared with £4,320,000 in 1910, whilst the figures for imports were respectively £3,076,309 and £5,122,000. Exports consisted mainly of palm products."[3] Originally, palm trees in Nigeria grew in the wild and Nigerians were able to harvest the fruits and produce the oil that for many years serviced European industries. By the middle of the 1920s, steps were taken by the British government in West Africa to secure and improve production. This new direction in the production and export of palm products was in response to the greater competition that was coming from East Asia and the Belgian Congo.[4] To facilitate an increased production, the United Africa Company donated 250 hand press machines to the farmers.[5] These were to expedite the processing of the palm fruit.

Another major export from Nigeria was cocoa. This was first introduced to Nigeria at the end of the nineteenth century and soon became the major source of income for many farmers in the southern part of Nigeria. During the Great Depression, the price of cocoa fell drastically and many farmers abandoned cocoa farming. In addition to the economic depression, the swollen shoot and black pod diseases infected the crop. In 1944, the British West African governments opened a research institute called the West African Cocoa Research Institute at New Tafo, Ghana to deal with cocoa diseases.[6] A substation of this institute was established in Ibadan, Nigeria in 1950. Given that cocoa was a major export from Nigeria, it was important to establish a research center to study diseases that affected production and to mitigate them. This research institute was used for investigations and trials with the goal of improving cocoa production.

Cotton and groundnuts were the other major agricultural products exported from Nigeria in this period. Though cotton had been grown in Nigeria for centuries, commercial growing only began in the first decade of the twentieth century. The British Cotton Growing Association, as well as some trading firms such as the Messrs. Elder Dempster & Co., encouraged this. This company bought seeds from New Orleans and distributed them to farmers in Nigeria.[7] Groundnuts were cultivated in the northern part of Nigeria in the precolonial times, but it was only after 1900 that it became an important cash crop.[8] The colonial government distributed groundnut seeds free to farmers.[9]

The expansion of cash crop production in Nigeria by peasant[10] farmers was important to the British colonial administration because they saw trade as a necessary instrument for the implementation of its "Dual Mandate."[11] The establishment of foreign-owned plantations was discouraged because colonial agricultural policy was not geared toward the expansion of plantation agriculture due to Nigeria's land tenure system.[12] At this time, land was communally owned and adult males were guaranteed access to it for farming. The introduction of plantation agriculture would have meant removing land from the community and placing it in the hands of private companies. The question then is, if trade in agricultural products was a vital component of colonial rule, why did the British not introduce plantation agriculture? Anne

Phillips in her book, *The Enigma of Colonialism*, puts it succinctly: "If colonialism was a project of capitalist expansion, then in Africa it significantly failed in its task."[13] She argues that the contradictions of colonial power are rooted in the makeshift character of British rule due to the constraints that were created by the local conditions. Initially, the British wanted to move toward a capitalist market in land and labor, but they retreated because of the resistance and turmoil this stirred up. The political weakness of the colonial state meant that it lacked the power to directly coerce labor and it had to form alliances with local chiefs:

> as the only reliable guarantors of labour, which in turn dictated the terms on which colonialism operated. The recurrent problems of land and labour revolved around this alliance with chiefs. Free access to land precluded the formation of a landless proletariat, and was ensured by relations of communal land tenure which installed the chiefs as agents of political order.[14]

This, Phillips argues, curtailed the power of the colonial state to alienate land for large industrial agricultural plantations. These local conditions forced the British to take the path of peasant production.[15] The stability and security of the colonial state depended on the cooperation of local rulers and the authority of these rulers rested in their ability to control both land and labor. Therefore, the local chiefs exercised control over land as they had over labor. By allowing big industrial agricultural corporations to expand, the British would have undermined the indigenous authority on which the colonial state itself ultimately rested.[16]

Up until the early twentieth century, the expansion of cash crop production and trade in West Africa was largely a spontaneous process of the expansion of capitalist market forces. Thus, farmers in Western Nigeria and Southern Ghana began the planting of cocoa not because they were directed or encouraged to do so, but because they saw the market profitability potentials of this new crop. It was a conscious economic decision on the part of these farmers. Similarly, the colonial state's ideologies of "Dual mandate" and "Indirect Rule," and the decision to consciously block plantation agriculture and large-scale farming in lieu of peasant farming under the tutelage of local rulers, were an intentional practice of development that Michael Cowen and Robert Shenton call a "doctrine of development."[17] They argue that the immanent process of development could be both constructive and destructive, for example, in the expansion of capitalist market forces. They do make a distinction between this process and the practice of development that arose as an intentional or conscious attempt by the state to intervene in market forces in order to deal with crises that will inevitably occur, such as the Great Depression or, more precisely, the problem of surplus labor due to unemployment and underemployment. The state becomes the trustee of development in order to respond to a perceived lack of the same. For Cowen and Shenton, development is different from natural progress. They write, "Development was the means by which progress might be ordered but it was not the idea of progress itself . . . the idea of development as an immanent process did not necessarily rest, as did the idea of progress, upon a conviction that the future would be an improvement upon the past."[18] If development always connoted natural progress, one would expect that the Obudu neighborhood discussed in the preface would be more advanced today than it was in the 1980s. Yet, the economic forces that have afflicted the country since the late 1980s have actually led to retrogression rather than progress. In this book, development is defined as intentional interventions directed by the state, with the goal of ordering progress toward an ideological end. These interventions do not happen by accident. The state intentionally intervenes because it has seen a need and its goal is to order society toward a certain goal. A good example of such interventions in colonial Africa was in the period after the Great Depression. Suffice it to state that such interventions have continued in the postcolonial period in response to Africa's poverty.

NIGERIA AFTER THE GREAT DEPRESSION

The period between 1940 and 1960 marked a high point in the practice of colonial development in Africa. David Low and John Lonsdale aptly describe this period as the "Second Colonial Occupation."[19] Colonies that had suffered many years of neglect were now seeing renewed efforts by both Britain and France to build infrastructure and prime the production sector. Though Joseph Chamberlain had argued since the 1890s that Britain had a responsibility to invest in its colonies, it took the Great Depression and the postwar economic crisis to move Britain in this direction. While the idea of empire had started waning in the period before World War II, there was new eagerness on the part of Britain and France to maintain their imperial holdings as these were considered essential to postwar economic recovery. The policies and programs that would constitute the bulk of the "Second Colonial Occupation" received their imprimatur in the period during the Great Depression when the colonial governments were grappling with the impact of this crisis on the colonial people.

In Nigeria, the British colonial government introduced significant policy changes in response to the Great Depression. For example, prior to the economic depression of 1929, the colonial government in Northern Nigeria was able to balance its budget through revenues derived from agricultural products and tin mining. These two industries were adversely affected by the economic slump. The decline in worldwide demand for agricultural products led to falling crop prices. The colonial state had to engage in severe economic adjustment policies to keep the budgets balanced. As Moses Ochonu notes, rather than the colonial state dealing with the problems resulting from the Depression by introducing a Keynesian economic model,[20] it engaged in strict austerity measures such as cutting down on public works projects, increasing taxation, enforcing high crop production, making pay cuts, retrenching workers, and introducing protectionist policies.[21]

In response to the Great Depression and the global geopolitics of the 1930s, the colonial government made three primary policy changes that had a significant impact on agricultural production and development in Nigeria.[22] The first was the establishment of government marketing boards in 1939 and 1940. The genesis of these boards was the realignment of the world market due to World War II. During the war, Britain took steps to prevent the export of Nigerian goods to the Germans and their allies and to only allow imports to Nigeria from Britain and its allies. A number of European markets were therefore no longer accessible to Nigeria. The U.S. market was also no longer easily accessible to Nigerian exports due to insecurity in the seas and the limits on shipping space. Britain was afraid that the Nigerian cocoa industry might collapse, potentially leading to political and social chaos in the colony. Thus, it decided to buy the entire cocoa crop and was willing to incur losses if necessary.[23] At their inception, the marketing boards had the task of issuing licenses to private firms to purchase locally produced goods that they in turn would sell to the colonial government. Though originally intended to stabilize prices, the boards had unintended consequences. Over time, they evolved into a system of indirect taxation of agriculture, exploiting peasant farmers who were already living penurious lives. Toyin Falola notes that "The underpayment to the producers enabled the firms to make profits and the government to raise money to finance the war without raising taxes."[24] This contradiction between intentions and outcomes is one that plagued development throughout the late colonial period. Though the colonial government intended to help the farmers during a time of economic crisis, the outcome of this policy change was the exploitation of the people the policy was intended to help in the first place.

The second significant change was the establishment in 1940 of a research system for studying export crops. Research had been an important component of British imperial development policy since the 1890s, with research centers studying crops and tropical diseases established both in the metropole and in the colonies. Carl Eicher observes that American scholarly research has ignored them, assuming that such centers were nonexistent before U.S. foundations helped launch the International Maize and Wheat Improvement Center in Mexico and the International Rice Institute in the Philippines.[25]

Before the Green Revolution of the 1970s, many European nations had successfully undertaken systematic scientific research efforts to improve agricultural production. At the turn of the twentieth century, "Several Central European states established plant-breeding stations whose express purpose was to make high-yielding plant varieties as well as the basic techniques of plant breeding available to the small farmers who predominated in those regions."[26] There were agricultural research centers in the British colonies prior to 1940. After 1940, these were substantially expanded with assistance from the Colonial Development & Welfare Acts of 1940 and 1945.[27] Examples of such centers were the Cocoa Research Institute in Ghana, which was founded in 1938, and the Oil Palm Research Station in Nigeria founded in 1939. By 1951, these research institutes were expanded and new ones were established around West Africa, bringing the total to ten.

The third policy change undertaken by the British at this time was development planning. This was in direct response to the Great Depression that had pillaged both the metropolitan and colonial economies. The stock market crash of 1929 and the ensuing economic crisis that resulted exposed the contradictions of British colonial rule. Though the Europeans had advanced colonial rule as a benevolent mission to civilize Africans, structural exploitation was at its core. The doctrine of financial self-sufficiency governed the relations between metropole and colony. This economic doctrine guaranteed that colonial people paid for their own exploitation through taxation. While revenues generated within the colonies were used to provide some essential and social services, the colonized were made to believe that these services were a result of the generous "mother country." With the colonial coffers drying up during the Great Depression, the colonial governments were unable to make the needed investments in public infrastructure and, more importantly, in social services. This unmasked the exploitative agenda of the colonial state, leading to social turmoil in the colonies. This unrest made the colonial powers the target of sharper criticisms within and outside the empire. Britain's response was the Colonial Development and Welfare Act of 1940. This legislation launched the era of a new developmentalist state, one this book refers to as the "Second Colonial Occupation." The legacy of this occupation, symbolized by the series of development acts passed by the British Parliament, has left a lasting legacy in Britain's former African colonies. After World War II, the 1940 Act was substantially enhanced in response to a growing decolonization movement and the need to give the empire a new lease of life.[28] Nigeria was one of the major beneficiaries of the development policies instituted by Britain during this late colonial occupation.

This book focuses on this third policy, examining the processes that resulted in the 1945 Nigerian Development Plan that was upheld as a model for other British territories in Africa. It also looks at the practice of development in this period, focusing on the Niger Agriculture Development Scheme, Mokwa. This book argues that poor planning inspired by imperial ideologies is responsible for the failure of development in late colonial Africa. These imperial conceptualizations of development transitioned to the postcolonial period, continuing this legacy of failure, and leading Africa to often be defined by pathological stereotypes such as corruption, disease, war, and poverty, or what Dambisa Mboyo calls "The Four Horsemen of Africa's Apocalypse." This book challenges some of the narratives that are proffered for the crisis of development in Africa, particularly the problematic image of Africans as corrupt and irresponsible, as well as others, such as the view that Africa's problems are caused by resistance to change on the part of the Africans, half-hearted commitment to development by the people, and Africa's environment. *The Second Colonial Occupation* invites readers to consider the ideological and material interests that colonial powers and Western governments have in the continent that inform planning and implementation. By locating this study in the late colonial period, the book is a response to this question: If corruption and ineptitude of African leadership are responsible for the crisis of development in postcolonial Africa, why did development also fail in colonial Africa when Europeans were the architects and implementers of development policy? Nigeria is the focus of this study because it was the most populous British colony in Africa and had a unique colonial experience, in which three territories were amalgamated into one. Nigeria was also rich in primary agricultural products that were vital for the British industry and therefore successful development in the territory was in their interest. For these reasons, Nigeria was ahead of the other African colonies in drafting a development plan, and the documents originating from Nigeria were thoroughly discussed in London and advanced by the secretary of state for the colonies as a model for other British territories.

In examining Nigeria's 1945 plan, the emphasis of this book is on the process that led to the plan documents. The practice of development as state intervention has been studied by social scientists, most notably modernization theorists. They have attempted to explain the success or failure of development in any given locality. Rather than attempting to study development by using some of the classical theories such as modernization, dependency, or world system theories, *The Second Colonial Occupation* historicizes development as a planning process. This approach, as Nick Cullather argues, conceives development as discourse and puts "the context, personalities, and politics back in."[29] In historicizing development planning in late colonial Nigeria, this book situates the documents in the trajectory of official colonial thinking. Though not precluding a discussion on the implementation of plans, the focus of the book is on the painstaking process leading to the official documents. It shows the discourse and conflicts in Nigeria and the metropole, as well as the negotiations that took place as attempts were made to craft a development plan for Nigeria.

By focusing on the development process, the book reveals how the historical debates on colonial development shaped the final plan document. One such debate that consumed the planning process was the question of whether metropolitan funds should be invested in the development of the colonies. Joseph Chamberlain had championed metropolitan investments in the colonies in the 1890s. Chamberlain's view was that of constructive exploitation. Rather than plundering the colonies without any investments in them, he wanted Britain to prime the resources of the colonies by making key investments. He argued that Britain, like a landlord of a great estate with abundant financial resources at its disposal, should invest in the colonies, opening them up for the extraction of resources.[30] For him, such investments should not be limited to the development of public infrastructure such as roads, rail, and ports but must be made equally in the area of scientific research. His imperial vision opened up a debate in London, one that continued into the 1920s. His imperial doctrine came up against the Treasury's historical position that colonies should be financially self-sufficient.

Although Chamberlain's ideas on metropolitan investments did not become the canon for Britain's relationship with its colonies, they continued to permeate the thinking at the colonial office (CO). Between 1890 and the economic crisis of the 1920s, rather than give free money to aid the development of the colonies, London guaranteed some development loans. Then, with Britain's economy in crisis and the resultant high unemployment, there was a gradual shift in London toward Chamberlain's vision. The result was the 1929 Colonial Development Act, a jobs program directed at helping the metropolitan economy. Casting the debate in these terms helped the passage of the 1929 Act. The Act's passage however did not end the ongoing debate in London over whether metropolitan funds should be used in the development of the colonies. The Treasury remained unconvinced and obstinate in their refusal. This debate recurred when Parliament debated the 1940 and 1945 Colonial Development and Welfare Acts. By this time, Chamberlain's vision of development had become the official thinking at the CO. These ideological debates helped to shape the outcome of the Development Acts as well as the plans that were introduced in light of them. Chamberlain's imperial vision shows us that ideas are important, even when they are not immediately implemented. The ideologies and debates surrounding such visions often live on to inform development trajectories.

By the 1940s, there was a major shift in Britain's development policy, with the metropole now willing to invest millions of pounds in the colonies. Treasury's question was no longer whether Britain should put money in the colonies but how much money and in what investments? By looking at the planning process that resulted in the 1945 Nigerian plan, *The Second Colonial Occupation* provides a proper context for understanding the shifts and policy decisions that were made. Two important events provide the larger context for this plan: the Great Depression and World War II. The development discourse shows the efforts made by both London and Nigeria to expand production during the war, which had the two-prone goal of supporting the war efforts and helping deal with Britain's postwar economy. At the end of the war, Britain's acute need to deal with its balance-of-payment problems forced it to emphasize the expansion of colonial production in its development policy. The agricultural bias of the development plan is a result of this context and is the reason that this book focuses on agricultural development.

Nigeria's 1945 plan shows the radical shift in colonial development policy in the 1940s. While the 1929 Colonial Development Act budgeted only £10 million for the development of the colonies, Nigeria's 1945 plan cost £55 million. This figure is staggering given that only £120 million was allocated for the development of all of British colonial holdings. Though only £23 million of this money was to be provided under the Colonial Development and Welfare Act, it still shows the faith that Colonel Oliver Stanley and his colonial office had in the Nigerian plan. Given the number of investments that was to be made in Nigeria and the value of the territory to London, the Nigerian plan was marred in politicking that is only revealed when one pays close attention to the planning process. One key question in the planning process was: Who should control the development of the colonies? Nigerian officials wanted control over this process given that they had a better understanding of the local conditions, while some in the CO favored a metropolitan-centered approach where development was controlled from London. This political jockeying between Nigeria and London almost torpedoed the Nigerian plan. The plan was delayed until a compromise was reached: the creation of yet another bureaucratic structure in the CO to oversee development.

Such politicking was not limited to the interactions between London and Nigeria. There were internal debates in Nigeria, between the political/administrative wing and the technical departments of the colonial state, over who should control local development. Some of these conflicts escalated into personal conflicts. One notable example was the conflict between the director of the agriculture department, Captain James Mackie, and the governor of Nigeria, Sir Arthur Richards. The governor wrestled power from the department and placed it in the hands of political officials. The escalation of the conflict forced Mackie to resign from Nigeria's agriculture department before the final approval of the agricultural plan that he had written. These kinds of conflicts expose the human side of development that are not always apparent in the plan documents themselves. This book reveals how these human elements in the planning process had an impact on the outcomes.

Focusing primarily on the planning process offers us a new perspective from which to look at the failure of development in Africa. Plenty of studies have explored the implementation of development plans or policies. These studies are insufficient to understanding this crisis. Planning is as important as implementation and poor planning inevitably leads to poor implementation and outcomes. Development plans in Africa are often designed or guided by international experts who are convinced that they know what Africa needs and how to achieve it. It is not surprising that when these plans fail, Africans are often blamed. Scholars associated with Western universities and think tanks have corroborating studies to support their deeply inaccurate notions about Africans and to justify the belief that Africans are to blame for the failures. Most of these studies focus on development in the postcolonial era and erroneously assume that Africans are in control of the development machinery during this period. Though political leadership is vested in the hands of Africans, the control of the economy and resources is still guided by the invisible hand of Euro-American states and institutions such as the World Bank/ IMF. For example, after independence in 1960, the Nigerian government launched six development plans that mirrored the 1945 colonial plan; in some cases the newer plans expanded upon the projects that were established by the 1945 plan. Because of this, it is important to consider the legacy of the plans developed by the British when judging the success or failure of those made postindependence, which shared many of the same principles. For this reason, rather than studying the postcolonial period, this book returns to the late colonial era to show that even when development was under the management of Europeans, it failed. The Niger Agriculture Development Scheme, Mokwa (NAP) in Nigeria is used as a case study to show how poor planning in the colonial era led to bad outcomes. This scheme is emblematic of other development projects in Nigeria and colonial Africa in the postwar period. By investigating this late colonial period, *The Second Colonial Occupation* will provide insights toward understanding postcolonial development.

In understanding the problems of development in Africa, we need to stop blaming Africans who are already victims of a world economic system that is historically exploitative and rigged against them. As Jeremiah Dibua has argued, the modernization paradigm plays a central role in the creation and perpetuation of the crisis of development in Africa. He does not discount Africa's internal problems such as corruption, ineptitude, authoritarianism, and the patrimonial nature of some states. However, these are not the primary causes of the crisis. The crisis is rooted in the attempt to export and plant Western modernization models or paradigms in places where the sociocultural realities are different from in the West. For Dibua, the reason for the failure of modernization-inspired programs in Africa is the paradigm itself and not Africa's internal problems.[31] He argues that development planning in

Nigeria, as evidenced in the 1962 plan and beyond, was a product of "Eurocentric diffusionism through modernization, which only attributes history to European societies while denying history or any form of meaningful autonomous development to African societies, fostered ethnocentrism and false universalism that negatively affected development planning in Nigeria."[32] This is the reason that development programs for Africa are often designed by expatriates with little or no input by Africans, with locally produced knowledge often rejected in favor of "imported" knowledge.

Nigeria's 1945 plan has not received the scholarly attention that it deserves because of the argument that it is not an actual development plan. In his *Foundations of an African Economy: A Study of Investment and Growth in Nigeria*, Ojetunji Aboyade studies the history of the Nigerian economy, measuring its growth and identifying the economic problems that are responsible for Nigeria's underdevelopment. Paying close attention to the Nigerian context, he offers a new direction for development planning. Nevertheless, Aboyade argues that the 1945 ten-year development plan instituted by the British in the late colonial period cannot be properly called a development plan, describing it instead as "more a catalogue of little interrelated proposals with ill-defined goals and no coherent statement of policy."[33] This argument is one that has been repeated by other nationalist economists who argue that the 1945 plan did not have any systematic model or guiding principle, but was rather an amalgam of different projects or schemes that became a plan.[34] *The Second Colonial Occupation* argues that the 1945 ten-year development plan was an actual plan. Careful thought and deliberation went into designing it. Several committees at the local and national level in the colony, and many other committees at the metropole, discussed, debated, and analyzed the ideas that would become the plan. To dismiss this plan is to also dismiss the postcolonial plans, which were built upon its foundation.

Another argument used to dismiss the 1945 plan is that development was invented after World War II. This view results in the incorrect assertion that plans designed in the early 1940s and implemented from early 1945, like the Nigerian plan, cannot be said to be development plans because development had not yet been invented. Adherents of this view have argued that the practice and theory of development arose when President Harry Truman, in his January 20, 1949 speech, announced his "fair deal" and set forth a doctrine that offered a new way of understanding world affairs. The transfer of global power from Britain and France to the U.S. following the war launched the American century in which that nation became more assertive in world affairs. American social scientists propagated a new style of development called modernization, which was financed by U.S. government and foundations. Nils Gilman notes that modernization was an invention of the U.S. in response to postwar challenges and opportunities.[35] His argument misses the fact that what was sold as "modernization" was merely theory. In practice, modernization was no different from development policy practiced under the British and the French. While Arturo Escobar does not see Truman's speech as solely responsible for the creation of development, he argues that it was invented in the postwar period by the West as an instrument for the exportation of Western moral and cultural superiority to the "Third World": the imposition of Western knowledge and ideas upon these people whom the West treated as "a child in need of adult guidance."[36] Like Gilman, Escobar's argument fails to account for British and French development policy in Africa prior to the war. David Ekbladh challenges the view that modernization is a postwar invention and pushes the origins of modernization to the prewar period. He argues that there were emerging new ideas of development in the 1910s and 1920s that coupled modern applied technologies with the new social sciences. Though these ideas originated from outside the U.S., they had strong adherents in America.[37] Ekbladh ties development to the ideological struggles of the twentieth century: Liberalism, Communism, and Fascism. The intervention by the U.S. in world affairs was part of an ideological struggle over whose "ideologies were best suited to deliver the benefits of modern life."[38] The ideas that would later be termed as modernization were not 1945 inventions; neither was modernization theory created by the Cold War. Rather, these preexisting ideas worked their way into Cold War policies.[39] *The Second Colonial Occupation* shows that there was continuity between British-led colonial development and American-led modernization.

ORGANIZATION OF THE BOOK

The Second Colonial Occupation is laid out in five chapters. The first chapter looks at the early years of British colonial development. It begins with Joseph Chamberlain's call for Britain to invest its resources in the colonies, with the goal of extracting the resources of the colonial people. The chapter discusses Chamberlain's doctrine of constructive imperialism and reveals how its primary goal was the exploitation of Africa. Chamberlain's call for Britain to use public funds to invest in public infrastructure and scientific research placed him ahead of his time. The prevalent belief was that private capital, and not government funds, should be used in the development of the colonies. Chamberlain faced fierce opposition from the Treasury. This chapter shows that though Chamberlain did not see his vision actualized, he laid an important ideological foundation within the CO and this thinking later influenced colonial development policy as Britain struggled with the economic slump of the 1920s and rising unemployment. In the 1920s, L. S. Amery, who was the parliamentary undersecretary of state for the colonies, and Lord

Milner, who was the secretary of state for the colonies, embraced the vision of Chamberlain and attempted to institutionalize colonial development. By returning to the 1890s, the chapter helps us to better situate the historical roots of the debates that the CO and the Treasury had over the development acts. It enables us also to see how London's thinking on colonial development shifted over time. By examining this earlier period, the chapter shows that implementation alone cannot be the primary vehicle for assessing the trajectory of development. Ideology is very important.

The second chapter explores the debates leading to the passage of Nigeria's 1945 development plan. The Nigerian administration was eager to produce a development plan and thus created new institutions to aid this process. It was through these bureaucratic institutions and thoughtful discussions in Nigeria that the first blueprints for a ten-year development proposal were produced. This chapter will also analyze those discussions and ideological debates that took place in London and in Nigeria leading to the 1945 plan. Examining such debates is important as it exposes the hidden effects of the planning process on development policies. Nigerian colonial officials were well intentioned in their efforts to develop the colony. Despite the strengths of the plan that was produced by Nigeria, this chapter argues that it had limitations and shortcomings. One of the primary problems the plan faced was insufficient financial investments to carry out the kind of development that was envisaged. The plan was also affected by the systemic racism of the colonial state, which excluded Nigerians from playing an active role in the design of the plan.

The 1945 development plan also reflected an agrarian bias. The colonial state relied on revenues from agriculture to finance development in the colony and thus was attempting to frontload most of the grants it received from the Colonial Development and Welfare Fund toward expanding agricultural production. Agriculture was seen as the path to Nigeria's economic prosperity. Therefore, in the third chapter, the focus is on the agriculture plan. This plan was the creation of Captain James Richard Mackie, the most influential director of agriculture in colonial Nigeria. Mackie served in the agriculture department of Nigeria for twenty-four years before he retired in February 1945. Mackie's policy of agricultural development emphasized careful research and field trials before farmers were asked to change their methods of farming. Mackie's policy was too cautious and conservative and it also failed to change the social and political systems that were associated with African farming. Like colonial rule itself, Mackie's policy was blinded by the color line, as it failed to incorporate the farmers' local knowledge. The chapter also examines the conflicts between the agriculture department and the political department of the colonial state for local control over development. This chapter shows how process is important to understanding the success or failure of development plans.

In the period after the war, there was a shift in the agricultural policy that was instituted by Mackie in Nigeria. This shift occurred because of the Sterling Crisis in London and the policies of the new Labour government. The Mackiean policy of careful experimentation and field trials was abandoned for a more rapid policy of agriculture that ended up becoming an expensive social experiment in modern agriculture. The fourth chapter of the book focuses on a specific scheme, the Niger Agricultural Scheme, Mokwa. The scheme is analyzed and some of the problems that plagued it are identified. This scheme failed because of poor planning. The scheme offers an excellent example of the practice of development and the ramifications of poor planning.

The legacies of British colonial rule in Nigeria are discussed in the fifth chapter. While the overarching legacy of colonial rule is colonial mentalité, in terms of development planning there are three specific legacies: multiyear centralized planning, agrarian bias, and a reliance on international experts for development.

The question why there were regressive changes in my neighborhood in Nigeria is addressed in the conclusion. The changes were a result of the IMF/World Bank–imposed Structural Adjustments Programs of the 1980s. Africa's crisis of development does not exist in a vacuum. History, geopolitics, and economics are important. This book reveals that in development, process and context matters and we better pay attention to it when we are planning or implementing development policy.

NOTES

1. The European traders did not venture beyond the seaports into the interior parts of Nigeria. They relied on their business partners in Nigeria to bring goods from the interior to them.
2. Philip Ehrensaft, "The Political Economy of Informal Empire in Pre-Colonial Nigeria, 1807–1884," *Canadian Journal of African studies* 6, 3 (1972): 456
3. Michael Crowder, *A Short History of Nigeria* (New York: Frederick A. Praeger, 1966), 233.
4. Great Britain. Colonial office, *Committee on Improved and Increased Production of Palm Oil and Palm Kernels in West Africa.* (London: HM Stationery Office, 1925), 10.
5. R. Olufemi Ekundare, *An Economic History of Nigeria 1860–1960* (New York: Africana Publishing Company, 1973), 166.
6. Ibid., 168.
7. Bade Onimode, *Imperialism and Underdevelopment in Nigeria: The Dialectics of Mass Poverty* (London: Zed Press, 1982), 46.
8. Ibid., 44.

9. Ekundare, *An Economic History of Nigeria,* 168.

10. The term "peasants" here refers to smallholder farmers who cultivated for their own consumption and for the markets. Their production was always small scale and relied mainly on family or communal labor. A small number of peasants retained paid labor but this was never at the scale of industrial agriculture. This word "peasants" has negative connotations. It is used because it captures the demeaning attitude of the colonial rulers toward the African farmers.

11. The "dual mandate," a phrase coined by Lord Lugard, one of British colonial governors in Africa, captures British imperialism in Africa. It is an imperial principle that the resources of the colony should be exploited for the benefits of metropole and colony.

12. Ekundare, *An Economic History of Nigeria,* 158.

13. Anne Phillips, *The Enigma of Colonialism: British Policy in West Africa* (Bloomington, In: Indiana University Press, 1989), 3.

14. Ibid., 11.

15. Ibid., 11–12.

16. The colonial state was not as powerful as it is sometimes purported to be. Fred Cooper argues that "the much celebrated policy of 'indirect rule' in British Africa . . . represented an attempt to make retreat sound like policy." See Frederick Cooper, *Decolonization and African Society: The Labor Question in French and British Africa* (Cambridge: Cambridge University Press, 1996), 11. On how African labor undermined the authority of chiefs and white administrators in Kenya, see Bruce Berman, *Control & Crisis in Colonial Kenya: The Dialectic of Domination* (Athens: Ohio University Press, 1999), 61.

17. See Michael Cowen and Robert Shenton, *Doctrines of Development* (New York: Routledge, 1996).

18. Cowen and Shenton, *Doctrines of Development*, 7.

19. This was a concept coined by Low and Lonsdale to describe the expansive development policies introduced by the British after World War II. Massive projects were carried out in the field of agriculture, with the intention of holding onto the colonies while at the same time boosting Britain's economy. See, D.A. Low and J.M. Lonsdale, "Introduction: Towards the New Order, 1945–63," in *History of East Africa vol. 3*, (Oxford: Clarendon Press, 1976). The title of this book is derived from this coinage by Low and Lonsdale.

20. John Maynard Keynes argued that the solution to the problem of the Great Depression was to stimulate the economy by cutting interest rates and government investment in infrastructure. Ochonu argued that, rather than the colonial state investing in infrastructure, they cut public investment.

21. Moses E. Ochonu, *Colonial Meltdown: Northern Nigeria in the Great Depression* (Athens: Ohio University Press, 2009), 28–29.

22. Carl K. Eicher, "The Dynamics of Long-Term Agricultural Development in Nigeria," *Journal of Farm Economics* 49, 5 (1967): 1161.

23. Toyin Falola, *Economic Reforms and Modernization in Nigeria, 1945–1965* (Kent: The Kent State University Press, 2004), 79.

24. Ibid., 21.

25. Eicher, "The Dynamics of Long-Term Agricultural Development in Nigeria," 1162.

26. Jonathan Harwood, *Europe's Green Revolution and its Successors: The Rise and Fall of Peasant-Friendly Plant Breeding* (Abingdon: Routledge, 2012), 2.

27. Hereafter, CD&W Act.

28. More details on these acts are provided in the second chapter.

29. Nick Cullather, Development? It's History, *Diplomatic History*, 24, 4 (2000): 648.

30. Joseph Chamberlain, "Speech at Walsall," July 15, 1895, in Joseph Morgan Hodge, *Triumph of the Expert: Agrarian Doctrines of Development and the Legacies of British Colonialism*, (Athens: Ohio University Press, 2007), 21.

31. Jeremiah I. Dibua, *Modernization and the Crisis of Development in Africa: The Nigerian Experience* (Brookfield, VT: Ashgate, 2006), 19, 27.

32. Jeremiah I. Dibua, *Development and Diffusionism: Looking beyond Neopatrimonialism in Nigeria, 1962–1985* (Palgrave Macmillan, 2013), xii.

33. Ojetunji Aboyade, *Foundations of an African Economy: A Study of Investment and Growth in Nigeria* (New York: Frederick A. Praeger, 1966), 150.

34. Pius Okigbo, *National Development Planning in Nigeria, 1900–1992* (London: James Currey, 1989), 154. Edward Ayo also makes the argument that this plan is hardly a development plan in any serious sense. Like Aboyade and Okigbo, he argues that it was just a list of projects. See, Edward Jide Ayo, *Development Planning in Nigeria* (Ibadan: University Press Limited, 1988), 2.

35. Nils Gilman, *Mandarins of the Future: Modernization Theory in Cold War America* (Baltimore: John Hopkins University Press, 2003), 61.

36. Arturo Escobar, *Encountering Development: The Making and Unmaking of the Third World* (Princeton: Princeton University Press, 1995), 4 and 30. For more on this argument see also Gilbert Rist, *The History of Development: From Western Origins to Global Faith* (London: Zed Books, 1997).

37. David Ekbladh, *The Great American Mission: Modernization & the Construction of an American World Order* (Princeton: Princeton University Press, 2010), 7.

38. Ibid.,2.

39. Ibid., 4. For more on prewar modernization origins, see Michael Latham, *The Right Kind of Revolution: Modernization, Development, and U.S. Foreign Policy from the Cold War to the Present* (Ithaca: Cornell University Press, 2011), 4–5.

Chapter 1

Joseph Chamberlain

Constructive Imperialism and Colonial Development

In the period before the scramble and partition, Britain's official interest in Africa was declining. However, private enterprises saw economic potential and were willing to penetrate Africa's interior. The scramble generated great interest among European nations as they rushed to sign treaties with African chiefdoms and plant national flags symbolizing their "trusteeship" over the vast African regions. This did not change Britain's economic relationships with the African territories within official circles. The governance of these territories remained in the domain of private companies that were granted charters by the British government. When it did occur, the evolution of colonial administration from chartered companies to the British government took different forms in different British possessions. This was because of the chartered companies' inability to administer the colonies. In Nigeria, for instance, the Royal Niger Company's charter was revoked in 1899 because the company lacked the resources to defend against French attacks on the region or to keep the indigenous rulers under control.

While the companies controlled the administration of the different British territories, a strong voice in the metropolitan government advocated for Britain to be more vested in its territories. From the start, Joseph Chamberlain was suspicious of the activities of the chartered companies in the territories and opposed to Britain granting a charter to Cecil Rhodes's South Africa Company. Chamberlain considered empire builders such as Rhodes and George Taubman Goldie of the Royal Niger Company to be people who looked after their own personal interest over those of Britain. Though critical of these empire builders, Chamberlain also made investments in and reaped profits from their companies.

In the late 1880s, Chamberlain reluctantly accepted the need to grant Rhodes's company a charter. Rhodes had signed a treaty with a local chief in the territory north of the Transvaal, in what is today Zimbabwe. Granting Rhodes the authority he needed would enable him to carry out development in the area at no cost to the British tax payers. Above all, if Rhodes's company occupied that territory, they would ward off the encroachment of foreigners such as the Boers. Chamberlain wasn't one to fully trust Rhodes and thus he advised one of his associates, Albert Grey, to take a seat on the board of the South Africa Company in hopes of monitoring Rhodes's activities.[1] The Company was granted a royal charter in 1889. Chamberlain's relationship with Rhodes remained precarious even as they cooperated on imperial projects that Rhodes considered beneficial to his business enterprise and Chamberlain saw as beneficial to the mother country. Ideological motivations were laid at the root of the tensions between Chamberlain and the likes of Rhodes and Goldie. This chapter focuses on Chamberlain's imperial vision, "constructive imperialism," and the ideological shifts that occurred between the 1890s and the Great Depression.

THE EVOLUTION OF AN IDEA

Joseph Chamberlain formed his imperial vision through his own experiences, both as a businessman and as a politician. Joseph Chamberlain was born on July 8, 1836, in London. He shared his name with both his father and grandfather. The Chamberlains had owned a leather business in London since the later part of the 1700s. After he turned sixteen, Joseph Chamberlain was removed from school to begin an apprenticeship as a cordwainer in the family business and never had the opportunity to attend university. At the end of his apprenticeship, Chamberlain's father had him learn accountancy to enable him manage the family's finances. This new apprenticeship was cut short within a year as he was dispatched to travel on short business trips to Birmingham, where he overlooked his father's investments in a wooden screw business owned by his uncle, John Sutton Nettlefold.[2] Chamberlain's father had already invested £10,000 in this business, which was aimed at mechanizing the production of wood screws. The future prospects of this new enterprise enticed the senior Chamberlain to sell his own cordwaining business in 1863 and move to Birmingham where he invested his proceeds and took on an equal partnership with Nettlefold in the wood screws business.[3] This move was instrumental to young Joseph Chamberlain's future both as a businessman and as a politician, as he would later become mayor of Birmingham, a strong industrial and manufacturing base and England's fourth largest city.

Joseph Chamberlain came of age as the Industrial Revolution was taking off in England. He ascended with this revolution and gained a global business perspective. As an industrial city, Birmingham's population was growing rapidly, rising from around 74,000 at the turn of the eighteenth century to about 600,000 by 1887.[4] By the early part of the twentieth century, the city of Birmingham had grown to become one of the largest cities in the British Empire, boasting a population of 840,000 people. The growth of the city expanded with the rise in industry. It was dubbed "a city of a thousand trades" because it was an industrial hotspot that provided wide-ranging opportunities for entrepreneurs and those who were willing to sell their labor. Birmingham was, as Simon Heffer writes, "a place of small manufacturing businesses, where the enterprises rapidly grew. If it became well known for anything it was the gun trade, and the city prospered abnormally during the Crimean War. But it also specialized in all sorts of metalwork, from the bibs for fountain pens to the screws made by the Chamberlain family. It was a city that flourished on free trade, but which had to ensure it kept ahead of its rivals."[5]

The city's population growth and economic prosperity led to an expansion of the government, with the local city government expanding in this period from 72 council members to 120.[6] The continuing rise in the demographics meant that the city had to build a stronger government and provide more services. The question which Birmingham and other nineteenth-century policy makers in Britain faced with regard to services is one that continues to plague municipalities today: Who can more efficiently deliver public services, the government or private enterprise? Take as an example the provision of gas. Before the 1860s, gas was always under private ownership. The municipal government only stepped in when the private enterprise could not provide the service. As J. Chandler notes, "For the most part local authorities left the supply of gas in private hands until the municipal 'take off' of the 1870s, but by 1882 there were 148 local authorities with municipal undertakings."[7] Joseph Chamberlain, as mayor of Birmingham, was instrumental in this "take off" in which cities became more involved in the provision of utilities.[8]

Chamberlain's ascension to the seat of mayor was occasioned by his desire to improve the state of education in Birmingham. As his biographer Peter Marsh notes, his foray into politics is not something he had intended to do or had prepared for; he was an interested bystander.[9] In 1867, some citizens of Birmingham, including Chamberlain, were invited to the home of the city's mayor, George Dixon. Dixon informed them of the destitute state of education in the city, sharing that over two million of the city's school-age children did not attend school. This piqued Chamberlain's interest because he saw education as a means toward bridging the gap between the working and middle classes. This idea was not original to Chamberlain but rather, as Asa Briggs has shown, "a persistent element in civic life."[10] Founded in 1829, Thomas Attwood's Birmingham Political Union had the aim of "bringing together the middle and working classes."[11] In the Union's first annual meeting, held in July 1830, Attwood "stressed the need for cooperation between the working and middle classes."[12] Briggs identifies four reasons for this cooperative relationship between the middle and working classes in Birmingham:

> First, there was a great diversity of occupation. . . . Second, work was carried on in small workshops rather than in large factories. . . . Third, a large proportion of the Birmingham labour force was skilled and therefore relatively well-off economically. . . . Fourth, there was considerable social mobility in Birmingham, or at least considerable local optimism about the prospects of "rising in society."[13]

Because of these factors, the working class in Birmingham did not develop the kind of class-consciousness that would have led to conflicts with the middle class. Chamberlain saw education as a worthy investment that could potentially pay itself back and help "secure industrial peace and prosperity."[14] For Chamberlain, and many others who gathered that evening with Dixon, education was not the prerogative of the church alone but something in which the government should have a greater stake. It was obvious to them that education solely administered through religious affiliations was failing the young children of Birmingham (and England as a whole) and therefore government should play a greater role in the provision of education. Chamberlain argued, "It is as much the duty of the State to see that children are educated as to see that they are fed . . . the enjoyment of this right ought not to depend on the caprice of charity or the will of parents."[15] It was this ideology that drove Chamberlain to cofound the National Education League, an organization that arose from the like-minded group that had gathered in Dixon's home. The League's plan was to promote an unsectarian and a national system of education and bring together all who shared the vision of a "system which shall secure the Education of every Child in England and Wales."[16] Chamberlain and ten other members pledged £1,000 each to the League, to be paid in annual installments over ten years.[17]

Chamberlain's desire to reform education in England plunged him deeper into politics. Together with the members of the League, he fought the education bill that was designed by W. E. Forster and was to be introduced to the House of Commons in 1870. The bill was unacceptable to the League because it promised the religious denominations another year of government financial support to build schools. Chamberlain's reaction to this bill was swift. He organized protests against the bill in Birmingham. Together with Dixon, he led a delegation to 10 Downing Street where he spoke against the bill before the prime minister, William Ewart Gladstone.[18] Though the final passage of the bill in 1870 did not result in the changes to education that the League had wanted, they continued to advocate strongly for education reform, engaging in spirited debates in city councils. Chamberlain's activism in education led to his nomination and election to the Birmingham city council in 1869, representing St. Paul's ward. Before 1870, his impact on the council was negligible. His election to the school board, created in November 1870, gave Chamberlain a platform upon which he could advance the League's arguments for reform. Commenting on his tenure in the school board several years later, *The Fortnightly Review* opined: "Tireless in committee, ever on the alert to take advantage of an opponent's blunder in tactics, eloquent and resolute at the meetings of the Board, Mr. Chamberlain, in the three years, made a great impression on both friends and foes, and made possible the personal triumphs which, although then probably unsuspected by his warmest admirers, were so quickly to follow."[19] Although Chamberlain was a reluctant politician when he was first elected in 1869, the events surrounding the Education Reform Act and his perceived impact on the school board catapulted him from a reluctant to a passionate politician. By the time of his reelection in 1872, his council seat had become very competitive. The views he espoused on the school board pitted the Conservatives against him. In the end, Chamberlain prevailed in the election by only sixty-two votes. By the time the votes were counted, the Liberals knew whom they wanted to be their mayor. The bitter contest had fragmented Birmingham strongly: this was the turning point after which elections were fought along political lines.[20] In later years, Chamberlain was unapologetic about this political turning point. In an 1880 speech in Birmingham he said:

> It is of the essence of our representative institutions that we should have party government, and the lines of party, if they are not defined by politics, will be fixed by something less honourable and less definite. They must be fixed by local prejudice or personal preference, and if you have lesser issues in place of the greater I believe you will find that there will be less extended interest in the work which has been done. There will be inferior character in the representatives. You are likely in such a case to have a more apathetic constituency and less efficient representation.[21]

These reflections are rooted in Chamberlain's own electoral politics. He saw the shifts from the pre-1870 municipal politicking, which was not strongly ideological, to the post-1870 Birmingham politics where elections were highly ideological and competitive. As people began to vote along political and ideological lines, voter apathy diminished and the electoral process was strengthened.

IMPROVEMENT SCHEMES AT HOME

Shortly after his 1872 election, at the age of thirty-seven, Joseph Chamberlain was almost unanimously elected mayor of Birmingham, only four years after he was elected to the city council. Though education reform was the driving force for his political evolution, other issues would soon preoccupy him. Chamberlain's education reform activism was not about secular education for its own sake. He saw in education a vital key to unlocking the economic potentials of the city and unshackling the chains of poverty. The Birmingham that Chamberlain inherited was a sanctuary of poverty. Despite the industrial production that was taking place, for many citizenry, there was a pervasive sense of hopelessness as they lived in squalor with their lot not improving. Robin Hambleton, a professor of city leadership, described the grungy Birmingham of the pre-Chamberlain mayoral years as "a bleak and forbidding place."[22] The conditions of Birmingham and Chamberlain's plans to improve the municipality became a model for what he would later propose for British "imperial estates."

Upon assumption of office as mayor, Chamberlain set out to improve the public utilities and the city took over public works projects such as gas and water supply. Under Chamberlain, the city earned recognition as a "municipal mecca."[23] The decay in public utilities that Birmingham experienced prior to Chamberlain's years as a mayor was as a result of a "laissez faire" economic ideology that did not support the investment of local government funds in the improvements of utilities. Previous officials had argued that private investors, rather than the government, should provide these. However, private investors were not prone to investments in areas where the prospects for profits were not great. The failure of both the private sector and the government to make key investments in social improvements led to a dilapidated city. As mayor, Chamberlain wanted to reverse this downward trajectory by investing government capital in public utilities. Thus, he "initiated a very ambitious improvement scheme including clearing of the worst slums, impressive public buildings, public parks, improved city lighting and cleaner drinking water."[24] His primary agenda was the implementation of what has come to be known as the civic gospel.

Most of Chamberlain's municipal improvement schemes received the favor of the council members and the citizens. There were no notable objections to the local government taking over the provision of water. The only objections from the Conservatives regarded the government takeover of the provision of gas. They believed this was a gamble with taxpayer's money that was bound for failure. The Conservatives were mistaken in their prophecies of doom: by 1875, the municipality's owned gas corporation was generating an annual revenue of £42,000 while saving consumers 33 percent in cost, and daily water supply was doubled and still providing citizens a savings of £33,000 a year.[25] Under Chamberlain's stewardship, not only were the utility corporations effectively run but they were done so at huge savings to taxpayers and consumers. His record in Birmingham debunked the Conservative ideology that private enterprises are better equipped to run utilities. This example is pertinent today when there is a growing trend to privatize all government services, from public utilities, to post offices and even prisons. The belief is that private investors will do it more effectively and cheaply. The example of Birmingham tells a different story. In an 1870 article entitled "THE BEST-GOVERNED CITY IN THE WORLD," Julian Ralph, a *Harper's Magazine* writer, chronicled in detail the reforms that were carried out during the Chamberlain years and thereafter. He argued that Birmingham was a model for other cities in the world, writing

> To-day it is a city whose people possess the highest and most varied and thorough educational facilities anywhere within the reach of all classes. It is a city wherein the difficult problem of the disposal of sewage is believed to have more nearly approached solution than elsewhere. It is a city that builds its own street railroads, makes and sells its own gas, collects and sells its water supply, raises and sells a great part of the food of its inhabitants. . . . It is, above all else, a business city, run by business men on business principles.[26]

CONSTRUCTING AN IMPERIAL IDEOLOGY

In 1874, Chamberlain ran for Parliament under the Sheffield Reform Association and lost. Then, with the retirement of George Dixon as MP in 1876, Chamberlain ran for his seat unopposed. In Parliament, he found an ally in William Gladstone, whom he believed, as leader of the Liberal Party, would be good for the Radicals program. This program "aimed to transform Britain into a popular middle-class democracy, completely unrestrained by tradition and free from the power and privilege of Anglicanism and landed elite."[27] After the defeat of the Liberal Party in 1874, Gladstone had resigned as the party leader and Lord Hartington, a Whig, was making a play for the leadership of the party. Chamberlain was opposed to Hartington's bid and so he called for the restoration of Gladstone to the leadership of the party. Through his instrumentality and the help of the Radicals, Chamberlain was returned as the leader of the party. Chamberlain's larger vision was to transform the Liberal Party in the image of the Radicals. To achieve this, he abolished the National Education League that had launched him into politics and created a new organization called the National Liberal Federation (NLF). This organization grew rapidly and by 1884 about 88 of the 198 local Liberal Associations were affiliated with it. He used the association as a tool for purging "the Liberal Party of its more moderate members, especially the aristocratic Whiggish elements."[28] The NLF became a formidable grassroots force within the Liberal Party. With its aid, the Liberal Party defeated the Conservative Party in the 1880 election, bringing the Liberals back to power. Chamberlain accepted a position as chairman of the Board of Trades in Gladstone's government. His relationship with Gladstone and the Liberal Party ended in 1886 over the question of home rule. Chamberlain was opposed to Ireland gaining home rule as he saw it as destructive to the long-term viability of the British Empire. With the Whigs in the Liberal Party, he created the Liberal Unionist Association to oppose this. In the 1886 election, the Liberal Unionists ran as a separate party and the Liberal Party had candidates contesting seats held by Liberal Unionists, including Chamberlain's own seat.[29] After the elections, the Liberal Unionists attempted a reunion with the Liberal Party but the talks failed. Meanwhile, the Liberal Unionists began to align themselves with the Conservative Party. After the 1895 elections in which the Conservatives returned to power, the Liberal Unionists joined the Salisbury government.

It was expected that when Chamberlain joined the Salisbury government, he would ask for a more prestigious position, given the political influence he had garnered within the Liberal Unionists and in the alliance with the Conservatives. He maintained enough political capital that Salisbury wanted to offer him the position of either the home office or the chancellor of the exchequer. Instead, Chamberlain requested the colonial office (CO), which was not very influential at the time. Many were surprised by Chamberlain's request for an office that had such a low profile. As Travis Crosby has suggested, Chamberlain saw in the colonial office "the greatest possible scope for his undoubted energies to pursue his goal of supreme power."[30] Chamberlain's goal was to transform this office and make it more influential in imperial policy. His own experiences in Birmingham undoubtedly influenced the way he envisioned the CO.

His national political journey in the late 1880s and early 1890s had shifted from education reform to Home Rule for Ireland. The primary basis for his denial of home rule was the fear that it would lead to the decline of the British Empire. If Ireland had home rule, which colonial territory was going to be next? Would it be India and the Asian territories next? Chamberlain thought that such changes would lead to the demise of the British Empire. He believed that the colonies had a significant place in the revitalization of Britain's manufacturing and economy, which was coming under the heavy scourge of late-nineteenth-century economic depression. Britain's imperial holdings could play a dual purpose in this economic climate. Firstly, like many other nineteenth-century European imperialists, Chamberlain saw Africa and other imperial holdings as Eldorados blessed with abundant raw materials that could be harnessed to revitalize Britain. British colonial territories, he reasoned, were a place to extract raw materials that were needed by British industries for manufacturing. The second important economic purpose that the territories could serve was as places where British manufactured goods could be sold. At this time, the growing competition among continental European countries and America led to protectionist policies.[31] British industries were having difficulties exporting their goods and this created an economic contraction at home. Chamberlain's business background and his position as chairman of the Board of Trades taught him the importance of finding new markets for goods and he saw in the colonies the market needed for British manufactured goods. Chamberlain saw the empire as waning and considered the colonies as the solution to Britain's economic decline.

In order for the territories to provide the economic relief that Britain needed, they first had to be developed. Thus, shortly after he became the S of S, Chamberlain said in a speech:

> Great Britain, the little center of a vaster Empire than the world has ever seen, owns great possessions in every part of the globe, and many of those possessions are still unemployed, entirely undeveloped. What would a great landlord do in a similar case with a great estate? We know perfectly well, if he had the money, he would expend some of it, at any rate, in improving the property, in making communications, in making outlets for the products of his land, and that, it seems to me, is what a wealthy country ought to do with regard to these territories which it is called upon to control and govern. That is why I am an advocate of the extension of Empire.[32]

This speech was an outline of Chamberlain's imperial doctrine, which advanced state intervention in the colonies, through what he termed "constructive imperialism."[33] His goal as S of S was not the further geographical expansion of empire but the economic profitability of the territories already held. The different colonies provided him with two contrasting economic outlooks. There were some tropical territories that were thriving and others that were both figuratively and literally decaying. Chamberlain believed that the key to the restoration of Britain's power, wealth, and prestige, which he feared were waning, was imperial union and development.[34] Colonial possessions were not simply a prize that Britain won for its military valor and diplomatic strength, but "an enormous potential source of national wealth and economic security."[35] For Chamberlain, colonial investments were a smart economic move for Britain. His own experiences in Birmingham had taught him that when the government makes key investments in utilities, they had long-term economic benefits. The investments in Birmingham saved the municipality money and facilitated its economic growth. Likewise, Chamberlain believed the investments made by Britain in the colonies would pay a hefty dividend. Thus, as S of S, he pushed the Salisbury government "to provide the necessary financial and technical assistance for the extension of imperial communications, especially railways, and other infrastructural projects in order to facilitate the mobilization of the largely unexplored wealth of Britain's tropical colonies in Africa and the East."[36]

As vast as Britain's territorial holdings were in Africa and Asia, Chamberlain's proposal required both substantial human and financial costs. He recognized the enormous commitments involved in defending and maintaining these territories, but believed that these costs paled in comparison to the potential profits that could be channeled from the territories to support the "mother country." In his opinion, Britain could manage these colonies by making sure that their colonial subjects felt contented and were prosperous. Under favorable conditions, the abilities of the colonial people would be unleashed to not only defend the empire against attacks, but also "to generate sufficient investment capital to set their domestic economies on a path of self-continuing growth."[37] His vision for colonial development was a novel one. Rather than leave the colonies in the hands of economic spectators such as Rhodes, Britain has to take active part in the development efforts by investing imperial funds to better the conditions of the colonial people and Britain.

The spending of imperial funds in the development of the colonies was anathema to the Treasury, which constantly fought Chamberlain's efforts. The prevailing view at the time was that colonies should be financially self-sustaining and economic development should happen through private capital infusion. Changing this mindset and policy was not an easy task as Lord Grey, the colonial secretary from 1846 to 1852, had advanced it. He argued that "the surest test for the soundness of measures for the improvement of an uncivilized people is that they should be self-sufficing."[38] In order for Chamberlain to change this policy, he needed to persuade the Treasury and use novel approaches toward funding colonial development. Given the Treasury's resistance to metropolitan-sponsored development, Chamberlain devised a clever approach. In 1875, Benjamin Disraeli had bought about £2 million worth of shares in the Suez Canal. These had appreciated to about £24 million by 1895 and were generating an income of £670,000 annually. Chamberlain's plan was to use this money to set up a fund that would guarantee loans for development in the colonies.[39] Though Chamberlain had the backing of Lord Salisbury, his plans were rebuffed by Sir Michael Hicks Beach, the chancellor of the exchequer. Hicks Beach argued that the revenue generated from the Suez Canal investment was public money and to divert it toward colonial development was tantamount to raising taxes on the British people to replace that lost revenue. This argument won the day and Chamberlain couldn't use the money for colonial development.[40]

Despite these setbacks, Chamberlain kept pressing on to find the capital he needed from other sources. The CO opened negotiations with the Treasury on low-interest development loans. An agreement was reached in 1900 when the Colonial Stock Act was enacted by Parliament. Through this Act, the colonies could borrow from the imperial government at favorable interest rates rather than from the market where interests were higher.[41] Though letting colonies borrow at low interest rates did not go as far as Chamberlain wanted, it marked a turning point in the financial and economic relationship between the colonial and metropolitan governments. The colonial governments now had a source through which they could "obtain capital to improve their basic systems of communication, transport and land utilization."[42] Whereas the high interest rates at the open market had discouraged the colonies from borrowing to invest, they could now borrow at rates that were partially subsidized by the metropolitan government. By facilitating this, Britain was intervening in the economic development of the colonies, a departure from the noninterventionist policy that had left these development efforts in the hands of private investors.

Chamberlain's most remarkable legacy as the S of S is his push for research into tropical diseases. He believed that science and technology could be a potent key in unlocking the potentials of Britain's imperial possessions. He reckoned that an investment in scientific education would be beneficial to Britain extending its control to the interior of its holdings. At a time when the conditions in some of the colonies were catastrophic to the "white man," leading to high mortality rates among imperial servants, Chamberlain believed that reducing the death rate among them "would do more for the sinews of imperial control than cables and steamships, more for the imperial armed forces than the addition of regiments, more for the construction of imperial railways or the sinking of colonial mines than navies and diggers."[43] Such a reduction could only occur if Britain made investments in the study of tropical diseases and medicine. Though British universities had been offering training in tropical medicine, the first dedicated institution for this study was the London School of Tropical Medicine, founded in 1899 by Chamberlain and Dr. Patrick Manson, the medical adviser to the colonial office. In 1886, the University of Edinburgh was the first European university to offer courses in tropical medicine. Chamberlain and Manson believed that a dedicated school was needed to effectively deal with the plaguing problem of tropical diseases.[44] This school and many others that would follow, both in England and in Europe, exercised a great deal of enthusiasm not only from government officials but from the private sector, because their research helped to protect British citizens who were carrying out the cause of empire in far remote ends of the world. It was also good for commerce. Understanding tropical diseases had the corollary effect of bettering the health of the indigenous labor needed to help their imperial masters extract colonial resources.[45] Chamberlain's support for research in tropical medicine wasn't altruistic. It served one and only one cause, Britain's imperial consolidation.

CHAMBERLAIN'S SUCCESSORS AT THE COLONIAL OFFICE

While Joseph Chamberlain's decade old leadership of the CO created a framework that advanced imperial development, such a project was not sustained by his successors, who returned to the laissez-faire imperial ideology under which the doctrine of colonial financial self-sufficiency was the guiding principle. After Chamberlain's resignation in September of 1903, Lord Balfour wanted to appoint someone to the CO who would continue his legacy. Alfred Lyttleton replaced Chamberlain in October of 1903. Writing about this appointment, Lyttleton's wife said:

> The offer was as great a surprise to him as anybody: he had never worked in a Government office, nor ever been concerned in any kind of administration; he was full of doubts of his own ability. . . . At that time the Government were not expected to remain in office for more than a few months, and Alfred feared he would disturb his legal career, lose his earning power and probably fail egregiously at his task. This was his mood; very far indeed from the exultation and delight which office is supposed to bring.[46]

Upon assumption of duties at the CO, Lyttleton was doubtful of his ability to do his duties. His time at the CO was consumed with the Chinese labor question in South Africa.[47]

The unpopularity of the Liberal Unionist government over the Chinese labor ordinance caused the Conservative leader, Arthur Balfour, to resign as prime minister in December of 1905, calling for elections in January of 1906. He had hoped that the Liberal Party was too divided to be able to form a government. King Edward VII asked the minority party led by Campbell-Bannerman to form a government. In the January elections, the Liberal Party gained an eighty-four seat majority over the combined seats of all the other parties.[48] Lord Elgin was appointed colonial secretary and Winston Churchill, the colonial under secretary. The Liberal government was opposed to the Chinese labor scheme. For them, it was a stain on the British Empire as it treated human beings as implements, a practice akin to slavery.[49] In December of 1905, the importation of Chinese laborers was halted. The question still remained: What to do with the Chinese citizens who were already in South Africa and the over 14,000 who had received licenses to travel there? With regard to these questions and other issues affecting Chinese labor, the government had by February 1906 formulated four distinct policies: "First, they would respect existing licenses, but issue no more. Second, they would modify regulations to remove, in Churchill's phrase, "all danger of cruelty, of impropriety or of gross infringement of liberty." Third, they would repatriate those who wished to go. Fourth, and most important, they would allow the Transvaal itself to take the final decision whether Chinese Labour should or should not be continued, after it had obtained self-government."[50]

Churchill's visit to East Africa in the Autumn of 1907 converted him to a follower and an advocate of Joseph Chamberlain's constructive imperialism. Though his visit to Africa was supposed to be a private vacation, he turned it into an official tour in which he had listening sessions, gave speeches, and wrote memos to send back to London. By witnessing the problems on the ground in Africa, Churchill was able to make policy suggestions to Elgin. Churchill was convinced of the future economic prospects of East Africa and suggested that improvements be made to the welfare of African contract laborers. He also advocated for a dam to be built across the Victoria Nile at Jinja.[51] During Elgin's time at the CO, Ronald Hyam says, two decisions seemed to have evolved with regard to policy on British territories in Africa. The first was to gather knowledge on the political views of the Africans. The second was "to support all attempts to secure 'the development of native institutions on native lines' throughout Africa, partly as a means of realizing the first objective and coping with the basic problem."[52]

When Asquith became prime minister in 1908, the Earl of Crewe replaced Lord Elgin. Like Lyttleton and Elgin, Crewe's influence in the CO was nominal. He maintained the conventions that were obtainable in the office and had "no particular interest in imperial affairs."[53] Lord Harcourt, who was colonial secretary from 1910–1915, did not bring to his office the aggressively exploitative vision that Chamberlain had advanced. In fact, he was determined to protect some of the colonial areas from exploitation.[54] In a speech delivered in the House of Commons, he likened his office to that of a "despot." He said, "The position of the Colonial Secretary on the Crown colony side of his Department carried with it the powers, duties, responsibilities and anxieties of a practical and laborious despot controlled only by the forces of nature, by his own discretion and by the sporadic curiosity at question time of friends or opponents inspired either by imagination or information."[55] The despotic nature of colonial governments and the exploitative imperialism championed by Chamberlain met resistance in the colonies, as they were dealing with crises such as the Sierra Leone's Hut Tax of 1898. The Radicals and Liberals assaulted Chamberlain's imperial ideology and considered it destructive to the "mother country." In its place was a new doctrine of development "along native lines" championed by Mary Kingsley, an ethnologist who visited Africa twice in the 1890s.[56] She argued that "Africans were an entirely different species who should follow their own separate cultural path of development."[57]

INDIRECT RULE

This new doctrine of development by Mary Kingsley had the support of some in the Liberal Party. It would metamorphose into the principle of indirect rule, which later became a form of government in many British territories. At the most basic level, this policy of indirect rule was a pragmatic attempt by the British to run a vast empire on a shoestring. Britain lacked the resources to carry out the direct administration of its colonies. Lord Frederick Lugard, the governor of Nigeria, together with one of his Residents, Charles Temples, were strong advocates of this policy. Temples wrote a book in 1918 supporting indirect rule, describing it as "the government of natives through their institutions, possibly modified to some extent in order to avoid practices which rightly or wrongly we consider repugnant to reason and humanity."[58] The policy of indirect rule was no more humane to the colonies than Chamberlain's "constructive imperialism." It was in fact double exploitation. Colonial people were now a cog in the wheel of the imperial power as they assumed an active role in their own colonization. This was expedient to the British who would have found it impossible to command the same level of authority over the colonial peoples as had been enjoyed by the traditional rulers. Traditional authorities became instruments for extending and concatenating imperial rule while the actual powers remained vested in the hands of the European overlords. This new policy was colonialism dressed in new clothes, but with far greater consequences for the ruled. Despite the rhetoric of the Liberal Party, the imperialism of Chamberlain was furthered and expanded. British imperialism that could have potentially collapsed beneath the weight of its own ineptitude was sustained for many more decades through the integration of an efficient traditional system of administration.

This policy, combined with World War I, gave British officials the impetus to further align the colonies with the metropole. The colonies were no longer seen as merely arenas for economic spectators such as Cecil Rhodes, but instead as strategically important to the metropole. In Africa, for example, the war expedited political and economic change, as "a largely haphazard colonial world became an increasingly centralized affair. . . . In many ways the War marked the period in which 'pacification' of both African and metropolitan critics of colonialism ends and colonial rule proper begins."[59] During the war years, an economic synergy was created between metropole and colony, from which Britain was the beneficiary. The colonies were not only recruitment grounds for soldiers who fought and gave their lives for the empire, but were also places where primary products as well as tariffs were extracted to support Britain's war efforts. The number of British officials in most of the colonies declined during the war and indirect rule was what stabilized the colonies during this time.

The contributions of Africa and some of the colonies during the war did not bring them expanded economic and infrastructural development. Though most African farmers produced more, they received depressed prices for their products as the price controls favored imported goods over African productions. In terms of infrastructural development, Africans fared poorly during the war. In many of the colonies, the budgets for development were slashed. As Richard Rathbone has argued, though taxation was increased during the war, "public sector capital expenditure in most colonies, which in any case was very modest before 1914, fell by as much as a third between 1914 and 1918 in money terms and in real terms of course a great deal more dramatically. Africans paid a heavy price for maintaining the colonial governance of their countries in war-time."[60] Africa's development during the war years was stunted. Chamberlain's vision of developing the "imperial estates" was beginning to pay off. While Britain did not invest metropolitan funds in the colonies as Chamberlain had proposed, it continued to support research in science and technology that was important for Britain's mastery over its imperial holdings. These kinds of investments in science and technology became even more pronounced following the Great Depression. While World War 1 changed Britain's relationship with its colonies, the postwar period saw greater changes as Britain responded to the ensuing economic crisis. Before this change occurred, however, a crucial ideological fight over investments of metropolitan funds in the colonies had to be fought first.

POSTWAR ECONOMIC CRISIS

World War I not only took away too many lives, it also wreaked havoc on the economies of Europe. Though Britain experienced some economic depression in the late nineteenth century, it was a relatively prosperous nation at the beginning of the war. The long war took an enormous economic toll on Britain. While its European allies were financed with money borrowed from the United States, Britain financed some of its trade deficits by selling off the securities of its citizens.[61] This meant that Britain was carrying a heavy balance sheet of private debt. Also, the economic glory of Britain was its strong industrial base and its global trade links. The war disrupted not only Britain's manufacturing but also trade. Britain's manufacturing base was retooled to support the war. Ships that served British trade networks were now diverted to military purposes. As a result, Latin America and Asia were starved of Britain's goods, creating a trade advantage for the United States and Japan. Britain saw its exports to Latin America and Asia decline significantly between 1913 and 1928, while U.S. and Japanese exports grew.[62]

The war's disruption of European manufacturing and trade had serious repercussions for the economy of Britain, Germany, and other European nations. The depressed economies gave expressions to totalitarian ideologies and movements such as Fascism and Nazism. In Italy, Benito Mussolini's Fascist Party was brought to power because of the masses' discontent with the declining political prospects of the nation. The expectations were that the Fascist Party would stabilize the economy. In Germany, the Nazi Party rode the waves of the economic downturn to power. The inability of the Reichstag to control hyperinflation paved the way for the Nazi Party to be voted to power to1932. The rapidly collapsing economies of the European countries gave rise to shifting political contours. In Britain, the 1923 elections led to the short-lived Labour government. This was the first time that a minority Labour Party formed a government. The government collapsed after only nine months, bringing the Conservatives back to power. Stanley Baldwin's Conservative government had the task of tackling the economic crisis in which Britain was enmeshed. Britain's economy was stagnant, resulting in high unemployment. In the 1920s, Britain's industrial unemployment was about 15 percent. In 1921, unemployment in Britain's mines and factories stood at about 1 million and even those who had jobs saw their wages declining.[63]

To further complicate matters, Winston Churchill, the chancellor of the exchequer, announced in his 1925 budget speech to the House of Commons that the government was going to revert to the international gold standard because of the financial situation of Britain.[64] Returning to the prewar gold standard equivalence would strengthen the pound, making British exports less attractive in the international market. At a time when Britain needed to export more goods in order to reduce unemployment, it saw its exports declining, further increasing the unemployment rate. This calamitous decision by Baldwin's government exacerbated the financial crisis and was partly responsible for the 1926 general strike that lasted for nine days. The strike had a long-lasting impact on the mining industry, as a good percentage of the miners who returned to work accepted longer hours and lower wages. Just as Joseph Chamberlain had in the 1890s seen the colonies as Britain's solution to its economic problems, Leo Amery, the S of S, looked to the empire as a Band-Aid to Britain's post-war financial challenges. In 1926, he established the Empire Marketing Board to help promote trade within the empire. This idea was recommended by the Imperial Economic Committee, which in its July 30, 1925 meeting suggested that "£1 million should be turned over to a Board, which could spend freely on research, and on the promotion of Empire goods, thus creating a 'non-tariff preference.'"[65] This Board, chaired by Amery, attempted to stimulate trade within the empire through propaganda. Though it has been mostly remembered for its film, radio, and posters, the Board did make some contributions toward research in the colonies. For example, it arranged £10 million for "transport works and scientific research in East Africa; this was justified as a way of stimulating British exports, and thus employment."[66] The economic malaise in which Britain found itself led to a heightened importance being placed on the empire. The activities of the marketing board were geared toward using the vast British Empire as a trading network, free of competition from other countries, to tide Britain over during economically hard times.[67]

While the metropolitan government looked toward the colonies for economic redemption, the health of most colonial economies was poor. Prior to the late 1920s economic crisis, Nigeria, for example, was able to balance its budget through the export of agricultural products and tin mining. In the 1920s, half of Nigeria's exports were palm products.[68] The postwar boom of the 1920s led to agricultural growth and prosperity for Nigerian farmers. Some were able to diversify their income investing in trade and transportation.[69] This period of boom, however, gave way to a period of busts as European economies began to contract. The economic weaknesses experienced in Europe were bound to become a problem in the colonies as well. Given that Nigeria, and in fact many colonies, relied on the export of primary products to generate revenues, a fall in European demand had a corollary effect of lower prices in the colonies. It was not too long before the world demand for primary products fell by 50 percent, leading to falling prices for exports from the colonies. This reduction in prices had a caustic impact on the economy of Nigeria and the colonies that were dependent on the production of primary products. L. J. Butler notes that "the price paid to Nigeria's palm-oil products dropped by almost 80 per cent between 1928 and 1934, and the total value of Nigerian exports fell from £16,927,000 in 1928 to £8,560,000 in 1933."[70]

Beyond the lost revenues from exports were those from imports. The declining prices in goods decreased the coffers of the colonial people and governments. It is normal that financial restraints are introduced during a financial crunch. The people in the colonies had to cut down on their demand for European goods, leading to a decline in the quantity of European goods that were imported. This led to financial losses for the colonial state, which depended on custom duties as an important source of revenue. Another important source of revenue that began to dry up was the hut and poll tax. Without a robust export regime of primary products, it was difficult for the people to sustain themselves. Collecting colonial taxes in the late 1920s and early 1930s became an insurmountable task for the state.[71] The colonial states were so indebted due to loans collected for development that the limited revenues generated through export trade was used to pay debt charges. The local colonial governments could not get bailouts from London because the doctrine of financial self-sufficiency was still operative. The implication of these factors is that colonies like Nigeria were unable to carry out development.

In fact, it was even challenging to maintain infrastructure that was already in place. The converging economic problems of metropole and colony gave rise to two problems: unemployment in Britain and stunted socioeconomic development in the colonies. It was thus not surprising that these imperatives found expression in the first attempt to institutionalize colonial development.

INSTITUTIONALIZING COLONIAL DEVELOPMENT: THE 1929 COLONIAL DEVELOPMENT ACT

Though Chamberlain had placed colonial development on the table in the late nineteenth century, it was only in the 1920s that attempts were made at institutionalizing it. Early in the 1920s, L. S. Amery, who was the parliamentary under-secretary of state for the colonies, and Lord Milner, who was the S of S, championed colonial development as a means of alleviating the postwar economic problems. Fresh sources of revenue were needed to service the rising British debt, which required £210 million annually. Without these revenues, industry and the investment class would see an increased burden of taxation, an act that would visit negative economic consequences on Britain's economy. An important benefit of colonial development, Amery argued, would be full employment in Britain.[72] Amery made a case for the "extension of tariff protection with imperial preferences and the sustained funding of empire settlement programs."[73] Not surprisingly, the Treasury opposed Amery's views on colonial development. Treasury officials argued that money invested in the colonies by way of development would never be recovered. Treasury continued to push the policy of providing loans and not grants to colonies, while the CO continued to push for development grants.[74] The struggle between the CO and the Treasury was intense. In 1928 Amery sent a letter to Stanley Baldwin, the prime minister, in which he wrote:

> Four years bitter experience have convinced me that any attempt to help the employment situation here by accelerating Colonial development is hopeless as long as matters are left to the Treasury, which is at bottom against all expenditure, whether on development or on anything else, and whose powers of obstruction are infinitely greater on an Imperial subject than on a domestic issue where there is constant parliamentary pressure.[75]

As the 1929 elections drew near, there was pressure on Winston Churchill, the chancellor of the exchequer, to support the policy of colonial development because otherwise the Conservative Party would be severely criticized by the opposition parties for doing nothing to reduce unemployment in Britain. While Churchill, a former S of S, dismissed the CO's pressure, by

May of 1929, Baldwin "included Amery's recommendation of a colonial development fund and advocated the extension and expedition of development policy in Africa, but in accordance with a cabinet decision he left open the question of the machinery for the administration of the fund."[76] However, Baldwin's government suffered defeat in the elections and had to resign on June 4, 1929. The Labour Party, which formed a minority government, had campaigned on the platform of tackling the problem of unemployment. The colonial secretary of Labour's government, James Henry Thomas was an enthusiastic supporter of the idea that colonial development would alleviate unemployment in Britain. Amery found an ally in Thomas and drew his attention to a Conservative Party proposal that called for the creation of a development fund. The Labour Party adopted this proposal and quickly turned it into legislation.[77]

There is no doubt that Labour's enthusiastic support for the 1929 Colonial Development Act rested on the belief that it would alleviate unemployment in Britain. In his introduction of the bill, Thomas said, "This Measure has been introduced by a Labour Government, not only because we believe in Colonial Development and because it is urgent, but because I think it will assist me in carrying out my idea of dealing with unemployment."[78] The thinking was that spurring the development of infrastructure in the colonies would generate demand for British machinery and supply and this would in turn expand production at home, thereby leading to lower unemployment. The policy was a jobs program for Britain with improvements in the colonies as a residual effect. In order for the colonial governments to embrace this new policy, Britain had to incentivize them. Stephen Constantine writes that "Since the purpose of the scheme was to induce colonies to undertake works, with which they would otherwise not at present burden themselves, in order to accelerate the revival of industry at home, it was essential that there must be an element of free gift to the territory. This should take the form of a contribution of the whole or part of the interest on a loan for a certain number of years."[79] Though the Treasury remained skeptical of the value of this scheme in reducing unemployment, nevertheless, on June 24, 1929 J. H. Thomas requested the CO, the Treasury, and the parliamentary counsel to prepare a bill. This bill was completed within two days. It went quickly through parliament and received the royal assent on July 26, 1929.[80]

The resulting 1929 Colonial Development Act had little impact because of the paltry sum allocated and its deficient structure. Only £1 million was available annually to fund the ten colonies that were part of the scheme. Between 1930 and 1940, Nigeria received about £330,000. Of this amount, "£114,450 (or 34.7 percent) was granted to pay interest on loans for the construction of the Minna-Kaduna railway, £51,000 funded the organization of ground facilities for air services, and £95,000 facilitated research and treatment of sleeping sickness. Agriculture received £3,400 to encourage mixed crop farming and another £1,500 on tsetse fly research, while the rest went for other small expenses."[81] True to its intention, it was a jobs program for the British, albeit a bad one, that neither brought about any significant development in the colonies nor solved Britain's unemployment crisis. £330,000 for a colony the size of Nigeria was very small. This Act is in stark contrast to the 1945 Act discussed in the next chapter, in which £55 million was earmarked for Nigeria's ten-year development plan. The 1929 Act, however, served an important purpose because it signaled the Treasury department's yielding and acceptance of Chamberlain's doctrine of constructive imperialism. It also laid the foundation for the future investment of greater sums of metropolitan funds in the development of the colonies.

CONCLUSION

The passage of the 1929 Act was the beginning of the institutionalization of Chamberlain's imperial vision that had, since the 1890s, remained in the background of Britain's relations with its colonies. By abandoning the policy of financial self-sufficiency and investing metropolitan funds in the colonies, Britain was rediscovering Chamberlain's idea that "imperial estates" should be developed for the benefit of Britain and the colonial people. This chapter shows that the ideology of development that became central to Britain's second colonial occupation in Africa was originated by Joseph Chamberlain. By looking at the policies of his successors at the CO, the shifts in this development ideology become more apparent. This ideology never completely disappeared, but found expression in different colonial policies and practices. The debates over colonial development policy that began during Chamberlain's time at the CO continued through the 1940s as Britain attempted to develop its colonies, which at that point had suffered several decades of neglect. The next chapter reveals how these ideological debates shaped the 1940 and 1945 Colonial Development and Welfare Acts.

NOTES

1. Peter T. Marsh, *Joseph Chamberlain: Entrepreneur in Politics* (New Haven: Yale University Press, 1994), 318.
2. Ibid., 9.
3. Ibid., 12.
4. J. A. Chandler, *Explaining Local Government: Local Government in Britain Since 1800* (Manchester: Manchester University Press, 2007), 76. See also Gordon

Emmanuel Cherry, *Urban Change and Planning: A History of Urban Development in Britain Since 1750* (London: G. T. Foulis & Co Ltd., 1972).

5. Simon Heffer, *High Minds: The Victorians and the Birth of Modern Britain* (London: Random House, 2013), 709–711.

6. P. J. Waller, *Town, City, and Nation: England, 1850–1914* (Oxford: Clarendon Press, 1983), 315.

7. Chandler, *Explaining Local Government*, 78.

8. Ibid.

9. Marsh, *Joseph Chamberlain,* 29.

10. Asa Briggs, *Victorian Cities* (New York: Harper & Row, 1970), 187.

11. Ibid.

12. "Birmingham Political Union," United Kingdom Parliament, accessed November 30, 2016, http://www.parliament.uk/about/living-heritage/transformingsociety/electionsvoting/chartists/case-study/the-right-to-vote/thomas-attwood-and-the-birmingham-political-union/birmingham-political-union/

13. Briggs, *Victorian Cities*, 186–87

14. Ibid. 31.

15. Heffer, *High Minds,* 711.

16. Report of the First General Meeting of Members of the National Education League: Held at Birmingham on Tuesday and Wednesday, October 12 and 13, 1869 (Birmingham: The Journal Printing Offices, 1869), 25.

17. Ibid. 26–27.

18. Marsh, *Joseph Chamberlain,* 43–44.

19. W. L. Courtney (ed.), *The Fortnightly Review, Vol. LV11* (London: Chapman and Hall, 1895), 905–06.

20. Ibid. 906.

21. Joseph Chamberlain, "Speech at Birmingham," October 27, 1880, in W. L. Courtney (ed.), *The Fortnightly Review, Vol. LV1,* 906.

22. Robin Hambleton, *Leading the Inclusive City: Place-based Innovation for a Bounded Planet* (Bristol: Policy Press, 2014), 55.

23. Mark S. Micale and Robert L. Dietle, *Enlightenment, Passion, Modernity: Historical Essays in European Thought and Culture* (Stanford: Stanford University Press, 2000), 147.

24. Peer Pelzer, Musterd Sako and Bontje Marco, *Inventive City-Regions: Path Dependence and Creative Knowledge Strategies* (Hamshire: Ashgate, 2012), 181

25. Courtney, *The Fortnightly Review, Vol. LV1,* 910.

26. Julian Ralph, "The Best-Governed City in the World" in *Harper's Magazine*, Volume 81, January 1, 1890, 99.

27. Joseph Morgan Hodge, *Triumph of the Expert,* 22.

28. Travis L. Crosby, *Joseph Chamberlain: A Most Radical Imperialist* (London: I. B. Tauris & Co Ltd, 2011), 24.

29. Chris Cook and John Stevenson, *A History of British Elections Since 1689* (Oxon: Routledge, 2014), 83.

30. Crosby, *Joseph Chamberlain*, 111.

31. Hodge, *Triumph of the Expert*, 22.

32. Joseph Chamberlain, "Speech at Walsall," July 15, 1895, in Hodge, *Triumph of the Expert*, 21.

33. Joseph M. Hodge, Gerald Hodl & Martina Kopf, eds. *Developing Africa: Concepts and Practices in Twentieth-Century Colonialism* (Manchester: Manchester University Press, 2014), 6.

34. Michael Havinden & David Meredith, *Colonialism and Development: Britain and its Tropical Colonies, 1850–1960* (London: Routledge, 1993), 87.

35. Melvin E. Page (ed.), Colonialism: An International Social, Cultural and Political Encyclopedia (Santa Barbara: ABC-CLIO, 2003), 107.

36. Hodge, *Triumph of the Expert*, 22.

37. Havinden and Meredith, *Colonialism and Development*, 87.

38. John M. Carland, *The Colonial Office and Nigeria, 1898–1914* (Stanford: Hoover Press Publication, 1985), 101.

39. Havinden and Meredith, *Colonialism and Development*, 88

40. Ibid., 89.

41. P. J. Cain and A. G. Hopkins, British Imperialism: 1688–2000 (Routledge, 2011), 570.

42. Marsh, *Joseph Chamberlain,* 412.

43. Ibid., 415.

44. Deborah Neill, *Networks in Tropical Medicine: Internationalism, Colonialism, and the Rise of a Medical Specialty, 1890–1930* (Stanford: Stanford University Press, 2012), 20.

45. David Arnold, *Imperial Medicine and Indigenous Societies* (Manchester: Manchester University Press, 1989), 15

46. Edith Lyttleton, *Alfred Lyttleton an Account of His Life* (1917; repr., London: Forgotten Books, 2013), 287.

47. To deal with the shortage of labor in South Africa following the Boer War, Alfred Lyttleton and many in the government supported the importation of Chinese laborers to South Africa. They were accused by many in the Liberal Party of enslaving the Chinese and bringing shame to the empire. Between 1904 and 1907, 63,695 Chinese laborers were imported. The Chinese question would lead to the defeat of the Conservatives in the 1906 elections. See Rachel Bright, *Chinese Labour in South Africa, 1902–10: Race, Violence and Global Spectacle* (Palgrave Macmillan, 2013);

48. L. C. B. Seaman, *Post-Victorian Britain 1902–1951* (London: Methuen, 1966), 16.

49. Ronald Hyam, *Elgin and Churchill at the Colonial Office, 1905–1908* (London: Macmillan, 1968), 63.

50. Ibid., 76.

51. Ibid., 357–58.

52. Ibid., 369.

53. Carland, *The Colonial Office and Nigeria,* (Stanford: Hoover Institution Press, 1985), 15.

54. Neal R. Malmsten, "British Government Policy Toward Colonial Development, 1919–39," *The Journal of Modern History* 49, 2 (1977): 1250.

55. Lord Harcourt, "Speech at House of Commons," June 12, 1912, in Lilian Charlotte Anne Knowles, *The Industrial and Commercial Revolutions in Great Britain during the Nineteenth Century* (London: George Routledge & Sons, 1922), 328.

56. Hodge, *Triumph of the Expert*, 48.

57. Ibid.

58. C. L. Temple, *Native Races and their Rulers: Sketches and Studies of Official Life and Administrative Problems in Nigeria* (London: Frank Cass & Co., 1968), 49.

59. Richard Rathbone, "World War I and Africa: Introduction" *The Journal of African History*, 19, 1, 1978: 4.

60. Ibid:, 8.

61. Barry Eichengreen, "The British Economy Between the Wars," in Roderick Floud, Jane Humphries and Paul Johnson (editors) *The Cambridge Economic History of Modern Britain, Volume 2* (Cambridge: Cambridge University Press, 2014), 319.

62. Barry Eichengreen and Douglas A. Irwin, "The Role of History in Bilateral Trade Flows" in Jeffrey A. Frankel (editor) *The Regionalization of the World Economy* (Chicago: The University of Chicago Press, 1997), 38.

63. William Brustein, *Roots of Hate: Anti-Semitism in Europe Before the Holocaust* (Cambridge: Cambridge University Press, 2003), 234.

64. Winston Churchill, Speech to the House of Commons, April 28, 1925, *Parliamentary Debates*, Vol. 183, cols. 52–58.

65. Ian M. Drummond, *British Economic Policy and Empire, 1919–1939* (London: Routledge, 2015), 66.

66. Andrew Roberts, "The Imperial Mind," in, A. D. Roberts (editor), *The Cambridge History of Africa, Volume 7* (Cambridge: Cambridge University Press, 1986), 47.

67. Ochonu, *Colonial Meltdown,* 27.

68. L. J. Butler, *Industrialisation and the British Colonial State: West Africa, 1939–1951* (London: Frank Cass, 1997),15.

69. Sara Berry, *No Condition is Permanent: The Social Dynamics of Agrarian Change in Sub-Saharan Africa* (Madison: University of Wisconsin Press, 1993), 72.

70. L. J. Butler, *Industrialisation and the British Colonial State,* 15–16.

71. On some of the challenges of tax collection during the economic crisis, see Moses Ochonu, *Colonial Meltdown.*

72. Stephen Constantine, *The Making of British Colonial Development Policy, 1914–1940* (London: Frank Cass, 1984), 36–37.

73. Ibid., 164.

74. Malmsten, "British Government Policy": 1250.

75. Amery to Baldwin, November 26, 1928, The National Archives, Kew, Colonial Office Records (Hereafter TNA CO) 323/1016/51165, Quoted in Constantine, *The Making of British Colonial Development Policy,* 168.

76. Malmsten, "British Government Policy," 1265.

77. Constantine, *The Making of British Colonial Development Policy,* 183.

78. Hansard, Parl. Deb. (Commons), 5th serv. Ccxxiv, 1300, July 12, 1929, in George C. Abbott, "A Re-Examination of the 1929 Colonial Development Act," The Economic History Review, 24:1 (1971): 70.

79. Constantine, *The Making of British Colonial Development Policy,* 184.

80. Ibid., 185.

81. Falola, *Development Planning and Decolonization in Nigeria*, 14.

Chapter 2

Negotiating Development

Nigeria's 1945 Development Plan

During World War II, the British Parliament continued to debate the Colonial Development and Welfare Bill that had been drafted in the period after the Great Depression. This bill, which would eventually institutionalize colonial development and welfare policy, was vigorously debated in Parliament, showing the commitment of the members to investing metropolitan funds in the colonies, albeit for different reasons. Some parliamentarians saw such investments as a means of developing primary industries in the colonies that would support the war efforts, while others insisted on investments in the social and welfare needs of the colonial people. Malcolm MacDonald, who was an ardent supporter of colonial development, appealed to the Members of Parliament to pass the bill, arguing that Britain had a "duty" to the colonized. The passage of this bill and the developmental state that emerged after the war was akin to a new colonial occupation. Though Britain came out of the war economically broke, there was a new energy as it tripled its investments in the colonies in an attempt to revive an empire that was already in its death throes. New development institutions were set up in Britain and in the colonies and the services of many "experts" were engaged to guide development efforts. Many discussions and negotiations took place between metropole and colony and between different apparatuses of the state within each.

This chapter historicizes the planning process that resulted in Nigeria's 1945 ten-year development plan. The focus of the analysis is the negotiations that took place between officials in the colony and in the metropole. At the heart of these negotiations was the question of who should design and control development. Sidney Caine, who was in charge of colonial development policy at the colonial office, argued that this form of planning should be controlled from the CO because the local governments "did not have the time, and in many cases the experience and expertise, necessary to carry out the daunting task of continuous, systematic planning."[1] While Caine's view of a metropolitan approach to development was under consideration, some other senior staff of the CO believed that it was important to bring the local governments to the planning process because they had a better understanding of the local conditions. Officials in Nigeria and some other colonies favored the latter view and not the former. In order to bridge the gap between planning in the metropole and in the colonies, it was decided that a planning section should be created within the CO and that technical staff from the CO would make regular visits to the colonies and provide them with expert advice. It was also decided that regional development organizations should be created and territories should set up planning councils that would carry out long-term planning.[2] This chapter argues that the metropolitan-centered development mission favored by Caine was limiting to development in Nigeria because the local administrators had a better understanding of the local needs. In planning, the local officials had to take into consideration the attacks emerging from the local press and the nationalist elites, all of which helped shape the development agenda.

By focusing on the process and the development discourse, the chapter shows that local colonial officials in Nigeria were well intentioned in their attempts to develop the colony. The officials had given serious and considerable thought to development in the colony and they took concrete steps to establish development institutions at the district, provincial, and national level. These institutions were set up to generate ideas and to propose schemes that would be beneficial to the colony. Agriculture was identified as the key to the economic success of the colony. For this reason, officials frontloaded resources toward the expansion and advancement of this sector in the early years of the plan. They hoped that production would be stimulated and revenues generated to sustain development beyond the ten years that were earmarked. Despite the strengths of this plan, it had serious limitations and shortcomings. It was grossly underfunded because of the financial challenges Britain was facing as a result of the war and it excluded the active involvement of Africans in the process, exposing the racial biases of the colonial state. Though the decolonization movement was growing, the development polices of the period deeply reflected a colonial occupation in which Britain controlled and determined the future of the colonized. Unlike the first occupation, which was characterized by the colonial people paying for their own exploitation, the second occupation had Britain investing some metropolitan funds in its quest for the exploitation of the colonial people. While the second occupation was more humane, as it took the people's welfare needs into consideration, it still reduced them to an inferior class lacking in the ability to shape and determine their own future.

PLANNING DEVELOPMENT, THE 1940 ACT

The economic depression that began in 1929 created deplorable conditions in the colonies. As the Depression deepened, the social and economic welfare of the colonial people worsened. During the Depression, the limited social services that the colonial state provided became extinct due to fallen commodity prices and the inability of European nations to generate the revenues needed for the day-to-day administration of their colonies. Since the colonies were expected to be fiscally self-sufficient, the colonial administrators responded by retrenching staff, broadening the tax base, and suspending public works projects.[3] As horrifying as colonial rule itself was, the global economic malaise created conditions in the colonies that became embarrassing to the whole colonial project. Critics argued that these deteriorating conditions "were evidence of years of complacency, neglect and exploitation."[4]

The extreme measures adopted by the colonial states in response to the Depression did not go unnoticed by the colonial peoples. Their response came in the form of riots and other mass actions. One major response in the colonies came barely a month after the stock market crash of 1929. Beginning in November of 1929, thousands of women in the southeastern part of Nigeria rebelled against the colonial state in what is now known as the "The Women's War." The grievance of the women was a tax that the colonial state planned to levy on them. By the end of the rebellion in 1930, over fifty "women [had been] killed by British troops and an unknown number [had been] wounded and otherwise traumatized."[5]

Other mass actions were soon to follow across the colonies, targeting the colonial economy specifically. One such action was the 1935 Copperbelt strike carried out by African mineworkers in Northern Rhodesia. Like the "Women's War," this strike was in protest of taxes that were being imposed by British colonial authorities. The new taxation imposed on the Africans only tells a part of the story. The Great Depression also created uneasiness in the Copperbelt. The decline in the price of copper in 1931 forced the mining companies to limit production and to retrench staff. One of the mines, Bwana Mkubwa, was shut down and work on three other mines was suspended. James Ferguson clearly captures this phenomenon:

> The impact on the labor market was accentuated by the fact that construction work at the two remaining mines was ending at the same time—in May 1931 at Roan Antelope and in December of the same year at Nkana. African employment on the mines, which had hit a peak of 31,941 at the height of the construction boom in September 1930, dropped to 19,313 by the following September, and to 6,677 at the end of 1932.[6]

The Great Depression exacerbated the problems faced by the people in the colonial territories. The Rhodesian strike and other actions taken by the colonial people between 1930 and 1939 in territories such as the Gold Coast, Mombasa, and Dar es Salaam, demonstrate that colonial rule had eventually "choked on the narrowness of the pathways it had created" and Africans were no longer willing to accept the limitations that were placed on them.[7]

These events in the colonies received wide and negative international media coverage in newspapers such as the *New York Times* and the *Daily Express*.[8] In Britain, the Christian Socialists and the Independent Labour Party, together with the Fabian Society, influenced the Labour Party to respond strongly to the social welfare needs of the colonial people. In Parliament, the Labour Party was critical of the events that were occurring in the colonies. Arthur Creech Jones questioned the language of trusteeship that had often been used by Britain to continue its dominance and exploitation of the colonial people. He said, "No longer do we regard them as our possessions. They are not places for easy profits for those who have the money to invest in them. We realize that our attitude towards them has to be constructive and positive."[9] Some of the criticism from the Labour Party was even more blistering. Reverend Campbell Stephen who represented Glasgow Camlachie accused the government of treating Africans as lower classes. He said, "I do not look for anything very much from the administration under the conduct of the Secretary of State for the Colonies, more especially the Secretary of State who has now been appointed [George Ambrose Lloyd]. I think his mind is very much like the mind of Hitler with respect to the primitive peoples. As he has expressed himself, his is the mind of a man who thinks of the native races as inferior."[10] The growing criticism of colonial rule within and outside of Britain and the crisis in the colonies evoked a response from the British government in the form of the Colonial Development and Welfare Act of 1940.

This Act marked a major shift in British colonial development policy. Unlike the 1929 Act that was passed on the eve of the Great Depression, the word "welfare" was now added to the Act. The significance of this was that colonial development now had as part of its mission, the improvement of the social conditions of people living in British territories. No longer was development solely an economic matter whose only beneficiary was Britain, it now encompassed the improvement of the lives of the people who had suffered Britain's neglect and exploitation for decades. With it, the British government placed importance on tackling the problem of colonial poverty. Alleviating colonial poverty became a major goal designed to inoculate Britain from the criticism it was facing both at home and abroad as a result of its poor treatment of colonial people. It is important to note that despite the fact that this Act was intended to be more humanitarian than mercantilist, measures that would bring about economic development were still promoted at the insistence of the Treasury. Treasury's argument was that economic development would enable colonial governments to provide essential social services. Many in the CO were not pleased with the idea.[11] Unlike the 1929 Act that allocated only £1 million annually for the development of colonies, the 1940 Act allocated £5.5 million. Of this amount, £500,000 per annum was earmarked for research in the colonies.[12] Research was an important part of this program, having been a core component of colonial development since the time of Joseph Chamberlain.

The governor of Nigeria, Sir Bernard Bourdillon, was excited about the passage of the 1940 Act. He had been instrumental to the vigorous debates that had taken place about it at the CO on the nature of the Act. In April 1939 Bourdillon had sent a long dispatch to the CO blasting "the established notions of financial self-sufficiency and damned the Colonial Development Act [of 1929] for its inefficacy. He lamented the problems of poor territories like Nigeria which, were burdened by debts, could not raise enough extra local revenue to meet the interest on new loans or to face the recurrent expenditure which development works often entailed."[13] Bourdillon's critique centered on the structure of the 1929 Act, in which a loan or a grant was made directly to a specific project or to defray interests on loans that the colony had raised. Colonies already saddled with heavy debt burden therefore faced difficulty in drawing from the funds made available through the Act. As D. J. Morgan notes, "The Nigerian Government had felt unable from the outset to add to its heavy debt burden, when there was no certainty that the ability to bear the burden would improve. So assistance for major schemes as, in Nigeria and elsewhere, of a kind which they sometimes could not afford to accept."[14] Bourdillon did not want the 1940 Act to suffer the same structural problems and he concluded his dispatch by making a few proposals. He requested that development loans should be granted by London on reduced interest rates and that the development of the Departments of Agriculture, Forestry, Veterinary, Geological Survey, and Co-operatives be fully financed by the imperial government.[15]

Bourdillon was enthused about the idea of a colonial development program that would expand social services in the colonies. This is understandable; it was the first time that the British imperial government had committed substantial financial aid to the colonies for their development and welfare. Bourdillon had long disdained the doctrine of financial self-sufficiency that was the hallmark of colonial governance and administration. When Parliament passed the legislation, he wasted no time in promoting it among his officials and asking the various Residents of the provinces to submit proposals for development. The CO did not provide much guidance, nor did Bourdillon provide his Residents guidelines on how to proceed. In turn, the Residents asked for statements of needs from the departments, district officers, etc.

These initial proposals were ambitious and not very well planned. However, they began a process of thinking within the Nigerian colonial state on how to make effective use of the financial resources available through the 1940 Colonial Development and Welfare Act. The lack of guidelines from the metropole and within the colonies is evidence of the novelty of this new approach. Britain had no experience with the long-term planning that the Act envisaged.

In the middle of 1943, Gerard Clauson, a career civil servant in the CO, and Sydney Caine, an economist with colonial experience, were tasked with the responsibility of creating a committee that would advise the S of S on development in the colonies. This committee had the responsibility of bringing together "expert economists and important businesspersons with knowledge of colonial areas and put them in dialogue with the most competent young economic experts at the Colonial Office."[16] In September of 1943, the CO established the Colonial Economic Advisory Committee (CEAC) to advise the S of S on economic policy as it related to the colonial empire. It was only after the formation of this body that guidelines were written on development planning in the colonies. These guidelines encouraged the formation of colonial economic advisory committees.[17] In compliance with these new guidelines, the Nigerian colonial state established the Advisory Committee on Economic Development and Social Welfare in August of 1943. This committee, which was headed by T. Hoskyns-Abrahall, assisted in coordinating the different proposals that formed the bulk of the ten-year development plan.

At this time, Lagos was the administrative center of the Nigerian colonial state and it was only proper that the headquarters of this new committee would be located there. However, the vast size of the Nigerian territory demanded that planning needed to move beyond Lagos to the local level. Important contributions needed to be drawn from those who were at the frontlines of colonial administration, for they better understood the local needs or economic problems. For this reason, provincial development committees were established in each of the twenty-three provinces of Nigeria. These committees were comprised of both official and nonofficial members. The official members were heads of departments, while the nonofficial members, who were mainly Nigerians, were chosen by the Residents to represent the different interest groups.[18] The role of the provincial development committees was to "coordinate the activities of the various departments, reduce the workload of the Resident in matters relating to the Colonial Development Fund, make suggestions on projects and prepare schemes on its own initiative."[19] Engaging the heads of departments at the provinces and including some Africans in the committees reflected the idea that development should be from the bottom-up, representing the local needs and conditions.

The devolution of planning from the central administration to the provinces was an important step toward identifying and advancing schemes that reflected varying requirements. The Nigerian government even took the planning one tier below the provinces, creating the divisional development committees. A district officer or DO, as they were known in colonial parlance, chaired each committee. Members of this committee included "a few high-ranking chiefs, the District Officer, and senior officers of the Health, Agriculture, and Public Works Departments. The divisional development committee also involved interest groups, such as the Christian missions, foreign firms, and a few educated elites."[20] This bureaucratic structure was in place by the end of World War II, and most of these committees had submitted numerous proposals to the advisory committee in Lagos with the hope of benefiting from the 1940 CD&W Act. The development plan that Nigeria would enact in 1945 was a result of the proposals that originated from the provinces and districts in response to the 1940 Act. Much of the thinking embodied in these proposals stretched back to the 1930s when the colonial state started seriously considering development in response to the Depression. By the early 1940s, these initial ideas had gradually crystalized into development proposals as London began thinking about wartime production and postwar economic and social development.

Unfortunately, the war obstructed the full implementation of the 1940 Act. As the war intensified, London's attention turned toward winning the war and production in the colonies focused on supporting the war efforts. The colonies had to wait until after the war to continue planning as envisaged by the 1940 Act. Nevertheless, the provincial committees in Nigeria continued to formulate development proposals during wartime. The proposals that were formulated at this time were not based on any carefully thought out long-term development strategy. This approach to development planning would change as Nigeria began to plan for the postwar period. With this new approach, the plans were prepared at the departmental level and then subsequently coordinated. In a nutshell, this is how the plans were put together:

> Each department had accordingly been asked to put up a ten-year plan based on what it considered to be essential development in its own sphere. In order that there should be no departmental competition, no department except the Public Works Department was allowed to know the financial implications of the other departments' plans. There had been no question of allowing each Department a percentage of a given figure. The proposals were then co-ordinated and modified as necessary.[21]

Planning development was a serious endeavor for Nigeria and the different apparatuses of the colonial state were actively involved in the process. The belief was that development would help strengthen the economic position of Nigeria and guarantee Britain an extended colonial occupation. The commitment of the Nigerian officials guaranteed that Nigeria had an avant-garde approach to this new development enterprise.

THE 1945 ACT AND DEVELOPMENT PLANNING IN NIGERIA

While World War II slowed Britain's commitment to developing the territories, in Nigeria, the officials continued to craft policies and schemes to further development. The Nigerian colonial state intensified its focus on agricultural planning during this period as it saw expansive production as necessary to support the war efforts. As the tide of war ebbed, London's attention was again turned toward planning for development in the postwar period. As plans were underway in Parliament for the 1940 Act to be enhanced and updated, Nigeria was also envisioning ways in which its initial proposals could be modified and improved. In May of 1943, the governor of Nigeria, Arthur Richards, set up a central planning committee called the Advisory Committee on Economic Development and Social Welfare. This committee had the chief secretary to the government (CSG) as its chairman. Other members of the committee included the commissioners of each of the three regions, the financial secretary, the director of medical services, the director of education, the director of agriculture, the director of public works, the chief conservator of forests, the commissioner of labor, the director of veterinary services, and three members of the legislative council.

This committee had its first meeting in August of 1943 to plan postwar development in Nigeria and devised a seven-point agenda for development:

1. The settlement of ex-soldiers. Nigeria and many other British colonies had contributed soldiers to the war. It was important for the colonial state to plan for the engagement of these soldiers postwar, so that they wouldn't create "social unrest" in the colony as a result of joblessness. Implicit in this was the fear that the soldiers would rise up against British occupation of Nigeria. Their experience during the war taught them that colonialism had short-changed Africans and they, like their Asian counterparts, could form a new movement to liberate their people from the shackles of colonial rule. The Nigerian colonial state was being proactive in dealing with future problems that may be caused by these veterans. It was decided that the development branch of the colonial government, in conjunction with the department of labor, should find ways to engage them.
2. Rural land planning and development. The focus here was land utilization and degradation, land settlement, and irrigation. It was decided this would be handled by the provincial committees.
3. Economic development of livestock. They decided that the directors of agriculture and veterinary services would form a subcommittee to work on this.
4. Urban land planning. It was decided that the work already done on this in Lagos would be expanded colony-wide.

5. Mineral development. It was decided that all that was possible in this regard was already being achieved as part of the war efforts.
6. Secondary industries. This subject had already been taken up with the Resident Minister.[22] This included the examination of all works and schemes proposed by any department of government. The task of the development organization was to take all the different programs of postwar reconstruction and prioritize them and advise on applications for CD&W grants.[23]

Governor Richards also established a development committee in each of the twenty-three provinces of Nigeria. Following in the footsteps of Bourdillon, Nigerian officials, including Governor Richards, were excited about the new Act that was being debated in Parliament and wanted the machinery of development to be ready once the new Act was passed. A special department was created: the "Development Department." The department had the responsibility of conveying instructions from the central government to the chief commissioners and provincial committees and also providing them with assistance and information. F.E.V. Smith, a man who Governor Richards had great confidence in, was appointed to administer this department.

In September of 1944, Governor Richards sent the first set of development proposals to London. These were sent to the S of S, Colonel Oliver Stanley to enable him and his advisers prepare for F.E.V. Smith and H. E. Walker's visit to London.[24] Governor Richards' letter to the S of S that accompanied the proposals demonstrates his confidence in Smith and his eagerness to begin development in earnest under the new Act. He wrote: "Mr. Smith has been instructed that he has my full authority and a free hand to discuss and modify the proposals in any way necessary in order to reach agreement with your advisers, and I trust that it will be possible for him to return with a sufficiently definite approval of these plans for action to be taken locally at the earliest date."[25] It is obvious that Richards did not want the proposals to be caught up in the bureaucratic system he was very familiar with. He wanted these proposals to be discussed, modified, and approved quickly so that implementation could begin immediately after the war. The initial proposals emanating from Nigeria laid out plans for a fifteen-year period. Initially, the plans were to last ten years, beginning in 1945. This was adjusted to a fifteen-year period because the planners feared a shortage of staff in the postwar period and saw the necessity of building each service gradually, thereby leading to a longer completion period.[26] While the CO accepted the Nigerian fifteen-year proposals in principle, it made clear that the CD&W Act as envisaged could only cover ten years. It was suggested that the Nigerian proposals should be divided into three sections, each lasting for a period of five years. The CD&W funds would cover the first ten years of the program but the last five years would be dependent on assistance from the CO.[27] Three main areas were covered in these preliminary proposals of development: capital works, government services, and economic development. Projects that fell under capital works were water supply, roads, telecommunications, electricity, and the improvement of African housing. Under government services, there were to be expansions of medical, agricultural, veterinary, forestry, research, and social welfare services. For economic development, the emphasis was placed on the provision of adequate marketing services covering as many Nigerian products as possible.[28]

These proposals did not place much emphasis on economic development. The writers were aware of this weakness, but the deficiency was in line with colonial development policy during the second colonial occupation, during which social welfare was emphasized over economic development. This did not mean that economic development was excluded, but there were many officials both in the CO and in the colonies who believed that improving the social conditions of the colonial peoples was important for long-term economic development. For example, the Nigerian planners argued that it was important to have some basic social services in place otherwise it would be difficult to have a good economic plan. In a meeting with the Treasury in London, Smith argued that "The fundamental necessity was not so much development as welfare and spectacular development could not be looked for until the basic necessities of life had been provided; when this was done the productive capacity of the people as a whole could be improved and could be absorbed into some form of economic development."[29] On the other hand, Sydney Caine[30] and the Treasury wanted a greater emphasis on increasing production and economic growth. Caine argued that, in the past, development was brought about through private individuals who were economic prospectors. In the future, this was not going to be possible because of conditions of taxation and control of capital markets. This meant that the state had to undertake the role of economic prospectors. He wrote, "If it is going to do that effectively and intelligently, it must develop machinery for doing the economic prospecting which was formerly done by large numbers of private persons acting on their own account."[31] Caine's view of development was one that was mainly economic in character.[32]

Today, Smith's view would be associated with the basic-needs ideology, while Caine's views reflect neoliberal economic policies. Though Joseph Chamberlain was an imperialist who had no remorse about the exploitation of the colonial people, he championed colonial investments in basic needs. Smith's basic-needs viewpoint was in line with Chamberlain's ideology of constructive exploitation because, in order to unleash the productive capabilities of the colonial people, it was important that the populace be provided with basic needs. If the people were contented and prosperous, then more could be required from them, with positive economic impacts. On the contrary, Caine's view was that the foundation of development was economic growth and productivity. Through these, resources would be produced that would allow the colony to invest in social services such as education, health, etc. The question was, and still is: What comes first welfare or economic development? For Caine, it was economic development and for the Nigerian officials, it was welfare. While the outcome of both Smith and Caine's ideologies was the exploitation of Nigerians, it is worth noting that Caine's view of development was narrow. Without a strong educational and health system, you cannot have a strong economic system. His views did not take into consideration the long-term economic development of the colony.

In late September, while the CO was still discussing the Nigerians proposals, the Resident Minister, Noel Hall, sent a letter to the S of S endorsing the Nigerian development proposals. He considered the general framework of the plans as being sound.[33] Meanwhile, Smith and Walker arrived in London and several discussions were carried out with officials at the CO. By late October, discussions had reached a point at which certain decisions needed to be made. The deliberations had raised seven substantive issues that were to be decided upon: first, the approval in principle of the outline development proposals and the revised rough estimates; second, an agreement in principle that Nigeria would receive £27 million during the period between 1946 and 1956; third, the approval of the general principle that the CD&W vote would service loans collected by Nigeria for development during the years covered; fourth, the provision of £375,000 from the CD&W vote for the period from 1944 to 1946 to enable initial preparations in anticipation of the main schemes being approved; fifth, an approval for the establishment of a development commission; sixth, an agreement for the hiring of development officers to begin immediately and that their salaries be paid by the CD&W vote; and, seventh, an agreement on the establishment of a department of commerce and industries to help foster and finance local industries.[34]

NEGOTIATING DEVELOPMENT: LONDON VERSUS LAGOS

The seven issues raised at the meeting at the CO became points of negotiations between London (the colonial office) and Lagos (the Nigerian colonial state.) Though Governor Richards had already delegated his authority to Smith to discuss and modify the plans as was necessary, the S of S, who was present at the meeting, did not consider it necessary to have detailed discussions on the issues since the governor himself was going to be arriving in London soon. He wanted to reserve the detailed discussion and decision on the development proposals to when the governor was present. However, the S of S was impressed with the general design of the development framework presented by Nigeria and wanted it to be crafted comprehensively. Though the details of the discussions were supposed to be spared, what ended up happening could be described as detailed discussions after all.

In the course of the deliberations, Frederick Pedler[35], one of colonial officials, felt that there was a difficulty in justifying the allocation of £27 million to Nigeria. His reason for objecting was based on the total amount that was available for development in all the colonies. At this time, the S of S was planning to ask for £150 million for development. Allocating £27 million to Nigeria constituted 18 percent of the total CD&W funds. Given the size of Nigeria and its significance to the empire, that amount was not excessive. In justifying the sum, the S of S rightly pointed out that Nigeria represented a third of the colonial empire. The S of S also agreed that an application should be made for the provision of £735,000 to cover the initial preparations in anticipation of the main schemes.

The meeting also addressed the Nigerian administration's proposal to appoint a development commission. The administration argued that such a commission would secure continuity of policy. They wrote, "The existence of a statutory body would ensure that changes in policy were not lightly made with every change in tenure of the higher offices of Government. The Commission would also be able to watch over the transition of policy into action and to ensure that continuity was also maintained in spite of changes at lower levels. There would be the added advantage that a commission would possess the standing and authority necessary for dealing with the Chief Commissioners."[36] In the event, the S of S expressed doubts about the appointment of a statutory board. He did not find the continuity argument convincing. The members of the commission would be as subject to change as individual government officials. He also had questions about the relationship between this commission and the chief commissioners. This was because recent constitutional proposals from Nigeria favored regional decentralization. The proposed commission would actually create centralization and not decentralization, thereby causing bureaucratic bottlenecks. He also noted that creating such a board would lead to Nigerians clamoring for unofficial representation and this demand would be impossible to meet because Nigerians were incapable of seeing the interest of Nigeria as a whole. Sir George Gater[37] agreed with the S of S that such a commission was not necessary and that creating it outside of the secretariat would create administrative difficulties. His reasoning anchored on the fact that it would be impossible to separate new development from existing services. It was decided that a decision should be postponed until it could be further discussed with Governor Richards.

The final point of consideration at this meeting concerned the appointment of development officers. It was agreed that they should be appointed on a short-term basis without any promise of permanent appointment to the administrative service.[38] Though the local administrators knew the circumstances under which they operated better, the metropolitan government attempted to make these decisions. It is however important to note that they deferred some decisions until the arrival of the governor in London, because they wanted to take his viewpoint into consideration. This was in line with an earlier decision to bridge the gap between metropole and colonies, yet it was a departure from the spirit of the Act. During the debates, the CO had made it clear that their role would be advisory and not an attempt to micromanage development decisions in the colonies.[39]

Upon Governor Richards' arrival in London in November, a meeting was held to discuss Nigeria's preliminary development proposals. The S of S was pleased with the proposals from Nigeria. He "fully approved the general design of the Nigerian scheme which [he thought] was excellent. It was much better to prepare a comprehensive framework on those lines within which detailed schemes could be co-ordinated subsequently than to continue to submit un-correlated small-scale schemes for individual projects."[40] The development proposals that Nigeria submitted and were under consideration required an assistance of £55 million to cover the fifteen-year period. When it was concluded that the CD&W Act would only cover a ten-year period, and after discussions between the CO and Smith, the financial cost of the proposals were readjusted. The S of S gave a general approval for the sum of £27 million from the CD&W vote. Nigeria was to finance a further £8 million through loans. The loans were expected to cover projects that would become self-supporting. The £27 million approved also included the annual charges on the loans covering the initial five years. A total of £35 million was approved for the projects which were to be financed through the CO. Nigeria was also to make a substantial contribution to the development of the colony through its own funds. It was to provide financing for the development of ports and marine, inland water transportation, postal service, police, labor, part of the geological survey, some administrative service, housing and pensions of African staff, accounting, audit, and African clerical services needed for the program.[41] The goal was that by the end of the ten-year period, Nigeria would be in a position to continue to fund the recurring commitments that the development program created.

Though the S of S gave his approval to the general outline of the Nigerian proposals, Governor Richards wanted more. He sought the approval of the S of S to have the general scheme published. He wanted to show the Nigerian public that colonial rule had brought them dividends. The rising influence of the nationalist movements and permeating influence of the local press were successfully convincing Nigerians that colonialism had no hopes for their future prosperity and that the key to progress was bringing an end to colonial rule. Publishing these schemes was a public relations move to suppress these agitations. The S of S agreed with him and said it was important for these proposals to be published as soon as possible because he thought of the Nigerian plan "as a model for comprehensive outline development schemes."[42] The S of S, however, told the governor that approval couldn't be granted at the present time because he had not settled the amount that would be made available in the 1945 CD&W Act with the chancellor of the exchequer. He also left open the possibility that the Nigerian plan could be scaled down if the Act did not make available the sums he had envisaged. It is important to note that all these discussions were taking place prior to the passage of the 1945 Act. The S of S was planning to ask for £150 million for development in the colonies for ten years. As we will see shortly, he was unable to secure that amount from the Treasury.

One issue left outstanding from the October meeting was the appointment of a statutory commission to oversee development in Nigeria. The governor, being aware of Gater's views on the statutory commission, decided to discuss it with him prior to the scheduled meeting with the S of S and other officials at the CO. Gater had expressed doubts about the value of such a commission even as he left open the possibility of a coordinating machinery that would oversee the development schemes. Governor Richards was able to come to an understanding with Gater and the idea of a statutory development commission was dropped. The governor said what he should have asked for was a development secretary that would be in charge of the whole development program and also a central coordinating committee that would have the development secretary as its chairman.[43] This position of secretary was an executive position with a considerable level of authority. These bureaucratic instruments that Nigeria was proposing to enable her to effectively carry out development were new to London. London had never done development like this before: investing significant metropolitan funds in the colonies for both social and economic needs spanning the period of a decade. That Nigeria was generating these ideas was evidence that the governor and his officials had been thinking about this for a while and were looking for an efficient way of carrying out development in the colony. As described earlier, the hesitancy of the CO to approving the statutory board requested by the governor hinged on the fact that such a board would create bureaucratic bottlenecks because constitutional developments in Nigeria had favored decentralization and not centralization. At the same time, it was important to have coordinating machinery in place to eliminate disparate and uncoordinated plans that might lead to unnecessary duplication and wastage of limited resources. Though the governor did not get his statutory board, he was willing to accept a committee with a significant amount of authority vested in Smith, his trusted ally. We can see here that good leadership is an act of compromises that enables the advancement of the agenda.

AFRICAN LABOR AND THE PROBLEM OF THE COLOR LINE

In his groundbreaking treatise on race, "The Souls of Black Folk," W. E. B. DuBois wrote that "the problem of the twentieth century is the problem of the color-line." Just as in America, race was very much a problem of colonialism in Africa. Colonial policies excluded Africans who were naturally confined by the colonial state to second-class status in their own land. Africans did not play important parts in the decision making, nor did they serve in the higher cadres of the colonial state. Even positions that did not require any advanced education were offered to Europeans while Africans who were qualified for these positions were excluded.

One of the major components of the Nigerian development plan was the appointment of development officers. Governor Richards saw them as an essential part of the development program. Smith thought that without them, it would be impossible to carry out development work in the provinces. While there were provincial development committees already in existence, the governor felt that there was need for development officers tasked with working out plans as well as seeing to their execution. These officers, who were to be appointed on a temporary basis, were to fill a gap that the administrative staff could not. The development officers, as envisioned by the Nigerian administration, had four principal functions: 1) to relieve administrative and technical staff of their routine duties; 2) to help with fieldwork in connection with local planning and execution of development schemes; 3) to supervise the execution of development schemes under the direction of the local administration or technical officers; and, 4) to train African staff in the duties of development officers.[44] The need for these development officers arose because it was estimated that there would be a dearth of European staff in Nigeria in the postwar period. In a memo, the Nigerian colonial government argued thus for the need for development officers:

> The administration lacks the resources in manpower under present conditions to deal with the vast amount of subordinate work, both in planning and the execution of plans, which will be required. It is already over twenty-five percent down on its established strength and will be further heavily depleted at the end of the war when large numbers of officers are due to retire. . . . It is clear therefore that it will take a considerable time after the war to bring the administration up to its necessary strength, even without taking into account any extra requirements for the development programme. It follows that, if adequate staff is to be provided in the immediate post-war period for the subordinate work on the planning and execution of development schemes, it will be necessary to resort to some other method of recruitment for the administrative service on a permanent basis.[45]

It was easier to fill the temporary positions of development officers than the administrative and technical staff positions. The net was to be cast as widely as possible to recruit the 100 development officers required. As wide as the net was, however, it was not wide enough to include Nigerians. Given that the war had not ended, the Nigerian colonial state believed that it was going to be impossible to recruit these men, as they were still on active duty. Thirty-five men were needed immediately and so they looked to the United Kingdom for recruitment. There was a general agreement between the CO and the Nigerian officials on the need to hire development officers. The only area of concern was that the CO thought the title of "development officer" was not ideal, yet it could not come up with another title that would be attractive enough to encourage good men to apply for the position.[46]

The qualifications for a development officer were set very low so that many European men would be attracted to apply. The Nigerian colonial government was looking for men of "good background and intelligence, with initiative, honesty and the ability to follow single instructions."[47] In Smith's earlier memorandum to the CO, he had given the qualifications outlined for a development officer as "a man of good background, preferably with a liking for a country life, but not necessarily possessing the full academic qualifications which would be required for permanent appointment."[48] Though the qualifications were low, Africans were not a major consideration. This was acknowledged in the memorandum as thus: "This work should properly be very largely entrusted to Africans, but at present there are exceedingly few suitably qualified Africans available."[49] Were there really too few Africans who could meet these basic qualifications? By the early 1920s, there were many Nigerians who had certificates from colleges and were teaching or engaged in other occupations in the colony. The compensation and benefits package was clearly designed with Europeans in mind. The answer to this disparity lies in the pervasive racial color bar that was indicative of the colonial state. In reality, many of the Europeans who were about to be recruited into this cadre of service actually lacked the prerequisite qualifications. The CO had agreed that Nigeria should cast a wide net and recruit development officers of a variety of "types." The intention was that some of these officers would be absorbed into the administrative service, and the government was willing to provide them the financial assistance they needed in order to obtain the academic qualifications for this type of service.[50]

This was a consideration that was not extended to Nigerians. Nigerians with a basic education could have been recruited and trained to obtain the necessary qualifications. However, the plan was that the European officers would teach the Africans the duties and then eventually hand over responsibilities to them at the end of their ten-year temporary appointment. The requirements stipulated that the development officer was to be from a good background, intelligent, able to take initiative, be honest, and follow a single instruction.

It is inconceivable that in 1945 Nigeria did not have one hundred people, or even thirty-five, who met these basic criteria. The job did not require any advanced degrees. The Nigerian administration's idea was also to bring some European men from the ranks of those who had served during the war with the West African troops. There were 243,550 members of the Royal West Africa Frontier Force during World War II and Nigeria contributed a majority of the soldiers. The British officials did not see fit to recruit some of these Nigerian troops who had fought alongside the British during the war and demonstrated their patriotism to the British Empire through their willingness to die in battle. Some of these returning troops would have been the most ideal candidates for the job of development officers. Yet no serious debate or consideration was given to this possibility. That the British officials in Nigeria opted for Europeans was not because of the dearth of suitable candidates for the position of development officers in Nigeria, but because of a racial ideology that claimed Africans were incapable of the most basic tasks, such as following a simple instruction. As a result, less educated and qualified Europeans were soon given jobs involving training Africans in the most basic tasks; tasks which Africans could obviously carry out without any education or assistance.[51]

The systemic racism that was inherent in the colonial state created a paradox for colonial development. While the development plans encompassed some ideas that could have potentially done a lot of good for the colonies, the racial limitations of colonial rule incapacitated these plans and hindered them from becoming successful. By limiting and underutilizing human capital for the simple reason that it belonged to the black race, the colonial state was invariably undercutting the fundamental key to sustainable development. In light of the historical trajectory at this time, the decolonization movement that was in its early years, and Britain's desire to hold onto the colonies, colonial development became a contradiction. The nexus of colonial development was the empowerment of the people in the colonies to realize their full potentials and for the colonies to become self-supporting. However, if the colonies achieved this potential, there would be no need for the expert services of the colonial state that saw the colonies as children in need of a mother's tutelage. The question then becomes: Is it possible to have colonial development without self-determination? It was the attempt to maintain this balance that made the colonial state limit and restrict the development of local human resources even when it knew that those resources were vital to the success of the development project.

DEVELOPMENT AND INSUFFICIENT FINANCIAL RESOURCES

The meetings and negotiations that were held between the Nigerian officials and the CO were in anticipation of the cabinet agreeing to increase the funds for colonial development. In November of 1944, Colonel Oliver Stanley submitted to the cabinet a request for a substantial increase in funding for colonial development. Stanley's appeal to the cabinet was couched in terms of the future prospects of the empire. His argument echoed those made by Joseph Chamberlain four decades earlier: that Britain should invest in its "imperial estates." Like Chamberlain, Stanley believed that the development of the colonies would determine Britain's future in regards to its empire. The colonies not only contributed substantially to the war, but they were now needed to help Britain's economic recovery. Stanley believed it was the wrong time for Britain to give up the colonies and the only way that Britain could sustain its empire was to carry out the work of social and economic development. Stanley argued that the war had two effects on colonial policy: first, it "increased our awareness of past deficiencies in our administration" and second, it greatly raised the colonial populations' aspirations for improved conditions, in particular those who, "in one branch or another of the Armed Services, have been enjoying a standard of living to which they have never been accustomed before [and] . . . have travelled thousands of miles from their native villages."[52]

The Nigerian soldiers, like those from other colonial territories, were returning home from the war to face deplorable social conditions. Before the war, development work had been mostly neglected in the colonies as a result of the Great Depression and substantial investments were now needed. As the CO acknowledged, during the economic depression of the 1930s, the small numbers of staff were further cut and services had been so reduced that they could only maintain present infrastructure and institutions. Though development was historically slow in the colonies, during the Depression, it was "practically eliminated."[53] The second problem Stanley anticipated was one that played out in India. Most of the soldiers, who had served in the war returned home to the same conditions they had left and, having enjoyed a better standard of living in Europe while in service, started agitating for freedom from British rule. As Yasmin Khan writes, "Troops housed in one camp twenty miles from Delhi, 'had become accustomed to a new standard of living in Germany . . . some had the conviction that they were coming to a free India' and others wrote to the newspapers."[54]

Stanley's proposal for extensive development in the colonies had a dual function: the improvement of the lives of the colonial people and the maintenance of the empire. To achieve this, he requested £150 million and an extension of the Colonial Development and Welfare Act for another ten years. Given the economic hardship that Britain was experiencing, the chancellor of exchequer agreed to only £10 million a year, plus an additional £1 million a year for research, making the total sum £110 million over ten years. Stanley argued that the colonies were worth the investments and that Britain stood to benefit either directly or indirectly from colonial development in the form of exports. He was of the view that Britain needed the Commonwealth and empire if it hoped to play a major role in world affairs. Winston Churchill agreed with the chancellor of exchequer. However, the cabinet decided that Stanley and the chancellor of exchequer would have to work out a compromise. In December of 1944, they reached a compromise of a total sum of £120 million over ten years with a maximum of £17.5 million to be used in any one year.[55] As Michael Havinden and David Meredith have noted, there was no rationale for Stanley requesting £150 million or accepting £120 million. Given the economic circumstances Britain was in, these figures just seemed like whatever the cabinet would be willing to approve.[56]

If Stanley wanted to carry out a strategic policy of social and economic development of the colonies, as he seems to portray in his statement, asking for £150 million and accepting £120 million even before the needs of the colonies were clearly assessed was akin to putting the cart before the horse. The more sensible approach would have been to let the colonies draw up their plans within broad financial guidelines, have the CO study these plans, restructure them, cost them, and then make a request to the cabinet for the money needed to execute them. The CO was requesting only £150 million for the development of the colonies when the Nigerian plans alone amounted to £55 million. In the end, Nigeria received £23 million from the fund; this was clearly insufficient considering the social and economic needs of the colony. Due to limited financial resources, development was concentrated mostly in the urban areas. The rural areas were only marginally touched through services such as agricultural extension and mobile medical clinics. The development plans did not invest heavily in capital-intensive projects such as building a nationwide electricity grid. For example, for the first five years of the plan, only £355,000 was earmarked for electricity. In Nigeria's 1962 plan, for example, the Kainji Dam electrical project alone received an allocation of £68.1 million. This one project was higher than the estimated cost of Nigeria's 1945 development plan. Thus, in addition to the racial biases and limitations of the colonial state, insufficient financial resources were a major deficiency of these plans.

BUREAUCRATIC STRUCTURES AND THE EXCLUSION OF AFRICANS

The agreement on the amount dedicated to colonial development by the cabinet paved the way toward the passage of the 1945 Act by Parliament. Parliament passed the Act in April of 1945. With its passage, the different British colonies were asked to submit a ten-year plan of development. This was the first time there was a systematic long-term development planning in the colonies. Nigeria was ahead of the other colonies in the drafting of its plan. Its proposals had even received a preliminary acceptance by the CO before the 1945 Act was passed.

As noted earlier in this chapter, it was agreed in late 1944 that there was no need for the creation of a statutory development board in Nigeria, but that there should be a coordinating committee with the development secretary as its head. However, in March of 1945, Governor Richards sent a letter to the S of S informing him that he had set up a new bureaucratic agency, called the Central Development Board. This board had the responsibility to consider, coordinate, and recommend all development projects to the government. He wrote, "Its main function will be to deal with overall development and to be the clearing house for recommendations coming forward from the Provincial Development Committees through the three Area Development Advisory Committees in order to ensure that a reasonable series of priorities should be set up for the whole of the territory."[57]

Richards' proposal for a development board met with stiff resistance and criticism in London. At the CO, D. J. Parkinson wrote a memorandum in which he disagreed with the arguments advanced by the governor for the new board. In his proposal, Richards explained that he used the title of "Board" for his new central organization rather than the title of "Committee" to distinguish this organization from the area and provincial committees and also because of the function this group would play. Parkinson disagreed with this reasoning. He wrote, "It appears from the explanation of the Board's functions, as described in the saving telegram, that they bear practically the same relation to the Area Development Committees as the functions of the latter do to the Provincial Committees; and if the central organisation is in fact the topmost of a hierarchy of committees, the introduction of a new name would seem more confusing than otherwise."[58] The function of the new board was essentially the same as that performed by the area development committees. It would have been more appropriate to retain the title of committee since people were already familiar with the role played by the area development committees. The governor was attempting to grant this new organization the kind of authority that the committees did not have.

Parkinson's objection to this new board was motivated by the racial limitations of the colonial state. He argued that by publicizing the names of this new board, there would be an immediate demand for unofficial African representation. Membership on this board, as envisioned by the governor, was not to include Africans. The governor's reasoning was that there were no Africans capable of viewing Nigerian interests as a whole. This argument reduced Nigerians to "tribalists" who were backward and could not think in terms of their own national interest. This argument would prove to be erroneous when the different regions fought together to end colonial rule. Parkinson was not convinced of the governor's rationale for excluding the Africans. While he conceded that the argument might be true, it was not sellable for several reasons. Firstly, two Nigerians were already on the executive council of Nigeria, on whose advice the governor legislated for Northern Nigeria. The second reason that Africans possibly would not find this argument convincing was the fact that the finance committee of the legislative council already had African representation. This committee had the important task of passing supplemental expenditures in excess of the ordinary estimates. Parkinson wrote, "If it is possible to arrange for the unofficial element in the Legislature to exercise control over the ordinary expenditure of the colony, it should also be possible to arrange for the Legislature to exercise control over development expenditure, which in the future is going to form a very considerable portion of the colony's budget."[59] Since the governor had already publicized the names of the members of the board in connection with the statement on development, Parkinson thought the damage had already been done, but left open the possibility of further discussion with the governor when he returned to London in the summer of 1945. The other staff at the CO agreed with Parkinson and so the board had to stand as conceived by the governor.[60] This was a case in which the governor twisted the arm of the CO to follow his bidding. By publishing the names of the board ahead of any consultation with them, they were forced to accept his decision.

The creation of this board ushered in a new bureaucratic structure, one that was different from the structure in place since 1943. Three area development advisory committees replaced the central advisory committee. Their task was to screen the recommendations made by the provincial committees and to advise the chief commissioners. The three committees were located in the three regions of the country: the western region, the eastern region, and the northern region. Governor Richards created the central development board, which was similar to the central advisory committee. The only difference was that Africans were excluded as members of this committee, although the governor offered a nonracial rationale. The reason he gave for omitting Africans was that it would be difficult for the central advisory committee to have regular meetings given that African representatives from all parts of the country would be represented. It would take time for them to travel and be present at these meetings. For the governor, this would render the work of the committee ineffective because the committee wouldn't be able to meet as regularly as it should. Parkinson disagreed with this reasoning. He said, "I do not see that it should be any more difficult for an African unofficial to get down to Lagos than for the Chief Commissioner."[61]

Given the unique role that the central development board played as the body vested with the authority to determine which development projects received funding and which ones were rejected, it is worth identifying the makeup of the board. This board had the development secretary as the chairman, the three chief commissioners of development, the financial secretary, and the director of public works. None of the six members of this powerful board were Nigerians. In addition to the reasoning mentioned earlier, the governor also claimed that Africans from the northern region of the colony would need to be appointed, and again, it would be difficult to summon them to meetings at short notice due to distance. The governor's solution to the question of African participation in development planning was to increase their presence at both the provincial and district levels. At this time, the total membership of the provincial development committees was 467, and of these, only 80 were Nigerians and these were nonofficial members. The reason for the small number of Nigerian members was owed to the fact that the committees were principally made up of official members and there were no senior African officials. The colonial state's rationale for choosing official members was "the necessity for having the technical advice which only these Government officers are able to provide."[62]

This argument for a limited number of African members in the provincial development committees is far from convincing. Just as there were many qualified Africans in the 1920s, by 1945, there were numerous Africans who had degrees from Europe and America and had returned to work in Nigeria. There were men like Nnamdi Azikiwe who studied in the U.S. and returned to Nigeria in the early 1930s to be a newspaper publisher, and Herbert Macauley who studied civil engineering in England in the 1890s and had a brief stint working for the colonial state in Lagos. These two men's growing distaste for colonial rule and its exploitation of Africans forced them to co-found the National Council of Nigeria and the Cameroons, a nationalist movement that fought for Nigeria's independence. Besides these Western-educated elites, there were some Africans that were locally trained in different technical skills and were also trained as teachers. A broad section of the African populace could have been engaged in these development committees in order for them to represent the interests of the local people. That the Africans were not involved in larger numbers on these committees shows how deeply ingrained the colonial ideology of European superiority was. The lack of presence of Nigerians, both on the area development committees and on the central development board, shows that despite Governor Richards's rhetoric that he was interested in more Nigerians being actively part of the development process, he did not want them to be able to make majority decisions on projects they felt would be more beneficial to them. Africans were excluded from both the middle and higher echelons of decision making, not because they were unqualified, but because the colonial state did not want the Africans to challenge their decisions.

One may erroneously argue that the colonial officials were right to make decisions on the development projects since they were administering and paying for them. This argument is not plausible because the projects were not a handout from a generous "mother nation" to Nigeria. Nigeria paid for a substantial portion of the projects and the loans that were subscribed for the projects were collected in Nigeria's name. Between £10 and 11 million was to be contributed to the development plans from Nigerian revenues and £16–17 million borrowed by Nigeria. The CD&W fund was to account for £23 million of the expenditures for development. Given that Nigeria was paying for a substantial part of the projects, a cross-section of Nigerian people, ranging from the Western-educated elites, to teachers and farmers, should have been given more seats at the development table to determine the projects that would be most beneficial to their people. This point cannot be overemphasized because it is a problem that continues to plague development planning both in Nigeria and other African nations, South of the Sahara. So often it is the foreign nation providing development "aid" that determines what projects it believes the country needs in order to improve their living conditions and the economy. These projects usually require the recipient country to provide a percentage of the cost of the project. In this way, the country is made to pay for projects that may not be immediate priorities, but which they may find difficult to reject because of the generous grants or aids provided. Today, remnants of equipment can be found throughout rural Nigeria from the many abandoned schemes that were imposed upon the local people by outsiders who wrongly believed the schemes were going to bring about development in these rural communities.

APPROVAL AND FUNDING OF NIGERIA'S 1945 PLAN

The development bureaucracy that had taken shape in Nigeria prepared a plan that was to be submitted to London for approval. In the initial discussions with the CO, the emphasis was on getting approval for the different projects that would become the Nigerian plan. No single "Nigerian Plan" document existed; however, approval was sought for a general framework.[63] The different schemes and projects that were approved by London would become the Nigerian development plan itself. In July of 1945, the Nigerian plan received a general approval from the CO. The letter of approval read, "We are in general agreement with the main outlines of the revised plan, which provides for a total expenditure over the ten years ending March, 1956, of about £56 million, of which total it is proposed that sums of the order of £16 million should be found from Nigerian revenues, £17 million from the proceeds of public loans, and £25 million from grants and loans under the Colonial Development and Welfare vote."[64]

Though a general approval was given, due to the requirements of the CD&W Act, Nigeria still had to get the approval of the CO for schemes that had received prior approval for shorter periods and that now had to be extended for the ten-year period. Such schemes from Nigeria included the proposals for agriculture, veterinary, health, forestry, and roads. The governor and the development secretary wanted to present the Nigerian plans to the legislative council in November of 1945.[65] They wanted to present them in installments as "Sessional Papers" because they felt that waiting to present one large volume containing all the different schemes might be indigestible to the members. Since the plans had between twenty and twenty-five major schemes in them, their strategy was to issue two or three plans confidentially each week. Smith sought approval for the pending major schemes as well as permission to release the plans in installments.[66] Officials at the CO told Smith, "We entirely agree that descriptions of approved schemes may be communicated to members of Legislative Council as they are ready and not be kept back till full development plan has been finalized. We should be glad to have up to 6 copies of each sessional paper as these are issued."[67] While Smith was given the approval to present these plans as sessional papers, he did not receive approval for some of the major schemes that were to be part of the Nigerian development plan. In the meantime, Governor Richards had taken annual leave and G. C. Winteley was acting on his behalf. In September, Winteley requested that the CO provide approval for the outstanding schemes because they could not draft the full ten-year plan without first having approval from them. His argument was that the members needed to receive the full plan with the total financial implications by the first week of November at the latest, otherwise the members would accuse the government of stampeding the council with financial issues.[68]

In a meeting at the CO later in September of 1945, the outstanding applications for health, agriculture, forestry, veterinary service, and roads were discussed with the goal of granting the approval sought by Winteley. Several points were raised during the meeting. The applications that were submitted by Nigeria did not have identifiable schemes. It was felt that by approving these applications, the CO was signing away very large grants to Nigeria, creating a later difficulty in identifying which services the money was spent on. The feeling was that it was preferable to have grants go to specific projects. The five applications sought a grant of £7.5 million over ten years. In the agricultural application, for example, £750,000 was allocated to "other charges." Members present at the meeting had serious concerns with figures like this.

Another issue raised was the payment of European staff with the CD&W grants and the payment of African staff by Nigeria. They foresaw that there would be problems at the end of the ten-year period when, suddenly, the Nigerian government would assume the payment of these European staff. That would potentially place severe stress on the Nigerian budget. Caine's opinion at the meeting was that CD&W grants toward the expansion of staff should be given in the form of a percentage. The Nigerian budget would assume a percentage of the cost while the CD&W grants would assume the other part. Over the years, the percentage of the CD&W's grant would be gradually reduced so that by the end of the ten-year period, Nigeria was paying the salaries of the entirety of the staff. In this way, the Nigerian budget would not be suddenly hit by a heavy recurrent expenditure for staff. This procedure had already been followed in a scheme that had been approved for Jamaica.[69] They prepared a draft letter to be sent to Smith stating that the schemes would be framed on a percentage basis. The letter was first to be approved by others present at the meeting and also shared with the Treasury for their views.[70]

Meanwhile, Governor Richards had returned to Nigeria from his annual leave and in a message to the CO reiterated the urgency in approving the outstanding schemes. He wrote, "Unless outstanding schemes can be disposed of at once, so that writing of draft full plan can proceed immediately, there will be insufficient time for this draft to be sent to you for approval and to be put in print by the first week in November, which I consider to be the latest date for the circulation to members if the Legislative Council is to meet on 10th December."[71] Neither the governor nor the development secretary was aware of the fact that there were discussions in the CO in late September about changing the procedure for funding the Nigerian plan. Given that Richards and Smith had discussed extensively with the CO and had even revised the plans according to their requests, Richards was anxiously expecting an approval so that he could present the plans before the legislative council.

The proposal to award the grant on a gradual percentage basis was changing everything at a very late stage in the negotiations. Parkinson was very critical of this decision and felt there wasn't enough time for Smith to recast and resubmit five of his most important schemes. Smith and the governor had only one month before the date they were supposed to present the plans to the members of the legislative council. Parkinson stated that the agricultural plan that drew much of the criticisms from the members was first submitted in June of 1944 and was fully discussed with the CO's agricultural adviser. After further discussions with the development department at the CO and the Treasury, it was revised and resubmitted in July. The same was true of the forestry plan, which had been revised and resubmitted in July of 1944 and likewise the medical plan, which had been revised and resubmitted. Parkinson felt that Smith was expecting an approval with only minor modifications. He said that it would be a huge shock to Smith if he received a letter outlining radical modifications on the way grants were going to be given for the development plans. Parkinson found the arguments for funding on a graduated percentage basis unconvincing. He pointed to the earlier approval of development officers and preliminary expenditure on medical and health services, which had provided for an expansion of staff with funds entirely from the CD&W grants without any objections. He also did not see any practical advantages for the graduated percentage, as the agricultural plan, for example, only called for a steady expansion of staff, combined with a proportionate increase of expenditure on other charges. He wrote:

> We do not object either to the total expenditure proposed for agriculture, or to the total amount to be provided from C.D. and W. schemes, or to the object on which the money is to be spent. . . . Our objection is to the way in which it is proposed to apply the C.D. and W. assistance. But even if the whole of the expenditure was met from C. D. and W. Funds in the early years, the money thereby saved to Nigeria would only have to be devoted to meeting the increasing deficit in the later years, as the C. D. and W. assistance tapers off, and at the end of the ten year period Nigeria would presumably be in exactly the same position financially as if the assistance had been provided as originally proposed.[72]

Parkinson recommended that Nigeria must be clearly advised on what they needed to do and the advantages of the new proposal.

Sir George Gater, while not disputing the wisdom of the new proposal, agreed with Parkinson that it was going to be a shock to Smith and may evoke a tremendous outburst from both Smith and the governor. Like Parkinson, he argued that the agricultural scheme was discussed with the agricultural adviser, Dr. Harold Tempany, and revised to his approval and full support. It was also discussed with the representatives of both the finance and development department and the Treasury and no objections were raised. Given the process this had undergone, Smith would have grounds for complaints. His suggestion was that the Nigerian plan should be accepted as it stood with provisions for some additional safeguards, since it required expenditures of money from the CD&W fund.[73] These discussions, disagreements, and decisions reveal that there was no clear process on how development should proceed in the colonies. As the country at the forefront of the enterprise, Nigeria made itself an experimental theater for the development ideas that were being concocted in both colony and metropole.

In October of 1945, the S of S sent a letter to Governor Richards granting approval for the basic proposals for the outstanding schemes. He did, however, inform Richards that modifications had been made to the precise form in which the assistance was to be given and also that there would be variations in the distribution of the funds between different services and over different years. Caine communicated the details of these modifications to Smith.[74] His letter anticipated Smith's likely reaction. From the outset, Caine informed Smith that although they had talked about the development plans before, they had to take another careful look at the applications. This was because of the magnitude of Nigeria's development plans in relation to those of the other colonies. Given the scale of Nigeria's plans, it was only prudent that the details of the schemes should be scrutinized. Two major applications that Caine identified were agriculture and forestry, which had something in common. In both areas, all the grants requested from the CD&W funds were for emoluments and recurrent charges in connection with the expansion of staff. While Caine believed that the funds requested for these applications were acceptable, he did not think that the method proposed for the use of these funds was the right one. He found two main difficulties with this. The first was that this amounted to handing a blank check to Nigeria and that wouldn't be a fulfillment of their responsibility to Parliament. The second was with Nigeria suddenly assuming these financial responsibilities at the end of the ten years, when CD&W grants would have been exhausted. He believed that this would create great difficulties for Nigeria. Caine suggested two solutions to these difficulties:

> The first is that C.D. & W. grants towards recurrent charges in these two applications (agriculture and forestry) ought, as far as practicable taper off towards the end of the ten year period, so that the transference of the residual is less burdensome. (This need not affect the total assistance, but only its distribution in time.) The second is that the C. D. & W. assistance might be given not to cover the full cost of the salaries and incidental charges for certain classes of new employees, but to cover a proportion, of the cost of all the new staff required for the development of these departments.[75]

Caine went on to suggest to Smith that these two schemes, together with all new applications for grants that involved the expansion of staff, had to be amended so that the grants would only go toward a percentage of the staff salary, while the rest would be assumed by the colonial state. The percentage should be graduated over the ten-year period with it peaking in the middle years and then beginning to drop toward the tenth year. At the end of the tenth year, Nigerian revenues should be fully paying for the staff. The amount of assistance that Smith had proposed was not changing, just the procedure by which this assistance was to be given.

While Caine's argument may sound logical, it did not take into consideration the economic power that came from investing such large sums in agricultural development at the initial period. Caine's main issue was distinguishing between "productive" and "recurrent" costs. He did not think that CD&W funds should pay for recurrent costs, because this was unsustainable and would create dependency on London. He wanted Nigeria to cover such costs. It is important to note that the Nigerian colonial government was not attempting to shift recurrent costs to London. It wanted to frontload resources, build up its agricultural extension services, and hire colonial personnel to help stimulate agricultural production. Their end goal was to generate the revenues that would be needed by the state to continue and expand development many years after the plan came to an end. Expanding agricultural staff was a pathway to expanding agricultural production, as it was the main source of Nigeria's revenues. Unlike some other colonial regions, Nigeria did not have large-scale industrial agricultural production. It was reliant on peasant agriculture. This system by its very nature required plenty of agricultural staff who offered extension services to expand production. By frontloading resources, the expansion of staff had the potential to expand production, placing Nigeria in a better economic position to absorb the staff at the end of the tenth year, without placing undue burden on Nigeria's budget or on the metropolitan government. This was one of the major strengths of this plan.

AFRICAN AGENCY

Although Africans did not receive proper representation in the development committees and in the central development board, they were still able to shape the development plan through the pressure that they exerted on the colonial state. The colonial officials in Nigeria were conscious of the reaction of the people to the development proposals. For example, five days after Smith received Caine's letter modifying the funding for the projects, he sent his own response to Caine arguing that radical changes to the way assistance was to be provided would create difficulties. He wrote, "We have gone on the principle of maximum assistance in the earlier stages, expecting that taxability of the people would increase as the plan develops."[76] The expansion of production by the farmers meant increased revenue from the government through taxes. Nigeria was not in a financial position to provide the kind of assistance that Caine was suggesting. By adopting Caine's position, Nigeria had to borrow more money because it could not impose more taxes on the people. In order to borrow more money, Nigeria would have to look to London and, because of the postwar economic crisis and the pressure on the Sterling, borrowing from London was highly discouraged. Smith faced a political problem, which Caine may not have clearly understood or appreciated. He had to deal with the African unofficial members of the legislative council, as well as the African press, which was very critical of the moves made by the colonial state. In his letter to Caine, Smith informed him of some of the local political factors he had to deal with:

> The local press is already stating that the development plan is merely a means of manipulated use for money intended for the benefit of Dependencies to find jobs for more Europeans. As in the early stages, we shall have to use many

> Europeans to implement the plan until the training of Africans has been suitably increased, you will appreciate the difficulties I shall have in introducing the plan and getting it passed if we have to deal in vague terms. In fact, we may very easily lose the present confidence of the Council completely in such circumstances, as Unofficial Members will be heavily bombarded by the press on the racial aspects, which are now becoming very pronounced.[77]

It was in Nigerian colonial state's interests to be seen as rapidly developing the colony. Though not completely altruistic, postwar development was a genuine attempt to develop the colonies. While attempts were made to source technical officers such as irrigation engineers from Britain and Canada, Africans were not given the opportunity to receive the kind of training that they needed to assume the positions that were now vacant. This was one of the contradictions of colonial rule. Over four decades of colonial rule had restricted the education of Africans and confined them to the realm of perpetual subordination. The effective use of the mass media by the African intelligentsia to advance decolonization and the social unrest erupting from the grassroots, best symbolized by the "Aba Women's War of 1929," challenged the colonial state's aura of inevitability as they advanced policies that had an impact on the Africans. In crafting development policies, the colonial state knew that Africans could challenge such policies and create social unrests should they see these policies as aimed at furthering the exploitation of African resources. Thus, the colonial state had to take into consideration some of the opinions of the Africans and appear as much as possible to be acting in the interests of the colonial people.

The strong reactionary language that emanated from the African press was not coming out of a vacuum. It was a cry against a system that had subjugated the colonial people and kept them in a state in which if they did not free themselves, they would forever remain "hewers of wood and drawers of water." For example, Africans trained at the Yaba College of Technology were provided a secondary education that did not qualify them to assume the special opportunities that late colonial development afforded. That was an opportunity missed. Nigerians were forced to agitate for more control through trade unionism and the national press, such as the *West African Pilot*. The Trade Union Congress of Nigeria (TUC), founded in 1943, published a quarterly bulletin called *The Nigerian Worker*, demanding the representation of labor unions in the legislative council. In an attempt to capture the plight of the Nigerian worker and convert it to positive action, the TUC called for a general strike in 1945.

This strike, which had strong support from the National Council of Nigeria and the Cameroons (NCNC), linked the nationalists struggle with the labor movement.[78] The strike created grave doubts in the minds of many Nigerians about whether the intentions behind the colonial state's economic and development plans were well-meaning. Toyin Falola notes that many "derided the Ten-Year Plan as a bourgeois document. . . . The plan was interpreted as a design to exploit Nigerians, an afterthought to justify the transfer of wealth out of the country, and admission of guilt that the people had been cheated. In their own campaigns for attention, the politicians among the intelligentsia warned the masses not to expect any positive outcome from the plan."[79] This was the reality that Smith and Richards faced in Nigeria. The trade unions and the nationalist movements such as the NCNC, the Nigerian Youth Movement, and the Zikist movement were becoming more involved in the public sphere and while they embraced the idea of development, they tried to use it to demand rights.[80] As one Nigerian, J. K. Ladipo, the managing director of a mill at the time, wrote to the CSG:

> In the days of our forefathers the farmer was the life of the country, to-day he is a poor man, and the clerk, who draws his salary from his sweat, is the richer and better man comparatively speaking. And yet often times you have the courage to ask us to "go back to the land." Undoubtedly in order to become poor . . . as far as I can see it is no business of the Secretariat if Nigeria is in debt, as long as the officials can be paid out of loans from the outside world and they can retire when the time is due leaving us, the Nigerians to foot the bills afterwards.[81]

This was the sense of frustration that the Africans felt and the one the Nigerian officials had to deal with. Flooding Nigeria with so-called experts that were going to be paid with Nigerian revenues or loans borrowed in the name of the government of the colony was a hard sell. The British government committing the money ahead to pay for the expansion of staff would show their commitment to developing the colony. It could also quell the criticism that development in the colony was only a jobs program for Europeans paid for with Nigerian revenues. This was especially true since Nigerian taxpayers were footing a substantial portion of the development bill. Smith concluded his letter to Caine in these terms:

> In these circumstances, and after all the discussions which have taken place, I trust that you will not show such lack of confidence in local administration of development as to remove local discretion, which is essential to its satisfactory and proper implementation. Any vagueness on your part will be a serious hindrance, and it is obvious that we shall have to take the Council and Local Administrations fully into our confidence to get the plan approved and to ensure that it is properly put into effect.[82]

Caine responded assuring Smith that there was no lack of confidence in the local administration. London's concern was not to tie Nigeria down on a very rigid plan of development when they could not foresee future circumstances. He wrote, "Indeed, I think it might help in presentation to council if you took the line that Government is not asking the Legislature to commit itself at once to all details over a long period ahead but is submitting a general plan on which the Council can give a broad approval now while leaving scope for all concerned, including the Council itself, to suggest modifications as parts of the plan come up for approval in precise form."[83] Caine's plan was in no way more flexible than the Nigerian plan; in fact, the Nigerian plan was more flexible. The primary issue for Caine was that the approval of the Nigerian proposals without having the details of expenditures for every scheme amounted to handing a blank check to the Nigerian government. The officials in Nigeria, on the other hand, wanted flexibility by not tying themselves too much to specifics on the expenditures of the schemes. Caine was undercutting his own argument by claiming flexibility. At the heart of this was a dispute over who should control the development planning process: a struggle between the local administration and the CO.

THE RIFT BETWEEN THE COLONIAL OFFICE AND NIGERIA

The disagreement between Caine and Smith opened a rift between the CO and Nigeria. This was not surprising as some in the CO, such as Parkinson, had warned that Smith and Richards might not take kindly to the changes. In light of the correspondences between Caine and Smith, Richards decided to hold off releasing the plan to the legislative council until he was able to reach an agreement with Caine. He offered some revisions to the Nigerian plan to meet Caine's demands. For example, in the last four years of the plan, the CD&W vote would only provide for 4/5, 3/5, 2/5, and 1/5 of the recurrent charges in agriculture, veterinary, forestry, and health schemes. The governor, however, raised an important problem that might arise with regard to staff. He feared he might have difficulty engaging good staff for only a short term. He needed assurance from the S of S that assistance would continue beyond five years so that staff would be aware of reasonable prospects for ten years of employment. Another area of concern was the recruitment of engineers. Given the scarcity of engineers, it was important to enter into agreements with them that were as long as possible.[84]

In the CO, there were discussions about the Nigerian plans and J. B. Williams even wondered if Richards' conception of development planning was the same as that of the CO. He disagreed with the approach Nigeria was taking as regards their applications. He was critical of the governor's conception of development planning and he wrote, "Our own conception has been that colonies should draw up a broad overall plan of development which should be considered by the Secretary of State's advisers and approved with or without modifications and then detailed schemes covering particular pieces or work should be submitted within the plan and approved separately."[85] Here, the CO was attempting to exercise control over the development process approving every single project or scheme that Nigeria undertook. The Nigerian officials had a different conception. Though Nigeria had received a general approval for a comprehensive plan, the governor wanted to place individual schemes before the legislative council. This was where the disagreement lay. In Williams' view, individual schemes with their expenditures still had to be approved by the CO but the governor wanted a blanket approval covering the schemes for which the expenditures had not been discussed and approved by the CO. Williams found it inappropriate to grant the governor an approval to spend such a substantial sum without showing the specific schemes and their cost. This meant that neither the governor nor the development secretary would need any more authority from either the S of S or the legislative council to spend the money for the next ten years. He doubted if this procedure of giving the governor unfettered access to Nigeria's allocation was in accordance with the conditions that were laid down by the CD&W Act. The Act, he wrote, "lays down that the authority for expenditure is that the Secretary of State should make schemes with the concurrence of the Lords Commissioners of the Treasury."[86]

Williams also responded to Parkinson and Gater's criticism that these schemes had been discussed and revised with the governor and Smith. He wrote, "The understanding in my mind then was that we were being asked to approve merely the comprehensive plan as a whole and that individual schemes could be gone into on their merits and if necessary remodeled, nor was it clear that there was any particular urgency to approve schemes covering the whole of the ten years. It was certainly not clear to me at that time that the Nigerian Government wished to lay schemes in cut and dried form before the Legislative Council."[87] While being sympathetic to the views raised by Williams, Caine believed that not giving an approval in principle to the Nigerian plan would be tantamount to going back on their word. He disagreed with Williams that the proposed procedure to be followed by Nigeria would be outside the scope of the Act. Another important point made by Caine was that they were still experimenting with planning. He wrote, "We must recognize that we are still feeling our way towards the kind of procedure which will enable due account to be taken of long-term planning without holding off all action until the ideal plan is produced, which may take years."[88] Frank Stockdale[89] agreed with Caine that the Nigerian plans had gone too far to attempt to begin a new procedure.[90] Caine's point is an important one when looking at development planning during the second colonial occupation.

Occupation was the easiest part; the difficulty was the management of that occupation. In this case, the difficulty lay in how this developmentalist state had to function. No one had a crystal ball to see how they should develop the colonies. Though some form of development had taken place in the empire for years, this was the first attempt at long-term development planning. Those who were fashioning these policies were not themselves experts with many years of experience in the field. They were themselves learning on the job, in an attempt to respond to development problems in the colonies. Given this knowledge, we can excuse some of the failures of this occupation and must resist using outcomes to judge intentionality.

At the end of the day, the individuals involved at the CO could not decide on how to respond to the governor of Nigeria. On the one hand, they wanted to approve in principle the schemes that were already discussed with the governor and the development secretary; on the other hand, they did not want to give the governor the authority to spend CD&W funds on these schemes without detailed examination and approval of such schemes by the S of S. The idea was to have schemes emanating from the colonies fully examined and vetted by London. The approval sought by Nigeria did not allow this because the governor did not have full details on the schemes in question. Caine's view was that an urgent meeting needed to be held to resolve the problem. The problem this meeting sought to resolve was whether the previous correspondence with Nigeria constituted a commitment that could not be broken or whether "it is now desired to re-examine the whole position, in which case, of course, a suitable explanation would have to be given to the Governor with the direct authority of the Secretary of State."[91]

This meant the decision was moving from the civil servants to the politicians. In the meantime, important political changes had taken place in London. There was a new Labour government in power and a new S of S who was very supportive of development and wanted it to happen rapidly. At this time, Arthur Creech Jones was the parliamentary undersecretary of state for the colonies and George Henry Hall was the S of S. When Creech Jones discussed the matter with the S of S and the officials concerned at the CO, he came to the conclusion that the previous S of S, Oliver Stanley, had already made a commitment to Nigeria and the Nigerian plans were drafted based on that commitment. It was decided that the Nigerian plans should be approved in principle. Creech Jones felt that there was need for adequate technical advice and this was to be emphasized in the telegram sent to Nigeria to inform them of the decision.[92]

In the letter, written in November of 1945, the S of S told Governor Richards that he was prepared to approve assistance in principle to the schemes. He insisted that the approval was based on the condition that annual estimates must be presented and he reserved the authority to review the schemes and modify them as needed. This, he stated, would allow for flexibility. He wanted Richards to make clear to the legislative council the fact that he reserved the right to modify the approved schemes after annual reviews. He also insisted on the importance of using adequate expert advice on all schemes in which experts were not already available. In response to Richards' concern about development officers, the S of S said, "The fact that scheme has not been approved for whole period of their service should surely cause no more uncertainty in minds of officers concerned than the fact that funds for salaries of ordinary Colonial Government employees are voted annually and not for a whole period of their careers."[93] Agreement was reached between Nigeria and London and the governor was ready to present Nigeria's development plan to the legislative council.

In December of 1945 Governor Richards sent a confidential letter to the S of S informing him that that he would be placing the Ten Year Plan of Development and Welfare before the legislative council on December 12 or 13. Together with his letter were six copies of the plan. These additional copies were meant for distribution to the London press such as the *Times*. Richards did not intend for the legislative council to carry out a vote on the plan. The intention was for a motion to be taken to refer the plan to a select committee that consisted of both unofficial members of the legislative council and a few official members who were directly concerned. The select committee, which sat in January of 1946, had the task of considering the proposals in detail. A summary of the plan was also provided to the S of S for distribution to both the local press and the international press. This one-page summary broadly outlined the different schemes that would be carried out. It also noted that a suggestion had been made that a board be established for the purpose of providing the means of financing approved schemes of local development. Finally, it discussed the cost of the plan. The plan was estimated at "£55,000,000, of which £23,000,000 will be provided under the Colonial Development and Welfare Act, £16,000,000 to £17,000,000 will be raised by loans, and the remainder progressively found from Nigerian Revenues."[94]

The plan was presented to the legislative council in December of 1945. A resolution was unanimously adopted by the members of the council, who thanked His Majesty's Government for the generous contribution of £23,000,000 for the development of Nigeria. The resolution read:

> That this council accords its deep sense of appreciation for the very generous allocation to Nigeria of £23,000,000 from the money provided under the Colonial Development and Welfare Act and requests that His Excellency the Governor should convey to H.M. Government and the people of the United Kingdom, through the Secretary of State, the (?gratification) and thanks of this Council, as representing the people of Nigeria, for this most generous and important contribution to the development of this country.[95]

The governor sent the resolution as a telegram immediately to the S of S.

The plan that was presented to the legislative council was missing schemes from some important departments. The plan did not include agriculture, veterinary, forestry, and medical schemes. The reason for the absence of these schemes was because they had not received full approval. They had only been approved in principle and the plan only included schemes that had been approved fully by the CO. The plans had not received full approval because they were not ready; the reasons for this will be discussed in the next chapter.

In December of 1945 Smith sent the estimates of those schemes that had not received full approval to the CO. Of particular interest to this book is the agricultural scheme. The proposal called for the establishment of a 250-acre experimental farm in Yola, Adamawa province. This farm would be used to test both local and introduced crops such as cereals and roots. A small number of animals were also to be kept there for draft purposes. Another experimental farm of about 300 acres was to be established in Maiduguri. This was to be used in the experimentation of date palms with the view of introducing them in the Bornu province. These two farms were to be the headquarters of "touring Agricultural officers for the districts concerned who will be able to carry out further experimental and expansion work in the outlying area based upon the results obtained on these two farms."[96] Part of the proposal was also to experiment with livestock such as cattle and poultry.

Some of the agricultural schemes that were to be introduced in the Northern region of Nigeria required good drainage and irrigation systems. The problem at this time was finding an irrigation engineer who would join the colonial service, tour Nigeria, and train special officers on the extension of irrigation and drainage work. It was proposed that £10,000 be allocated for this work, including salary and buildings. Given the topography and geography of Nigeria, it is surprising that the plan only called for one irrigation engineer. Any serious agricultural scheme in Nigeria requires a lot of irrigation and drainage work. Nigeria has two seasons: the raining and dry season. During the dry season, the soil becomes very hard as a result of lack of rains. In order to plant crops, you have to be able to channel water to the land. During the raining season, some parts of Nigeria are prone to floods. The rivers overflow and wash away the crops. The water around farmlands has to be channeled properly to avoid the farms being flooded. The irrigation engineer that the proposal suggested was not to be brought in on a full-time basis. They were to do one or two tours of duty training others. The writers of the proposal were overly optimistic that a few days in a location was enough for an engineer to train the local officers on all they would need to know about irrigation and drainage.[97]

On the last day of December, Governor Richards officially submitted the estimates for the four plans to the S of S. He wanted an approval before the estimates were to be presented to the legislative council in February of 1946. The estimates only covered the period 1946/1947. In these estimates, forestry received £18,140, agriculture £61,040, veterinary £48,050, and medical and health services £102,610.[98] Given the economic importance of agriculture to Nigeria, one would expect that agriculture would receive the greatest allocation. In a sense, there was a financial bias against agriculture, because most of agricultural cash crops from Nigeria were not produced by big commercial farms but by smallholder farmers. In fact, at this time, there were no large colonial agricultural schemes. Most agricultural schemes were mainly for research and experimentation. The second point to consider is that the CD&W Act did not only emphasize economic benefits, but also the welfare of the people. Medical services at this time remained very scarce and the mortality rates were high. It was perceived to be more important to commit resources to combat tropical diseases and to provide general medical services, than to focus on agriculture.

In February of 1946 the CO sent a letter to the Treasury including the estimates and informing them of the general approval in principle of the Nigerian plan.[99] The CO was willing to have further meetings with the Treasury about the plan. Three days later, the CO again wrote to the Treasury requesting a general approval of the Nigerian estimates to enable the governor to have this information before the opening of the legislative council in March of 1946.[100] The Treasury went ahead to grant an approval in principle while it continued throughout 1946 to work with the CO on modifications to the Nigerian schemes.[101] The S of S also approved the outstanding schemes in principle and informed Governor Richards that he may have to deal with some details later, particularly certain salaries.[102] Richards did not find any problem with later changes after the legislative council had approved the estimates. He pledged that these could always be carried out by an administrative control of expenditure.[103]

The Nigerian legislative council approved the "Ten Year Plan of Development and Welfare for Nigeria" later in February of 1946. It had first been presented to the council in December of 1945 and was immediately referred to the select committee. This committee met in January and presented their report to the legislative council on February 7, 1946. The council unanimously accepted the committee's report and the resolution of the legislative council read:

> Be it resolved: That this council adopts the Report of the Select Committee appointed to consider the Ten-Year Plan of Development and Welfare for Nigeria set out in Sessional Paper No. 24 of 1945 and approved the Plan as amended by the Select Committee and recommends its acceptance as the general development policy of the Government of Nigeria for the next ten years, subject to

> periodic review of details in the light of experience and the inclusion of such additional schemes as may prove to be necessary as the result of unforeseen circumstances.[104]

The last part of the resolution provided the flexibility that the S of S needed in order to make adjustments to the plan. Richards was happy with the fact that all the unofficial members commented on the desirability of the plan. This was important to the governor because he was afraid these members would be critical of the plan and incite the Nigerian press against it. Richards said that throughout the debate every unofficial member took part and they saw the plan as "a thoroughly constructive piece of work and a clear indication of the desire both of His Majesty's Government, through the generous allocation to Nigeria . . . to ensure that this country should be developed as rapidly as possible."[105] For Richards, this was a big win and he could not wait to share the Nigerian plan with all the colonial governors.

CONCLUSION

By focusing solely on the correspondences and discussions between colonial officials in Nigeria and London, this chapter reveals certain problems with development planning in the late colonial period. The British wanted to develop the colonies, but they did not have a coherent plan on how to go about it. They had to rely on ideas that originated from the colonies or generated by the colonial officials in London. After asking the colonies to draw up development plans for a ten-year period, about halfway through implementation, the CO asked that they be changed to five-year plans because of the difficulties of planning for a ten-year period. It is easy to look at the failure of these development plans and question the intentions of Britain to truly improve the conditions of the colonies. These efforts were genuine attempts to develop the colonies after many decades of neglect. However, the intensive efforts to develop the colonies when they were gradually slipping from their control as a result of the decolonization movement could be likened to a second colonial occupation in which Britain attempted to extend the life of its empire by appeasing the colonial people with basic social services and infrastructures. In the first colonial occupation, the agenda of exploitation had blinded the colonial overlords to the welfare needs of the people in their colonies. In the second occupation, though Britain continued to have its own interests at heart, the provision of social welfare needs became an important component of the colonial agenda in the developmentalist states that they were creating.

The second colonial occupation, like the first, failed to sustain Britain's extended colonial domination over its African territories. This developmentalist state failed in Nigeria and other colonies because of three interlocking problems: ingrained racial ideologies of the colonial state that manifested themselves consciously or unconsciously in the decision-making process; the two different conceptions of development between the CO and the colonial state leading to bureaucratic wranglings; and the lack of financial and human resources available for sustained development. The color bar was very much a part of the British colonial system as it was in the U.S. Though revenues generated from Nigerians through taxation comprised a significant amount of the development program, the Nigerian people had a limited voice in what schemes and projects were carried out. The few Nigerians who served as unofficial members in the legislative council and in the development committees had no votes. They could only hope that the ideas they put forward during the discussions shaped the plans. The attempt by the European officials in Nigeria to be the custodians of development was in line with the civilizing mission of European colonialism. Inherent in this ideology is the notion that Europeans were superior and this was reflected in their patronizing attitude toward Africans and their belief that they had a "duty" to civilize them. Colonial officials saw themselves as "trustees" over British possessions. A key tenant of this ideology was that Africans could not determine their own future. The Europeans had to create and determine both the future and the pace at which Africa would reach it. The idea was that the Europeans knew what was good for Africa better than Africans themselves. Africans were not given the choice, for example, between a school and an irrigation scheme. European agrarian biases directed at Africans meant that agricultural development always took precedence over schools. This agrarian bias remains a major problem in international development when organizations such as the World Bank design plans that insist that agriculture is the only pathway to the economic prosperity of African nations. Development plans that exclude the active participation of the local people in the process are pathways to failure.

The second problem that led to the failure of this developmentalist state were the bureaucratic wrangling between the CO and the Nigerian colonial state. This slowed the process and caused the plan to be rushed toward the end. Though the CO was originally intended to provide advice to the colonial governments, they ended up hijacking the process and attempted to micromanage it. As a result, some good ideas that had originated from the colonies were killed off. One example was the idea to frontload resources in the early years of the plan to expand agricultural development and production and then use the revenues generated to sustain the plan in its later years and beyond. This idea was dismissed by the CO for fear of creating dependency on Britain in the later years of the plan. The power struggle over control of the development processes limited the success of the plan.

Finally, the lack of financial and human resources hampered the success of development during this colonial occupation. Britain emerged from World War II with serious financial and economic problems. It was not in a position to make heavy investments in the development of its colonies. The figure that was agreed upon for colonial development was not a result of any serious economic research, but was one that sounded reasonable for the approval of Parliament. France had channeled some of the Marshall Aid money to its African territories; Britain did not do this. It was a missed opportunity as the U.S. was willing to provide such aid to the European's African territories because it wanted to strengthen their European allies economically. Such aid could have potentially furthered the development of Britain's African territories. In the same manner, Britain lost an opportunity to actively engage the returning African soldiers in the development process. These had fought valiantly with their European counterparts, yet many of their services were not retained by the colonial state in the postwar period, even when Britain had difficulties recruiting Europeans. The colonial system, which had provided mainly technical and subpar education to the colonialized, guaranteed that there were few colonized people who could assume senior cadre positions in the colonial service. Africans who had studied in the U.S. and other parts of Europe were excluded because of Britain's suspicions about their ideologies.

All three problems still create great interest as Africa's development continues to be considered. African nations today are a token of their colonial past. Their relations with the West and the language that characterizes their relationships is still in line with the colonial period but now with a new flavor. It is no longer the colonizer and the colonized, but the developed and the underdeveloped, first world and third world, center and periphery, rich and poor. The African nation's role in this language is subservient. Even though Africa was sold a political illusion called "independence," its economy remains tightly under the grips of the West and at the mercy of Western market fluctuations. Lack of economic independence means that African politics is controlled by those who control the economy. Thus, African leaders find themselves accepting and implementing economic policies that are bad for their nations in return for guarantees that they can retain political power. As a result of this, constitutions are changed to increase term limits, and dictators are propped up as international development agencies continue to provide loans and aid under the guise of being apolitical. African nations today are populated by all sorts of experts who claim to have solutions to Africa's problems while locally trained intelligentsia are sidelined. Their solutions have become very predictable as they always begin and end in agriculture as the pathway to lifting Africans out of poverty.

Is agriculture the way for Africa's development? The idea that agriculture is the pathway to Africa's prosperity is not new and that is why this book is specifically interested in agricultural policy. Colonial development policy in Africa focused on agriculture as the way to boost the economy and alleviate poverty. The goal of development was not to transform the colonies into industrialized centers like the metropole, but to create a sustaining agricultural economy that would maintain stability and provide for the basic social needs of the people. Colonel James Mackie, the colonial director of agriculture in Nigeria declared that Nigeria was and would always be an agricultural country. The next chapter will look at Mackie's ideas as well as agricultural policy and planning in Nigeria.

NOTES

1. Hodge, *Triumph of the Expert*, 199.
2. Ibid. 201.
3. Ochonu, *Colonial Meltdown*, 7.
4. Hodge, *Triumph of the Expert*, 145.
5. Marc Matera, Misty L. Bastian & Susan Kingsley Kent, *The Women's War of 1929: Gender and Violence in Colonial Nigeria* (New York: Palgrave Macmillan, 2012), 2. See also Toyin Falola & Adam Paddock, *The Women's War of 1929: A History of Anti-Colonial Resistance in Eastern Nigeria* (Durham, NC: Carolina Academic Press, 2011).
6. James Ferguson, *Expectations of Modernity: Myths and Meanings in Urban Life on the Zambian Copperbelt* (Berkeley: University of California Press, 1999), 51.
7. Frederick Cooper, *Africa Since 1940: The Past of the Present* (Cambridge: Cambridge University Press, 2002), 20.
8. In its May 30, 1935 issue, the *New York Times* reported on the Copperbelt Strike. It said the strike was "efficiently organized" and was against the government.
9. Arthur Creech Jones, HC Deb May 21, 1940, vol 361, cc 41–125.
10. Campbell Stephen, HC Deb May 21, 1940, vol 361, cc 41–125.
11. Butler, *Industrialisation and the British Colonial State: West Africa, 1939–1951*(London: Frank Cass, 1997), 21.
12. Falola, *Development Planning and Decolonization in Nigeria*, 24–25.
13. Constantine, *The Making of British Colonial Development Policy*, 244.
14. D. J. Morgan, *The Official History of Colonial Development: The Origins of British Aid Policy, 1924–1945* (London: The Macmillan Press Ltd, 1980), 60.
15. Constantine, *The Making of British Colonial Development Policy*, 244.
16. Robert L. Tignor, *W. Arthur Lewis and the Birth of Development Economics* (Princeton: Princeton University Press, 2005), 56.
17. Falola, *Development Planning and Decolonization in Nigeria*, 26–28.
18. Ibid., 29–30.
19. Ibid., 30.
20. Ibid., 30.
21. Planning & Reorganisation Development Proposals. Extracts from notes of a discussion with the Treasury on November 9, 1944, TNA: CO 583/271/4.

22. Noel Hall was the Resident Minister, West Africa and he was in Achimota, Ghana.

23. Richards to Stanley, January 7, 1944, TNA: CO 583/271/4.

24. F. E. V. Smith, C.M.G was the head of the development branch of the secretariat and H. E. Walker, CBE was the deputy director of public works. Walker had collaborated in the preparation of the proposals and he had a wide knowledge and a long experience in Nigeria.

25. Richards to Stanley, September 22, 1944, TNA: CO 583/271/4.

26. F. E. V. Smith, Memorandum on Nigeria's Preliminary Development Plan, October 3, 1944, TNA: CO 583/271/4.

27. Ibid.

28. Ibid.

29. Planning & Reorganisation Development Proposals. Extracts from notes of a discussion with the Treasury on November 9, 1944, TNA: CO 583/271/4.

30. Sydney Caine was appointed financial adviser to the colonial office in 1942 and was in charge of the colonial development policy from April of 1943. He was assistant undersecretary of state from 1944 to 1947.

31. Memorandum by S Caine, August 12, 1943, TNA: CO 852/588/2, in S. R. Ashton and S. E. Stockwell, eds. Imperial Policy and Colonial Practice, 1925–1945 (London: HMSO, 1996), 168.

32. Ibid.

33. Hall to Stanley, September 30, 1944, TNA: CO 583/271/4.

34. Minutes of a meeting held at the colonial office, October 20, 1944, TNA: CO 583/271/4.

35. Frederick Pedler worked in the finance department of the colonial office at the time of these negotiations on the Nigerian plan. Before this current position, he was British Economic Representative in Dakar, Senegal.

36. Notes of a meeting held in the secretary of state's room to discuss the Nigerian development proposals, October 25, 1944, TNA: CO 583/271/4.

37. Sir George Gater was the permanent undersecretary of state.

38. Notes of a meeting held in the secretary of state's room to discuss the Nigerian development proposals, October 25, 1944, TNA: CO 583/271/4.

39. In debating the 1940 Act, an issue was raised about the CO and its advisory committees trying to dictate development policy. Malcolm MacDonald stated unequivocally that "the plans will be examined by the committee with a view, as the White Paper says, to assisting and guiding, but not dictating to, the Colonial Governments concerned." Malcolm MacDonald, HC Deb May 21, 1940, vol 361, cc 41–125

40. Notes of a meeting held in the secretary of state's room to discuss the Nigerian development proposals, October 25, 1944, TNA: CO 583/271/4.

41. F. E. V. Smith, Memorandum on Nigeria's Preliminary Development Plan, October 3, 1944, TNA: CO 583/271/4.

42. Notes of a meeting held in the secretary of state's room on Nigerian preliminary development plan, November 6, 1944, TNA: CO 583/271/4.

43. Ibid.

44. Ibid.

45. F. E. V. Smith, Memorandum on Nigeria's Preliminary Development Plan, October 3, 1944, TNA: CO 583/271/4.

46. Ibid.

47. Ibid.

48. Ibid.

49. Memorandum on development officers in Nigeria, December 7, 1944, TNA: CO 583/271/4.

50. Ibid.

51. During parliamentary debates on the 1940 Acts, Sir Francis Fremantle's (representing St. Albans) arguments reflected this view. In referring to the colonial peoples, he said: "They are different from us in all sorts of ways. . . . Although we may bring them up to be equal in that respect one day . . . as regards intelligence, they are certainly not equal to us, though the standard varies a great deal." Francis Fremantle, HC Deb May 21, 1940, vol 361, cc 41–125.

52. Havinden and Meredith, *Colonialism and Development*, 226.

53. Notes of a discussion with the Treasury, November 9, 1944, TNA: CO 583/271/4.

54. Yasmin Khan, *The Great Partition: The Making of India and Pakistan* (New Haven: Yale University Press, 2007), 13.

55. Havinden and Meredith, *Colonialism and Development*, 227–28.

56. Ibid., 229.

57. Richards to Stanley, March 6, 1945, TNA: CO 583/271/4.

58. Memorandum by D. J. Parkinson, March 14, 1945, TNA: CO 583/ 271/4.

59. Ibid.

60. Ibid.

61. Ibid.

62. Ibid.

63. It is important to note that at this time, there was no single document that contained the whole plan of development for Nigeria with all the different projects. There were several plans that dealt with different departments such as health, agriculture, forestry, veterinary services, roads, and so on.

64. Creasy to Smith. July 6, 1945, TNA: CO 583/271/4.

65. The use of the plural "plans" here is to make clear that the Nigerian development plan was actually a conglomeration of different plans emerging from the different departments. The official documents used the plural "plans" and I retain that usage here.

66. Smith to Creasy. August 10, 1945, TNA: CO 583/271/4.

67. Creasy to Smith, telegram, August 28, 1945, TNA: CO 583/271/4.

68. Winteley to George Hall (S of S), telegram, September 20, 1945, TNA: CO 583/271/4.

69. Notes of a meeting at Frank Stockdale's room, September 24, 1945, TNA: CO 583/271/4.

70. Ibid.

71. Richards to Hall, telegram, October 9, 1945, TNA: CO 583/271/4.

72. Minute by Parkinson, October 1, 1945, TNA: CO 583/271/4.

73. Minute by Gater, October 3, 1945, TNA: CO 583/271/4.
74. Hall to Richards, October 11, 1945, TNA: CO 583/271/4.
75. Caine to Smith, October 10, 1945, TNA: CO 583/271/4.
76. Smith to Caine, October 15, 1945, TNA: CO 583/271/4.
77. Ibid.
78. Robin Cohen, *Labour and Politics in Nigeria* (London: Heinemann, 1974), 172–73.
79. Falola, *Development Planning and Decolonization in Nigeria*, 70.
80. Frederick Cooper argues that Africans took the assertions of the colonial rulers and turned them "into claims and mobilizing ideologies of their own." See, Cooper, *Africa Since 1940*, 15–16.
81. J. K. Ladipo to CSG, December 10, 1945, RH: MSS. Afr. S. 2124.
82. Smith to Caine, October 15, 1945, TNA: CO 583/271/4.
83. Caine to Smith, October 17, 1945, TNA: CO 583/271/4.
84. Richards to Hall, October 23, 1945, TNA: CO 583/271/4.
85. Minute by J. B. Williams, November 2, 1945, TNA: CO 583/271/4.
86. Ibid.
87. Ibid.
88. Minute by Caine, November 2, 1945, TNA: CO 583/271/4.
89. Stockdale was an adviser on colonial development planning at the CO, 1945–1948.
90. Minute by Stockdale, November 2, 1945, TNA: CO 583/271/4.
91. Minute by Sydney Caine, November 15, 1945, TNA: CO 583/271/4.
92. Minute by J. B. Williams, November 22, 1945, TNA: CO 583/ 271/4.
93. Hall to Richards, telegram, November 23, 1945, TNA: CO 583/271/4.
94. Richards to S of S, December 8, 1945, TNA: CO 583/271/4.
95. Richards to S of S, telegram, December 13, 1945, TNA: CO 583/271/4.
96. Smith to Williams, Memorandum on the estimates for Colonial Development and Welfare Schemes 1946/47 in connection with the extension of agricultural, veterinary, forestry, and health services with notes as to the form of latitude requested in connection with expenditure under certain subheads, December 24, 1945, TNA: CO 583/271/4.
97. Ibid.
98. Richards to S of S, December 31, 1945, TNA: CO 583/271/4.
99. J. E. Marnham to D. R. Serpell, February 25, 1946 TNA: CO583/271/4.
100. J. E. Marnham to D. R. Serpell, February 28, 1946 TNA: CO583/271/4.
101. Serpell to Marnham, March 20, 1946, TNA: CO583/27/4.
102. S of S to Richards, March 9, 1946, TNA: CO583/27/4.
103. Richards to S of S, March 13, 1946, TNA: CO583/27/4.
104. Richards to S of S, February 23, 1946, TNA: CO583/271/4.
105. Ibid.

Chapter 3

The Agrarian Bias

Mackiean Policy of Agricultural Development in Nigeria

How can Africa, South of the Sahara achieve development? This was an important question during the second colonial occupation and continues to occupy the development enterprise today. Policy makers in the period after the Great Depression insisted that the key to unlocking the wealth of Africa was through agriculture. It is not surprising that during this period, myriad agricultural development schemes emerged throughout Africa. The developmental agenda of the colonial state was clouded by an agricultural bias and thus the agrarian doctrines of development were considered the only way forward for Africa's prosperity. It is no surprise that many development policies emanating from international organizations such as the IMF/World Bank still insist on expanding African agriculture as the way to GDP growth and African prosperity. African countries have remained locked in the boom-and-bust cycles of commodities, cycles that often leave the majority of people poorer. The development programs of the second colonial occupation did not envision an industrialized Africa that reflected the economy of the metropoles. The agricultural systems introduced in the colonies were not intended to transform the colonies into industrial regions but to make them producers of primary products that would feed European industries. Thus, African agriculture was geared toward food production for internal consumption and cash crops for export. For example, Nigerian cocoa was exported but rice production was only for internal consumption.

The logic that guided the colonial agricultural departments was no different from the one enshrined in the colonial enterprise as a whole. The idea was that African farming was backward and devoid of any coherent organization. African farming systems were believed to be desperately in need of a European touch of progress in order to unleash their full productive capacity. Several approaches were introduced during the second colonial occupation.

In the first phase, which lasted until the end of World War II, agricultural policy was more cautious and conservative and the use of advanced machinery was limited. In the period after the war, Britain took a more aggressive posture, attempting to "upgrade" the traditional means of agriculture with mechanized farming.

The focus of this chapter is Nigeria's agricultural development policy before 1945. Focusing on this policy gives us a window into understanding the agrarian bias as well as the conflicts and contradictions of the colonial state during the second occupation. The Nigerian colonial state was sustained by revenues derived from agricultural production and expected such revenues to continue to support the goals of the occupation. To the colonial masters, Nigeria was an agricultural territory and always would be. This accounts for why the Nigerian planners were determined to front-load most of the resources that were available for the 1945 colonial development plan in the expansion of agricultural development. Despite this agrarian bias, the development of agriculture in Nigeria, as in some other British territories, was clouded with conflicts and contradictions. In most British colonies in the period before the second colonial occupation, agricultural development was expected to evolve along "native lines." While this policy seemed to be respectful of African practices, it had its racial biases and undermined the goals of the colonial economy. The argument of this chapter is that the agricultural policy that was pioneered and championed by James Richard Mackie[1], the Nigerian agriculture director, was too cautious and conservative to respond to the colonial agricultural needs in a period when high production was expected. Mackiean policy insisted on careful research and field trials before farmers were asked to change their methods of farming. This policy also required the decentralization of agricultural development and required the officers to build strong relationships with the local authorities.

A second contradiction is the failure of the Nigerian colonial state to create a new agricultural system that could have potentially sustained the colonial economy and its developmentalist agenda. Such an agrarian system would have required the colonial state to radically change the social and political systems that were associated with African farming. In Nigeria and some other African colonies, land was communally held and the authority to distribute it rested in the hands of the local authorities. Disrupting the system meant changing the land tenure system, an action that would have elicited great resistance from the colonized and could have potentially torpedoed the colonial state. The colonial state needed the local authorities in their colonization project and these authorities would have lost their power in their communities if the land was wrestled from their control. The state was forced to adapt to the local system of farming to accommodate the political interests of their local allies. Although the colonial officers collaborated with the local authorities in agricultural production, they failed in integrating the most important asset the locals could offer in expanding colonial agricultural production: locally produced knowledge. Instead the state was focused on the knowledge produced by the agriculture department through research and field trials and relied on using this knowledge to transform African agriculture. Centuries of wisdom accumulated as a result of Africans studying and adapting to their environments was rejected.

By focusing on agricultural policy and its development, this chapter also exposes the conflicts that were a mainstay of the colonial state. For development to be successful, the two main wings of the colonial state—the administrative and the technical departments—needed to work harmoniously. This was not the case in Nigeria. The Nigerian development agenda was caught up in the politics of the colonial state. The question became: Who has power and control over development policy in the regions or provinces? The political/administrative[2] staff such as the Residents who worked with the African authorities saw themselves as the employees of the African authorities and restricted how much access the technical staff had to the local administrations. This chapter chronicles the rocky relationship Mackie had with the administrative department. In the end, the governor moved toward centralization, wrestling power from the director of agriculture and handing it over to the administrative staff who were not necessarily knowledgeable about agricultural services.[3] This was detrimental to the development of agriculture, and Mackie's frustration with the perceived marginalization of the agriculture department by the governor was the reason for his sudden resignation from the Nigerian service.

THE STRUCTURE OF THE NIGERIAN COLONIAL STATE

Nigeria's colonial state was a tripartite organization consisting of the administrative department, the technical departments, and the "native" authorities. [4] The collaboration of these three facilitated the stability of the colonial state. Though the local authorities did not relate to the colonizers on equal basis, they were an essential part of the colonial system, as the Europeans relied on them to exercise direct control over the colonized. The Europeans had neither the staff nor the financial resources to directly administer their African "possessions." John Cell notes that in the period shortly before World War II, the number of British administrative officers spread across Africa was little more than 1,200 men.[5] The cooperation of the local authorities was needed for the successful implementation of colonial policy. The relationship between the three arms of the colonial state was marred by tensions as the colonial officials jostled for control of policy and the Africans. To understand how agricultural development evolved in the midst of these tensions, it is important to step back and briefly look at the structure of the Nigerian colonial state. This is significant because the technical departments in the 1930s were challenged by the fact that they had to work through the political officials assigned to the provinces and districts. They did not have direct access to the local authorities and Mackie's policy was an attempt to change this by finding ways to work within the entrenched system.

One of the primary challenges faced by British colonial officials in Nigeria was how to govern a territory so vast with a limited number of European personnel. It was impossible for colonial officials to directly collect taxes, adjudicate cases, and provide essential services. There was a devolution of power whereby the African authorities who controlled their subjects came under the control of the colonial officials. Taxes were not collected directly by the British officials but by the African authorities who then remitted the taxes from their communities to the colonial officials. The vast majority of colonial subjects did not have any direct interaction with British officials as colonialism was mediated through their own local leaders. This system of government, which was known in British colonial parlance as indirect rule, was first introduced across Nigeria in 1914 by Governor Frederick Lugard after his 1914 amalgamation of the Northern and Southern Protectorates. Indirect rule was created to maintain order and stability in the colony, and to maintain the sociopolitical structure of the people, a necessity for the success of British development policy. Sir Hugh Clifford, the immediate successor of Lugard, argued that indirect rule slowed the rate of progress.[6]

Working through the African political structure that was in existence meant that colonial rule remained remote to the people it was supposed to govern.[7] The people's daily experience was with the African local authorities. Lieutenant governors administered the northern and southern parts of the country and they reported to the governor general who reported directly to the S of S in London. In 1939, the South was divided into nine provinces and ten years later the North was divided into twelve provinces. Regionalism was instituted in 1939 with the South being divided into West and East regions and the North forming a third region; these regions remained in place till the independence of Nigeria in 1960.[8] The regions were created to help with the effective administration of the territory. With the institution of regionalization, each of the three regions had a chief commissioner who reported to the governor. Each province in the regions had a Resident who reported to the chief commissioners. Below the provinces were the districts, which had a district officer (DO). The emir or chief was the political head of a district. It was this bureaucratic structure that Mackie had to deal with in the 1930s and which limited his department's access to the African farmers.

CAPTAIN JAMES RICHARD MACKIE

No other person had as great an impact on Nigeria's agriculture in the late colonial period as Captain James Mackie. He served in the agriculture department of Nigeria for twenty-four years before retiring under controversial circumstances in February of 1945. After a career in the military and at Reading University in the UK, he was appointed superintendent of agriculture in September of 1921. His first post in Nigeria was at Moor Plantation, Ibadan. The director of agriculture at the time was O. T. Faulkner. To gain varied experience of the agricultural conditions in Nigeria, Mackie was later assigned to Ilorin, in the western part of the colony, and then to Yandev in the North. After seven years of service in the agriculture department, he was appointed deputy assistant director of agriculture. Only six months after assuming this position, he was named the assistant director of agriculture. His promotions were unusually fast for the colonial service. In most cases he was promoted over those who were more senior to him in the service. During his farewell party, the African staff wrote in their speech:

> Barely seven years after your appointment you were promoted Deputy Assistant Director of Agriculture, and the following year, that is six months after your first promotion, you were appointed Assistant Director of Agriculture, in each case superseding more senior officers. Those in-born qualities of which you are so remarkably possessed and of which you early gave evidence when you were serving as a Superintendent of Agriculture received adequate recognition when it was necessary for Mr. Faulkner to relinquish his appointment as Director of Agriculture, and you were considered, throughout the whole Colonial Agricultural Service, to be his fittest and worthy successor on the 31st of October, 1936.[9]

Though loved and respected by African authorities and the staff in the agriculture department, Mackie found himself in constant conflict with the administrative officials, a state of affairs that eventually drove him to early retirement from the Nigerian service. Though a great patriot of the British Empire, he fought for better conditions for African staff in his department. His agricultural policy is fourfold: 1) the training and education of African agricultural officers; 2) the expansion of research and experimental farms; 3) close collaboration with African authorities; and 4) the expansion of mixed farming. This policy perspective influenced his agricultural planning before and during the war. His policy was geared toward the expansion of production for both the benefit of Nigeria and the British Empire. He was very passionate about these goals and this passion was on most occasions the source of his conflicts with the administrative officials.

ELITE MEDIATION AND AGRICULTURAL DEVELOPMENT

By the time of Faulkner's retirement from the Nigerian agricultural service in 1936, no one in the agriculture department was a better replacement than Mackie. They had collaborated very well together and were pioneers in the investigation of agricultural systems used by peasants. They had strived to understand peasant cultivation and this had significant impact on expanded production, not only in Nigeria but throughout the British Empire.[10] In order to effectively understand peasant agriculture and build upon it for the expansion of production, they saw the need to work closely with the African authorities. Though this approach was peasant-friendly, it was restricting and limiting to development. This was because they were attempting to expand peasant production through innovations without making dramatic changes to the social structure and African farming organization. They sought the cooperation of African authorities in their quest to improve agriculture and expand production. Faulkner and Mackie's approach to the development of agriculture was similar in structure to the policy of indirect rule introduced earlier by Frederick Lugard. Through this policy, Faulkner and Mackie were adopting a form of elite mediation as a key to peasant agricultural development. Though at first sight this policy may seem friendly to the African farmers, it rested on the erroneous assumption that African farmers were insusceptible to change and thus should be handled delicately. These assumptions led Faulkner and Mackie to believe that dramatic changes should not be introduced into the agriculture system, as peasants would have difficulties adapting to these innovations. Such a belief was not unique to Nigeria, nor was it limited to the British territories. This was very much part of the colonial mentality. In Northern Rhodesia, the ecological survey that was carried out by the colonial administration concluded that agricultural development was "to serve the stabilisation of an existing balance of nature while the gradual introduction of ecologically sound improvements and remedies would guide an agricultural evolution 'on native lines.'"[11] The assumption here is that poor African practices were responsible for the ecological degradation. However, colonial governments didn't suggest any radical changes to be implemented immediately because they believed Africans needed to evolve according to their "backward" traditions. In her study of development in the Netherlands East Indies, Suzanne Moone provides a compelling case of this kind of ideology at work. She shows how the colonial state from the beginning of the twentieth century to the late 1920s was under the assumption that Javanese society is static and thus they developed their agricultural policies on the faulty premise that the people could not be relied upon to change, even though that was what the colonial state really wanted and needed. Instead the colonial state favored technologies that were not going to bring about any social reorganization of farming, while at the same time increasing yield. As her work shows, Javanese society was not, in fact, inept at change.[12]

Like the colonial officials in the Netherlands East Indies, Mackie and his agriculture department assumed that Nigerian peasants were incapable of change, when this was clearly not the case. The fallacy of the colonial state was the belief that slow adoption of policies by the colonial people meant inability to change. African farmers factored in the economics of labor and financial returns in their decision-making process. For instance, in the western part of Nigeria, the peasant farmers adopted cocoa farming by their own initiative because they saw the economic benefits that cocoa production brought. This idea that peasants were slow to change their agricultural practices had a negative impact on the planning and development of agriculture, as the planners were more interested in policies that would enshrine the status quo rather than those that would improve the system.

A SCHEME FOR THE EXTENSION OF AFRICAN AGRICULTURE

In August of 1930, as assistant director of agriculture, Mackie wrote a memorandum outlining a scheme for the extension of agricultural development by engaging fully the African authorities. This scheme, which was accepted by Faulkner and promoted vigorously by Mackie, deserves close study and analysis. Realizing the rocky relationship that existed between the agriculture department and the administrative department, Mackie's scheme was intended to build a closer working relationship between these two arms of the colonial state to enable an effective agricultural extension work. For example, the administrative staff that worked with the local authorities were suspicious of the activities of the agriculture department and restricted them from having direct access to the emirs and their officials. The officers of the technical departments were treated as enemies and outsiders who deserved to be kept at a distance from the local authorities. Though the administrative officer drew his salary from the government, he saw himself as an official of the African authorities, while at the same time treating the technical staff as government officials who should not exercise any role in the administration of African affairs.[13]

There were two reasons advanced by the administrative officers for the restriction of direct access to the technical staff by the African authorities. The first reason was that local administration was young and delicate and had to be protected. They saw the presence of the technical department staff as interference from the outside.[14] This interference, they believed, would force the African authorities to move at a pace that they were not capable of. The question then is: Did the African authorities need protection from the political officers? For the colonial state, this was an attempt to maintain stability. The principle of indirect rule in Nigeria was geared toward maintaining the status quo of a traditional African bureaucracy. As Harry Gailey argues, this form of rule was "simply to the advantage of the chiefs and the people to accept the 'indirect' form of government since it did preserve intact some of their laws and practices, and retained for the chiefs the right of low-level decision making."[15] The African authorities in the colonial state were instruments used in the colonization of the people. The role of the Residents or other officials appointed to serve the African authorities was to ensure that their rule conformed to the dictates or expectations of the colonial state. Thus, the direct access of the technical staff to the rulers was seen as interference in the colonial state's bureaucratic structure.

The argument that the technical staff would speed up the evolution of traditional agriculture is not convincing. The technical departments were cautious and conservative and the agriculture department did not see its mission as moving the African farmers at a pace they were not willing to. The department was slow in changing agricultural methods and it felt that having direct access to the local authorities would enable it to provide good technical advice that would be instrumental in expanding production for the benefit of the colonial state and the farmers. For the department, traditional farming methods needed to be improved upon through the use of new tested technologies that would not radically change the farming system that the peasants are familiar with. This view of careful technological intervention in the farming system rested on the assumption that peasant production was stagnant because of lack of innovation in the practices. By carefully introducing best farming and innovative practices to the farmers, a significant expansion would occur in production.[16] The conflicts were not limited to the agriculture department but affected other technical departments as well. These restrictions deprived the local authorities of expert advice from the technical staff.

According to Mackie, there was another reason why his department staff was restricted from exercising any form of official role in the local administration. The administrative staff believed that the technical departments were "trying to undermine the influence of the Native Administration by creating enclaves which were independent of it."[17] At issue here was the colonial state's goal of maintaining stability by subjecting all the people within the umbrella of the African authorities. They did not want the people whose livelihood and economic means were independent of the authorities to challenge the political structure that was now being maintained by the state. This policy was geared toward maintaining the stability of the state.[18] For these reasons, the political officials were vigorous defenders of the African authorities.

Apart from the goal of maintaining stability in the state there was also an unbridled desire for power and control. The political officers, who were often less experienced than the experts from the departments, wanted to exercise control over the African authorities. They did not want to see their own positions being undermined by the African leaders going directly to the technical staff for advice on their technical problems. The administrative staff wanted to mediate all relations that the colonized had, becoming "gatekeepers" to the world of the Africans. Mackie was disillusioned by this politics and thought the administrative staff was trying to usurp the role of the technical staff, becoming technical experts in domains they had no expertise in. He stated that though agriculture was the staple industry of Nigeria, "practically nothing is spent by Native Administration in trying to encourage it, and although every political officer has some little pet scheme for the development of Agriculture in his own particular Emirate the assistance of Agricultural Officers has with few exceptions never been welcomed, presumably because the Political Officers feared that they might gain too much influence with the Emirs etc."[19] While the political officers were not technical experts in the sense that the officials from the technical departments were, they were experts in their own way. Many of these officials often spent several years working in the same district or village, with the same emir or chief, and had a good grounding in the language, culture, and knowledge of the local people. Although their knowledge of the science of agriculture may not have been comparable to the experts from the agriculture department, they knew the local people. While the lack of consultation and inclusion of agriculture officials in the local schemes led to the failure of some of these schemes, it is also true that the arrogance of scientific men who thought that their ideas were the most rational and that local practices were primitive and backward also contributed to the failure of many others.

Mackie identified a problem that he felt could be easily resolved, and thus his proposal was intended to change the frosty relationship between the technical officers and the political officers, while also aiming at forming a closer working relationship with the traditional administration without making the political officers feel threatened. He saw the role of the agriculture department officers solely as that of offering technical advice to the African leaders without meddling in the affairs of administration. This was an unrealistic expectation because it was impossible to change the African farming system without affecting political affairs. The farming system was closely linked to the political system. The land tenure system, which the British had supported from the early years of colonization, vested authority in the hands of the local rulers. The farming system could only be changed to an extent because the policy of indirect rule limited the possibilities for such change. To radically change the system and increase production, the power over the control of land and labor had to be removed from these local authorities, which would invariably create cracks in the foundation of the colonial state, a risk that most colonial governors or officials would have been unwilling to take. Due to the contradictions of this colonial policy, by the 1940s, colonial developers and planners began to move toward using educated elites and capitalist farmers as intermediaries rather than continuing to collaborate with traditional rulers.

Mackie's proposals did not attempt to fundamentally change the status quo but clothe it in a new collaborative garment. In his memorandum, he laid out six proposals that may transform this relationship. He proposed that they should start an experimental farm under the authority of the local administration. The headquarters of the emir's agricultural adviser would be located on this farm and he would be responsible for demonstrating improved methods of farming and, later on, provide extension services. Mackie presented the Katsina Emirate as the most suitable place to start. He emphasized the point that the role of the agriculture official was purely advisory and he was not responsible for the farm itself. He wrote, "The executive officer in charge of the farm and all its staff should be Native Administration officials, paid by the Native Administration and responsible to the Emir and his council."[20] This proposal was necessary to placate the administrative officials who might have felt that the agriculture department staff would step on their terrain of authority. The agriculture officer assigned to the farm reported on technical matters to the assistant director of agriculture, just as he would in government-owned farms. It was the responsibility of the executive manager of the farm to send accounts and reports directly to the emir and his council and not to the assistant director of agriculture. Mackie also proposed that the farms owned by the local administration would not perform complicated scientific experiments but would follow the pattern of demonstration farms. The conducting of scientific experiments was to be restricted to government-owned farms. He saw a future in which these farms would become farm schools where people learn improved methods of farming.

PRODUCERS AND RECEIVERS OF KNOWLEDGE

For Faulkner and Mackie, emphasis was placed on the African farming system and technological interventions meant improving upon this system that was already in use by the people. For this reason, they were very careful in asserting that the farms they had established hand in hand with the African authorities must be demonstration farms, rather than farms that would carry out complex experiments. Whatever was shown in demonstration farms had to have been tried and proven to improve production. Faulkner and Mackie believed that without practical demonstration of the effectiveness of their new farming methods, farmers would be reluctant to adopt them. In Tanganyika, for example, the colonial officials pushed for the widespread adoption of cashew production by planting a few trees in courthouses and public centers. When the cashew began to bear fruit and people saw what they could potentially earn, many started planting cashew trees.[21] Planting these plants in such heavily trafficked places was a way of demonstrating the viability of this new crop. The idea of demonstration farms that was championed by Faulkner and Mackie was a new perspective in agricultural development and expansion not only in Nigeria but also the rest of tropical Africa. This policy eliminated the need for the officials to use force to coerce the African farmers to adopt a new crop. While this policy was more peasant-friendly, it was colored by racial attitudes. This policy was paternalistic and demeaning in the sense that it created a two-tier structure: the European scientists in the technical departments would conduct the scientific trials and research on stations owned by the government, while the local farms were only for demonstration purposes and for the dissemination of results. This discounted the ability of the locals to produce knowledge. They had to be reliant on the Europeans as the producers of knowledge which they had to consume. Through this policy, African farmers were effectively removed from the knowledge creation aspect of the agricultural development process.

The magnitude of the arrogance displayed by some colonial officials was appalling and offensive to the sensibilities of the African farmers. Farmers were blatantly accused of lacking good knowledge of farming. The traditional farming system was characterized as disorderly, wasteful, and chaotic. Colonial officials described Sierra Leone agriculture in this way:

> Agriculture is backward, and the best and most profitable results from the land are not generally obtained in the Colony or Protectorate. The cultivation of the land on the rotation of crops principle is not followed by the native, with one or two exceptions, and the efforts of the more intelligent individuals only bring out into stronger relief the wasteful methods which are generally followed. These consist in clearing the land of trees and bush by cutting them down about two feet from the ground, the roots being left in the ground. When dry, the bush is burnt, and the ground is considered ready for planting, no tilling is done. After the crop has been reaped, the land is allowed to lie fallow for from three to seven years before it is again planted. It will readily be understood that good results cannot be looked for from such a system, and that the labor devoted each year to the clearing of fresh land is, to a great extent, wasted.[22]

The practice described above was the African traditional agricultural practice that received the most attack from colonial officials. What looked like disorder to the British officials was actually a reflection of their own ignorance of the traditional methods. African farming systems such as bush-fallow rotations (Shifting cultivations) and intercropping were alien to the British and thus they considered them to be unproductive. This bush-fallow system was similar to crop rotation practiced in Britain but in the case of Africa, the plots were abandoned for several years to enable them to return to natural vegetation. This was different from the British approach in which during the fallow period, grass and legume were used to restore soil fertility. For those who were only familiar with British agriculture, the African system was a mess.[23] Farmers in West Africa were castigated "for 'wasteful' burning of vegetation, 'merely scratching the surface' of their soils, 'failing' to plough deeper, lazily mixing their crops in an arbitrary and unhygienic manner."[24] In actuality, African practices were innovative as they tried to adapt to their environment. Rather than "backward," the African system had evolved to meet the present circumstances. It has been argued that the burning actually helped to release phosphorus to the soil and this was a vital nutrient that was deficient in the savannah and forest regions of Africa.[25]

George Howard Jones, an agricultural officer in Nigeria, wrote a book in the 1920s challenging the colonial assumptions that African agricultural practices were disorderly. In describing the West African farmer, he wrote:

> There seems a reason for everything. The plants are not growing at random, but have been planted at proper distances on hillocks of soil arranged in such a way that when rain falls it does not waterlog the plants, nor does it pour off the surface and wash away the fine soil: the stumps of bushes and trees are left for the yams to climb upon and the oil palms are left standing because they yield valuable fruit: and although several kinds of plants are growing together, they were not sown at the same time nor will they be reaped together: they are rather successive crops planted in such a way the soil is always occupied and is neither dried up by the sun nor leached out by the rain, as it would be if it were left bare at any time.[26]

Jones made the point that Europeans should be cautious and thorough before passing any judgments on the Africans. He said that the African method of farming and the farmer's outlook is so different from the European that the latter might be tempted to dismiss it as foolish. He said the Europeans had made the same mistake in India. He wrote, "In assessing native agriculture, then, we have to guard against condemning native methods merely because they offend European temperate agricultural principles, and in addition we must be prepared to grant that there may be reasons for his peculiar methods of which we know nothing, even after we have considered them as carefully as we can with our present knowledge of tropical agriculture."[27]

In support of Jones's observation, let me draw from my own personal observation of intercropping among the Bette farmers in Cross River state of Nigeria. In a typical planting field, the Bette people have hips with yams planted on them. The hips are made in such a way that the land would not suffer from erosion. This is important, because in the past African practices have been blamed for causing erosions, when in fact African practices are often an adaptation to an environment that is already suffering from erosion or degradation. Depending on the soil, the hips have to be of a certain size and height. This is knowledge accumulated and perfected over many years. Four hips are crossed with wooden sticks to allow the branches from the yam tubers to grow and expand on them. This allows the yam tubers to receive the sunlight it needs. Apart from yams planted on the hips, other staple food crops are also planted: corn and cassava. Corn takes about three months to grow before it is ready for harvesting. It is planted alongside the yams immediately. The harvesting of the corn happens before it becomes a problem for the successful growth of the yams. Cassava, which is planted alongside the yams, takes longer to reach the point of harvesting. Usually the cassava is harvested about a year after yam harvesting has taken place. These crops are not planted haphazardly without order. Locally produced knowledge has convinced the people that they could plant all these crops alongside each other on one piece of land and still acquire a good harvest. As Paul Zeleza has noted, colonial officials once considered intercropping like that practiced by the Bette people as "a sign of Africa's agricultural backwardness. Now agronomists have discovered the advantages of intercropping."[28]

Intercropping was not a haphazard and irrational practice by Africans. It was motivated by the scarcity of labor and the desire to conserve land. In any agricultural system, labor and land are important factors to be carefully considered. African farming systems evolved in relation to the availability of labor. The peasant farmer did not practice industrial and mechanized farming and so was reliant on family and extended family labor for cultivation. The number of people within the family or a village unit often determined the amount of production that could be carried out. As Goran Hyden has argued, "Peasants are essentially self-sufficient and self-reproducing, either within the context of the household or the village. In other words, each unit of production is separated from each other, they are socially independent, united by no social division of labor, and depending on no other unit for their conditions of reproduction."[29] Due to the independent nature of peasant production and the family as the primary economic unit of production, labor had to be maximized. It is one of the reasons many peasant farmers embraced polygamy and had many children as a secure source for labor.[30]

Faulkner and Mackie give a good example that further buttresses this point in their book, *West African Agriculture*. When American cotton was first introduced to Southern Nigeria, the farmers were unwilling to adopt the new crop variety, even though it would have provided a better yield than the local cotton variety. The reason for their refusal was not because they were backward and slow to change, but because growing the new crop would entail clearing a new piece of land, as it had to be grown as a sole crop. Doing this required additional labor that the family did not have and could not afford to hire even if it were available. Families had to manage their production scale based on the amount of labor available to them. It was logical for the farmer to continue to grow the local cotton, which could be grown alongside other crops in an intercropping system. However, when the farmer was provided with an improved variety of the local cotton, he immediately adopted it because he could grow it alongside other crops.[31] For the European who looks from a distance, the peasant farmer is not adaptable to change, but the reality is that his decision to reject the American cotton was economically logical. The reason the African farmer had three or more crops in the same piece of land is it saved him the labor that could have been diverted into clearing another piece of land. Would he acquire a better output if he had each of the crops planted separately? Probably he would. However, the problem of labor would make him less inclined to do that.

Apart from labor, land conservation is another key reason that African farmers planted several crops on the same piece of land. Take, for example, the Bette farmer's choice to plant several crops on the same piece of land. This is necessary for the conservation of land. The Bette farmer traditionally allowed a piece of land to fallow for about five to six years before they cultivate it. This period of fallow was even longer in decades past when the pressure on land was not as intense as it is today. It was not uncommon for colonial officials to erroneously chastise African farmers for having no respect for land and destroying it through shifting cultivation or using the bush-fallow system. This system of farming, which was prevalent in West Africa, involved farmers slashing and burning a piece of land, cultivating it for a few years and then moving onto another piece of land. Colonial officials thought that this system was bad because it was "exploitative, untidy and misguided."[32] In their thinking, natural forests were constantly being destroyed in order to find virgin soil for cultivation.[33] For example, the Kenyan settler businessman, Major E. S. Grogan, testified to the 1933 Kenya Land Commission that "the African people, have never established a symbiotic relationship with land. They are, in the strict scientific sense, parasites on the land, all of them."[34] This was a bold statement from someone who was ignorant of Africans' generational relationship with the environment and land.[35] This was an argument that was often made during the early period of colonial rule. One common criticism was that African practices caused soil erosion. Helen Tilley devotes a fair portion of her book, *Africa as a Living Laboratory*, to showing that African agricultural practices for the most part were not as destructive of the land as some of the European settler farmers and colonial officials claimed. Most of the failure in crops did not result from what Africans were doing, but rather due to the tropical soil, which was not as fertile as had been initially assumed. Tilley writes, "In a discussion of the causes of soil erosion at the second conference of colonial directors of agriculture in 1938, C. J. Lewin of Northern Rhodesia remarked that the papers presented showed that, contrary to popular opinion, 'erosion was almost invariably due primarily not to the native but to the European who had introduced tillage in certain areas and had encouraged the production of economic crops.'"[36] While this is debatable, what is important to note is that African practices were not as destructive to land as it was claimed. Recent studies have challenged the argument that shifting cultivation is destructive to land when there is limited land and rapid population growth. In a case study of Machakos district in south-east Kenya, Mary Tiffen, Michael Mortimore, et.al write that the colonial government in the 1930s had deep concerns about land degradation and had ambitious plans to curb it. They falsely assumed that population growth was harmful to the environment because it meant fewer trees. These scholars, however, argue that when there is population growth in agricultural areas, there is a change that takes place in the farming and income systems. They write, "Farmers can adapt by innovation and investment and can develop new sustainable systems, but government policies can either impede or assist this process."[37] Even though the population of this region had continued to grow, erosion had also continued to reduce. This reduction was not a result of changes in the cropping system but due to improvements in terracing.[38]

THE ROLE OF COLONIAL SCIENTISTS REVISITED

Despite some of the colonial officials' faulty assumptions about African agriculture, a good number of colonial scientists respected African agricultural practices and worked to improve production. A fair share of African historiography today dismisses the role that European scientists played in the development of colonial Africa. These scientists are accused of being "oriental" toward African practices. They have been accused of proffering solutions to problems that they did not understand because of their lack of understanding of African environments and their dismissal of African practices as being backward or primitive.[39] While there is some evidence of these problems, it is also true that colonial science played an important role in the improvement of local agriculture and the elimination of disease. Not all colonial scientists were so arrogant to condemn the local practices of the colonial people. Some of the colonial scientists in the 1930s were voices of moderation, calling for the application of some of the best practices of the peasant farmers. The director of the Ugandan agricultural department, for example, recommended the incorporation of African customs into "regional policies, particularly in terms of crop rotations and soil protection measures."[40] John Smith, the secretary of agriculture in Northern Rhodesia was somewhat reluctant to wholeheartedly reject African agricultural practices even though he considered some of them to be wasteful. He thought some of the African methods are founded on sound ideas.[41] This change in attitude of the technical staff resulted from research and closer observation of African agricultural practices. Most of these scientists spent several years working in Africa or in other colonial states and they shared their research with one another through scientific journals and conferences. Some of these scientists may have moved regularly, "but they nevertheless accumulated experience and knowledge of particular issues, and their careers demonstrated a professional continuity. . . . Such scientific officials also drew on a wider range of experimentation and information than they could generate from their own research or from their particular colonial contexts. They shared information through correspondence, scientific journals, conferences, and government agricultural publications."[42]

Most of the interventions that took place during the colonial period were experimental and so the outcomes were unpredictable. The experimentation and networks forged by these scientists helped to provide the foundational basis for understanding African environments and diseases.[43] These networks of knowledge and transcontinental colonial experience formed the basis for the understanding of Nigeria's agricultural practices. Faulkner brought knowledge acquired in India to Nigeria and this was instrumental in his work in the agriculture department. Faulkner and Mackie were willing to share their own experiences of Nigerian agriculture with colonial officials working in other parts of the world. Their book was widely read by colonial officials, most especially those working in the agriculture departments.[44] They felt that an understanding of West African agricultural practices would enable colonial officials to be less judgmental, less arrogant, and more successful in their work. This book became so significant that it was included "in a list of books of 'first importance' for Malcolm Hailey to read when he assumed the role of director of the African Research Survey in 1933."[45]

Given the level of knowledge that African farmers possessed of their environments, it was important that European "experts" approaching African farmers did so with humility. The European official should not have thought that they had superior knowledge and practices to those of the Africans. Faulkner and Mackie note that the African farmer was suspicious of the advice that he received from the European, because "His own methods have been evolved and adapted during many generations, so that they suit local conditions and also suit his economic position, his social arrangements, his psychology and his tastes. It will generally be found that by them he obtains a maximum return from a minimum of labour."[46] It was necessary that the European official took all these factors into consideration as he tried to introduce a new crop to the farmers or advocate that they change their methods of farming. Faulkner and Mackie were not against the introduction of new methods or new crops in tropical Africa. They themselves had successfully implemented mixed farming in Northern Nigeria. What they called for was careful research and experimentation of crops before they were introduced to the African farmers. Given their argument that African farming practices were well evolved and adapted to the local environment to meet the needs of the farmer, the question then is: Why introduce change at all? Faulkner and Mackie believed that, although not necessarily inferior, the local practices could be improved upon or changed if necessary to improve production. In some cases, this meant improved seed varieties or other methods of improving soil fertility.

JAMES MACKIE AND WARTIME AGRICULTURAL PLANNING

With Faulkner's retirement in 1936, Mackie was his anointed replacement. Faulkner had groomed Mackie for his replacement and by doing this, left his imprint on Nigeria's agriculture. While the person heading the department had changed, agricultural policy and development had continued along the same trajectory since the 1920s. Mackie had worked closely with Faulkner and they both shared the same vision of agricultural development. The major shift the department witnessed after Mackie's ascension to the position of director was the impending World War II. Mackie spent these early years of his directorship planning to make sure that Nigeria met the wartime agricultural production needs. He demonstrated great vision and foresight in this direction. Even before the CO sent the circular to the agricultural departments of the colonies instructing them to begin reorganizing and planning for wartime production, Mackie had already taken the initiative. While the governor was still looking at agriculture in Nigeria from a business point of view, Mackie was raising the alarm that Nigeria's position as an important source of raw materials in time of war was being overlooked. In a memorandum to the CSG he wrote:

> The possibility of war cannot even now be overlooked and in such an event it should be noted that Nigeria could if properly developed supply almost every product which can be grown in the tropics; and moreover of the large tropical colonies she is nearer to England than any other. By speeding up the shipping services she could easily be brought to within 10 days of England and the sea route could be made comparatively safe. It seems to me therefore that the Agricultural development of Nigeria is a matter of vital importance to the Imperial

> Government, especially as she would not herself require supplies which are needed elsewhere for the prosecution of the war, for she could if necessary become self supporting for greater bulk of her needs.[47]

Mackie was attempting to position Nigeria for wartime supply of raw materials and this was an important strategy. The other large British colonies, such as Kenya and India, were closer to the combat zone than Nigeria. Ghana, also in the west coast of Africa and closer to London than Nigeria, was a smaller colony and had a population of less than four million in 1939. For Mackie, the size of Nigeria and the potential the colony had could not be ignored. Nigeria's strategic importance during the war and Mackie's efforts toward developing agriculture had as a primary goal the exploitation of Nigeria's resources for the benefits of Britain's war. The contributions made by Africans, not only in terms of troops, but also the resources that were exploited from Africa to support the war efforts, are often ignored in the historiography of World War II. Wartime agricultural planning in Nigeria is a window into understanding how the African colonial economies were linked to the successful execution of the war. Planning and efforts in the colonies were no longer focused on the economic growth of the economy but to help the "mother country" in its war efforts. Thus, Mackie's goal was to have a strong agriculture department that was capable of responding to the wartime needs of the imperial government.

In February of 1939, Mackie sent a letter to the governor of Nigeria inquiring if officers of the forestry and agriculture departments would be released for military service in the event of war. This question was important because he was interested in seeing how the department staff could be reorganized in preparation for war. He did not want production to be affected by the absence of these officers.[48] The CSG responded that as a general rule, officers of these departments would not be released for military service because of the vital role played by the two departments in the provision of raw materials.[49] That the staff of the department were not going to be released for war wasn't satisfactory for Mackie; he also wanted to position the department in a way that their work was recognized as a major contribution to the war. A few weeks later he wrote again to the CSG saying, "It will not be a very satisfactory position for us unless we can feel assured that the work we are doing is essential for the successful prosecution of the war. To those of us who are fit for military service and are quite prepared to take such service, merely carrying out our peacetime duties would be a very severe trial."[50] Mackie was not attempting to abdicate his position to join the military, but the looming war was an opportunity for him to expand the services of his department. If agricultural production was a vital aspect of the war efforts, then the imperial government should be willing to make the necessary investments for the expansion of production. The context of the war was an opportunity for colonial agriculture departments to expand their services. In Kenya, the acting director of agriculture, H. Wolfe, saw the war as "an excellent opportunity for a forward movement in the agricultural development in the European Highlands."[51]

For Mackie, merely maintaining peacetime production levels was a colossal waste of his effort at a time of great demand for both men in the military and agricultural production. The context of Mackie's assertion is his relationship with the political department, which he felt marginalized the role played by his department. He never felt satisfied with the support he got from the political officials and this feeling followed him throughout his time as director of the department. To reinforce his point, he continued in his letter: "I therefore feel obliged to ask whether the Government proposes to take any preparatory steps to ensure that we shall be in a position to increase production rapidly, and whether I may receive some indication of the products which Nigeria will be called upon to supply and whether the Government anticipates that in the event of war Nigeria will have to be self supporting as far as its own food requirements are concerned."[52] For example, in the first years of the war, the settler's production remained at the 1930s levels but by 1942, there was urgent need for Kenya's export commodities.[53]

Mackie wanted to position Nigeria in a way that the territory would be able to export needed commodities during the war. He also felt that without the rapid expansion of agricultural production, the department was not making a substantial contribution to the war. The level of food production had to be high enough to satisfy local consumption and export needs. Mackie's wartime agricultural planning was guided by four key assumptions: 1) the war would break out at a time when some parts of Northern Nigeria would be in partial drought; 2) shipping would be dislocated in some months and it would be difficult to rapidly receive foodstuff in large quantities from elsewhere; 3) the Europeans left in Nigeria would have to serve for two or three years without leave; and finally, 4) that the Mediterranean sea route might be closed and there might be an urgent need for Nigeria's surplus products at short notice. If his assumptions were correct, he argued, then it was important that there should be foodstuff reserves throughout Nigeria. He wanted these reserves to be kept immediately before the war broke out and he also wanted the welfare of the Europeans serving in Nigeria to be taken into serious consideration. If the war meant that Europeans would have to undertake longer tours of duty in Nigeria, then in order for them to remain fit, there was need for some extra essentials that Nigeria could begin providing. He wrote, "Thus if transport existed and preparation was made beforehand it would be possible to ensure that most Europeans situated within reasonable distance of the railway at any rate could be supplied with fresh milk, meat, and fresh vegetables from the North and fruit and fish from the South. Such amenities would do much to maintain them in a good state of health."[54]

For Mackie, the overarching question was: What contributions can the agriculture department make to the war efforts? He had given serious thought and consideration to this question. He was very knowledgeable of world geography and agriculture and he understood the impact of the war on production and export. He believed that Nigeria was in a strategic position to provide the wartime agricultural supplies to the imperial government and also to be self-sufficient in some things that at the present time were being imported. For example, though Nigeria was importing rice and sugar for local consumption, Mackie argued that Nigeria could be self-supporting in these two items by investing in local production. The climate was suitable for the cultivation of rice and also, Mackie argued, Nigeria, just like India, could be self-supporting in crude sugar such as the *gur* type. Sugar cane was grown in Nigeria but people mainly chewed it. Mackie's thinking was that the production of sugar cane could be expanded and all that would be needed to convert it to sugar was a simple crushing machinery and a boiling apparatus like those used in India. He was convinced that growth of oil seeds such as groundnuts and cotton could be rapidly expanded insofar as the department was properly organized for this kind of production. At the time, the department was incapable of instituting a rapid expansion agenda because of the dearth of supervisory staff. Staffing was viewed as one of the primary obstacles to the agricultural development in this period. This inadequacy was not limited to the European staff but the Africans as well. Mackie had developed proposals that were geared toward ameliorating this problem. He wrote, "An adequate staff is essential whether to improve Agriculture in peace time or to develop production rapidly in war time. At the present time our African staff is totally inadequate for either, and unless it is increased rapidly as possible I have no hesitation in saying that Nigeria will not be in a position to pull its weight in the event of war."[55] Mackie saw his proposals as important and wanted the colonial government to act on them. He even suggested that the governor could draw money from the Nigerian reserves to begin the implementation of these proposals and then discuss reimbursement with the imperial government at a later time.

In July of 1939, Mackie received a response from the CSG. He was told to organize his staff on a war basis so that in the event of a war Nigeria could facilitate maximum production of materials that would be of service to Britain. He was to report such a plan to him. The CSG's letter can be interpreted as either a gross misunderstanding of Mackie's letter, or just an attempt to play along to keep him satisfied. Mackie had suggested that the men in the departments of agriculture and forestry would opt for military service if they didn't consider their work in the departments to be an essential contribution to the war. The CSG's response to that was, "while his Excellency [the Governor] fully realises the Agricultural Officers would be anxious to participate in active military service in the event of war, he considers that they would be contributing their share of national service in a greater degree by increasing to the maximum extent the output of the raw produce of Nigeria."[56] As argued earlier, what Mackie and his staff needed was the support of the governor and the officials, support that was not always forthcoming. Whatever the intentions of the governor, Mackie found the CSG's letter reassuring. He was reassured by the stated intentions of the governor that the agriculture department would be offering national service by increasing Nigeria's agricultural production the maximum extent possible. With this assurance, Mackie set to work on crafting a policy and reorganization plan for the agriculture department.

AGRICULTURAL POLICY AND REORGANIZATION PLAN

In October of 1939, Mackie presented his department's policy of wartime reorganization to the CSG and to his senior officers. He made the point that if Nigeria was to maintain maximum production, all efforts must be in place to ensure that the fertility of the soil was maintained. To do this, he argued that the basis of their efforts must be mixed farming[57] in the northern region of Nigeria and work on green manuring and compost making in the southern region.[58] Faulkner and Mackie had long championed mixed farming in Northern Nigeria and devoted a chapter in their book, *West African Agriculture*, to discussing this practice. Their idea of mixed farming was

> one in which every farmer owns cattle of his own, say two bullocks and one or two cows, together with his usual head of sheep, goats and fowls. He would keep his cattle in a pen and supply them with bedding, thus making farmyard manure of the highest quality all the year round. His bullocks would be used for ploughing, thus solving the labour problem; and his cows would breed calves and supply him with milk for his family or for sale.[59]

They believed that such a system of farming was going to lead to the prosperity of the farmer and the country as a whole. Mixed farming had been experimented with in other colonies, such as Kenya, and had been successful.[60] Mackie and Faulkner were surprised that such a system had not been introduced in Nigeria earlier. In fact, mixed farming had not been widely adopted in Nigeria because of two problems. The first was the fear of epidemics such as Rinderpest. About three quarters of cattle were wiped out when there were epidemics.[61] The cost of keeping cattle and the product output that resulted from the farm animals was another difficulty. It was expensive to feed the animals and in some cases there wasn't substantial cleared land available for cultivation.[62] Faulkner and Mackie had tried mixed farming among a small group of farmers and they saw tremendous results. Farmers who adopted this system saw growth not only in the amount of land they cultivated but also better yields. Farmers who were cultivating only three acres of land could now cultivate ten or twelve acres because the bullocks helped with plowing and enough manure was produced for the fields.[63]

The second problem mixed farming faced was finding a suitable type of plow. Not only did the plow have to be technically suitable, it also had to be affordable because of the challenges African farmers faced in accessing capital. Several attempts that were made in the past by European missionaries and administrative officers failed because the type of plow chosen was unsuitable. Faulkner and Mackie felt that there was now a solution to this problem: the double-breasted ridging plow. Village craftsmen could easily make these plows of wood. They wrote,

> The wooden ploughs now in use can be made locally for less than £1. 10s. 0d., and they do quite satisfactory work. They have been used exclusively for all the ploughing on our experimental farms for the last three or four years, and those native farmers who have tried them have been well satisfied.[64]

In the southern part of the colony, Mackie advocated green manuring. Unlike in the North, land was a scarce commodity in the South and there was no cultural tradition of rearing cattle. The North had vast lands that the cattle could graze in. Mackie thought of green manuring as the best solution in the South because southerners were already practicing shifting cultivation. Green manuring is "the process of growing a crop simply for the sake of turning it all into the soil as a manure. The plants grown for this purpose were usually one of those belonging to the leguminous family—the family that includes beans, peas and clovers. The plants of this family have the unique property of collecting nitrogen directly from the air through the agency of bacteria which live in nodules on their roots."[65] The reason this system was more ideal in the southern region was because of the heavy rainfalls. It was common for the rains to wash and leach vital nutrients such as nitrogen from the soil. The agriculture department officials had been carrying out research and experimentations for about ten years and they had come to the conclusion that the fertility of the soil was best maintained through the use of green manuring. Faulkner and Mackie wrote, "The crops obtained at Ibadan now, after ten years of rotational green manuring and cropping, are as heavy or even heavier than were obtained from newly cleared bush; and they are heavy and very quick-growing crops by any standard."[66] Mackie's wartime agricultural reorganization proposal that mixed farming and green manuring should be used, was thus based on several years of investigations and experimentation.

In Mackie's view, the agricultural policy laid down in his memo was going to place Nigeria in a stronger position than it had been in the period before World War II and would consolidate Britain's colonial occupation of the territory. The first goal of the policy was to achieve food self-sufficiency. Thus, efforts had to be made to ensure that each part of the colony was as self-supporting as possible in the staple food crops, and if an area was not self-supporting, there must be distribution channels available to quickly and easily move supplies from one area to the next. Not only should the colony be self-supporting, food has to be stocked in reserves that could be drawn upon in the event of any emergency such as a drought or a partial failure of crops. The amount in reserves had to be documented to give a clear knowledge of what was available to be used at any given time. Mackie also insisted that in areas where cocoa was the main crop cultivated by the farmers, each farmer had to produce enough food for himself and his family. He was attempting to avoid a situation where farmers would invest all their resources into cash crops and then rely on imported food. This was an important measure to reduce the possibility of food being purchased that could have potentially gone into reserves in other areas. Large parts of Western Nigeria relied primarily on the production of cocoa. If they did not cultivate the food they needed for their consumption, they would resort to purchasing food from farmers in other regions of the country, undermining the policy that each region of the country should be self-supporting in food production. The policy of being self-supporting in agriculture was extended to individual families as well. Each family had to produce enough food needed for their consumption without resorting to buying imported food.

The second important policy goal was to increase local production. In this vein, products and food items that were previously imported had to be produced locally. As Mackie had predicted, during the war, they were major shipping disruptions leading to reductions in the imports and exports.[67] The agriculture officers in the different regions were to produce previously imported commodities that were suitable for their climatic conditions. Mackie summarized the duties of the agriculture department during war time as those of: being ready to help the imperial government with the production of crops that it may request; to ensure that Nigeria was self-supporting in foodstuffs that it usually would import; and finally to do what it could to make West African colonies as a whole self-supporting.[68] Mackie was convinced that his policy would stimulate industries in the manufacture of native products such as "sacks, baskets, rope etc."[69] These two objectives that Mackie set out to accomplish—being self-supporting in food and the production of crops for Britain—were potentially conflicting, since concentrating too much on one was bound to take away from the other. Nevertheless, his ideas were laying the foundations for the developmentalist state of the second colonial occupation.

Mackie's planning had anticipated the needs of the imperial government during wartime. By the time the S of S had sent a proposal to the agriculture departments advising them on what to do, Nigeria was well ahead in its planning. Mackie was quick to respond to this proposal:

> I think it is safe to say that we in Nigeria have anticipated the Secretary of State's proposals and I think that every important point mentioned in his circular is dealt with in my circular memorandum. . . . We have indeed gone rather further than merely to carry out the instructions to the letter, for we are also considering proposals for assisting the African to take a greater share in the processing of his own crops and the development of the internal trade in food stuffs.[70]

The major points in the S of S circular were that the colony should expand its production capacity and that the whole British colonies in West Africa should be self-supporting, directly mirroring Mackie's already well-formed plans on the matter. The expansion of production had already been the goal of the agriculture department and the colonial state; such expansion was good for the colony because it helped in raising revenues. The challenge for the department now was how such an expansion would be possible in the context of wartime Nigeria, given the bureaucratic wrangling that had stifled the efforts of the department. Be that as it may, Mackie wanted to make sure that he and his staff in the agriculture department made an essential contribution to the success of the war by producing sufficient quantities of commodities that may be needed.

After the war started, Mackie became quickly disappointed that demands were not made of Nigeria's produce. Though he acknowledged that Nigeria's first duty was to be as self-supporting as possible, he also felt that they had a duty to supply Great Britain with the tropical produce it needed. It is worth noting that Nigeria was actually struggling with its first wartime duty, despite Mackie's wider aspirations for assisting the empire. Rice, for example, was not being produced in a large enough quantity to stop importation. R. R. Glanville,[71] who was an expert on rice, toured some of the northern parts of Nigeria and reported that it was possible for Nigeria to be self-supporting in the production of rice if a special survey of the rice area was made and an officer was made available to work this. It was impossible to carry out such a survey during wartime due to the lack of human resources.

Mackie and his officers were disappointed with their work because the imperial government did not need the raw materials they had produced in large quantities. The different types of oilseeds they produced—palm, groundnut, beniseed, etc.—were not in need. The only demand that had been made of them was the Cameroon banana that was produced in the Cameroons. There, efforts had been intensified to meet the demand. Nevertheless, it was too early in the war for Mackie to start feeling disappointed that Nigerian produce was not needed. In the postwar period, there in fact ended up being a shortage of oilseeds and the colonial governments had to set up schemes to help ameliorate this problem. Mackie's own impatience with the colonial system may have undercut his own work. Shortly after the war started, Mackie was already expressing his disappointments with the British government for not requesting Nigerian products. Mackie was aware that he was perhaps being a little impatient. In a letter to the CSG he wrote, "We must still assume that the war will be a long one and there is still time to make preparations even if they may take some time to carry out. . . . I therefore beg to suggest that a definite enquiry should be sent to His Majesty's Government asking if there is any product which is likely to be required."[72] His goal at this point was no longer to plan for the immediate needs but also to start planning for what the future needs of the empire might be. He started to speculate about what products might be needed, writing, "I have heard unofficially that there is a real shortage of fibres of various kinds, and I note that Keyna [*sic*] has been asked to grow flax. We have never tried to grow flax, and so far jute has not done well in Nigeria, but we can grow sisal, ramie, or sun hemp. Similarly we can grow cotton. If any of these are wanted we could undoubtedly push up production quite quickly if seed supplies were available."[73] Finding adequate staff was undoubtedly going to be a major hindrance to carrying out any of these plans. For Mackie, Nigeria's agriculture could not carry on normally as during peacetime. It must make a useful contribution to the war and its contribution was not military but economic. This contribution, in his opinion, was not only limited to the agriculture department but was in fact Nigeria's contribution to the war. He went on to suggest that "if officers could be spared for military service now that they are not required for this purpose a few officers could be spared for Agricultural service."[74] For him, these officers need not have any agricultural training. They could help with office work to free up agricultural officers from such duties or they could help with some preliminary work that did not require any agricultural expertise. Given the pivotal role that agriculture was to play in the immediate success of the war and the period after the war, it is unfortunate that the colonial state did not see the need to immediately train and integrate Africans in the state service. The question is, if trained labor was such an essential component in the economic success of colonial agriculture, why was African labor excluded or underutilized? The answer to this question lies in the racial attitudes of the colonial state. The state was willing to sacrifice its economic success at the altar of its racial biases. The economic problems that arose in the postwar period could have been avoided if the colonial state had empowered the colonized through advanced education and training and had actively involved them in the development process. There is no system that worked so hard to undercut its own interests than colonial rule. If the goal of colonialism was the exploitation of the colonized, it was really bad at it and even the second colonial occupation with its change of policies and tactics could not save this inept rule.

CONFLICTS WITH ADMINISTRATIVE OFFICIALS

The ineptitude of colonial rule created a system in which the different organs of the colonial state were constantly in conflict with each other. These conflicts undermined the goals of development in particular and colonialism in general. Mackie felt a sense of noncooperation from some of the administrative officials. He had a long list of grievances, which he had put in a letter he intended to send officially to the CSG, Hoskyns Abrahall. He had some reservations putting this letter in the official records and thus he decided to attach it to a private letter to Abrahall. In this letter, he expressed his feelings that he was not allowed to pull his weight in Nigeria and felt that he would be more useful in other colonies or even helping with the war back in England. He reiterated that the other members of the agriculture department shared his feelings as well. He wrote,

> I should hesitate to write like this if it was merely a personal matter but all my officers feel the same. Also, it is not a new thing. The whole history of my Department since 1921 shows that almost every scheme which involved work among the farmers has been opposed or obstructed. As far as the North is concerned, in present conditions I can see no point whatever in putting up schemes for the Colonial Development Fund, for I know that I should not be allowed to carry them out.[75]

Mackie was distraught with the opposition his department faced from the administrative department of the colonial state. Were these two organs of the state not supposed to work toward the same goals? This is emblematic of the contradictions of the colonial state. The administrative department needed agriculture to be successful because it was the staple of the economy. So, why would they obstruct the department that was supposed to help in improving agriculture? The magnitude of the obstruction was so elevated that Mackie and his staff were not willing to submit agricultural schemes to be funded by the colonial development fund. He believed that some level of reorganization needed to happen in order for his department to function effectively. Despite the frustrations he felt, he was not ready to leave Nigeria because in his words, "I like the country and the people and am most anxious to do something for them."[76]

Mackie's difficulties were neither directly with the governor nor the CSG. His challenge was with the administrative officials in the provinces. One official in particular that he singled out was Sir Theodore Samuel Adams.[77] Some of his grievances with the administrative department centered on the lackadaisical attitude they had toward his requests. For example, in April of 1939 he wrote to the administrative department requesting that they begin preparations for the war. It took about three months before his letter was acknowledged. When he requested the appointment of a marketing officer, it took over a year before one was appointed and it required the backing of the cocoa marketing committee. He was also frustrated with the fact that, even though they were at war, the activities of the department were still governed by the financial secretary's ruling that "there must be no expansion of work and that I must not make work in order to give members of the African staff increased responsibility."[78] The governor had a proposal to increase the production of wheat flour, but the agriculture department's proposal for this scheme took more than six months before it was approved. Mackie said that correspondences kept constantly bouncing between the central secretariat, the northern secretariat, and the agriculture department, without any decisions being made. While the scheme faced the bureaucratic red tape, the wheat crop had ripened and there was no machinery available for milling it. These issues raised by Mackie were part of the dysfunctional nature of the colonial state as a whole. The different arms of the colonial order were trying to protect their own turf and they did not want any interference. However, was it realistic for Mackie to think that at a time of labor shortage, the administrative department would be able to appoint a marketing officer within a short time?

The British colonial order was extremely bureaucratic and generally very slow to act. Mackie, however, believed that what was happening went beyond the bureaucratic bottlenecks of the colonial state but was a deliberate attempt by some administrative officials to frustrate his efforts and those of his department. As evidence he highlighted how Sir Theodore had treated him. He said the commissioner held up his department's proposals for ordering sugar cane crushers and it took the intervention of the governor to have the approval granted. The commissioner also denied Mackie's proposal for the storage of food crops and demanded evidence that the soils of Kano were deteriorating before he would approve the proposals for the storage of groundnut seeds. Mackie's proposals for making Nigeria self-supporting in potatoes was also rejected by the chief commissioner of the northern Province, who informed him that what was wanted was expert advice and not "restrictive regulations."[79] The same commissioner obstructed the proposals for the production of rice and it again took the intervention of the governor for him to change his position.[80] These obstructions had so much impact on Mackie that, if he was deemed to be the problem in this conflict, he was willing to transfer to a smaller colony on a smaller salary or to work under someone else temporarily during the war. He was convinced, however, that he was not the problem: it was the organization. He wrote, "But whatever may be my shortcomings I do feel that there is also something wrong with the system of Government which permits of such delays and obstruction and I am fortified in this opinion by discussions I have had with Administrative Officers in both Secretariats and in the Provinces, many of whom feel as I do."[81] His feeling that Nigeria was not taking the war seriously, he argued, was shared by many Europeans who were in Nigeria and that the unnecessary red tape and paperwork that existed during peacetime was also continued during wartime when there was a need for things to be done at a faster pace. Mackie's request was that immediate steps should be taken to review the organization and to put Nigeria on a war footing.

Sometime between May 29 and June 18 Mackie had a meeting with the governor. We can only assume that the governor had a conversation with Mackie about the letter he sent to Hoskyns Abrahall. This assumption is based on the fact that on June 18 Mackie sent a circular to his officers in the agriculture department and he referenced a recent meeting with the governor.[82] The governor informed him at the meeting that for the duration of the war, the primary work of the department should be the production of foodstuffs. He also said that the governor had assured him that his administration would assist them "in this work to the fullest possible extent."[83] Feeling very optimistic about the support of the governor, in June Mackie gave his officers the free hand to carry out the work of expanding food production. He wrote, "I wish to give officers a very free hand and hope that everyone will use his own initiative. Each officer should formulate his own local proposals, discuss them with the Resident and then put them into effect. If however difficulties or obstructions are encountered I must be informed at once. The great thing is to get work done."[84]

Mackie was motivated by the words of the governor and he was now in the position to motivate his officers to get work done. This was necessary at a time when morale was low in the department. Without the meeting with the governor, Mackie would not have had the confidence to give this directive to his officers. When he instructed them to report to him immediately should they encounter difficulties or obstructions, he was counting on the support of the governor to intervene. In this memorandum, he reiterated the policy of the department that each province should be as self-supporting as possible and that it was impossible to overproduce essential commodities. To commit his officers to what was the most essential of their duties, the production of more foodstuffs, he put to an end the department policy in which the officers had to send a monthly report to the director. This was a bureaucratic step that took time away from the officers' work. Instead the officers needed to submit a monthly statement of expenditure. Relieved of the obligation to submit a monthly report, they could devote more time to food production; however, they were to keep Mackie informed of their work progress and report any important issues that arose.[85]

Three days after Mackie sent the memorandum to his officers, he met with the CSG and submitted a new request. He wanted one person to be put in charge of food production, to carry out any policy that was being enacted by the governor. He expressed his willingness to serve under such a person. There is no doubt that Mackie would have been disappointed if such a position was created and he was not put in charge. Later that same day, the governor met with Mackie and proposed to make him the director of food production (DFP) in addition to his position as director of agriculture. Mackie's idea of this new position differed from what the governor had intended. Mackie wanted a statutory position but the governor had intended it to be a ceremonial position that had no authority attached to it. For the governor, the sole purpose of the position was to draw attention to the state's emphasis on food production. When the governor communicated to Mackie that this position carried no authority, Mackie was not pleased and requested that the governor attach some authority to it. In what was presumably a way to dismiss Mackie's concerns, the governor told him he was going to discuss the position further with the CSG and get back with him. Almost one year after Mackie was named to the position; the governor did not grant him any powers. In May of 1941, Mackie wrote to the CSG: "The duties of the post of Director of Food Production have never been defined and up to the present time I have never been asked for or been given any special powers. I have no authority to co-ordinate the food production work of the Agriculture Department with that of the Veterinary Department and schemes put forward by the Veterinary Department are still treated as if the latter was a completely watertight compartment."[86] It is surprising that Mackie was so aloof to the politics that was in play here. If the governor wanted to attach some authority to the position, he did not need any further discussions with the CSG. It is obvious from the governor's long silence that he had never intended to attach any authority to that position.

After a year of not receiving any additional powers, Mackie used his letter to the CSG to restate his case. He argued that the Conference of Directors of Agriculture in 1938 had stressed that supply cannot be separated from production and that each colony should appoint a director of food production and supply with ample funds at his disposal.[87] Mackie continued: "If I am to carry out the functions of the Director of Food Production as envisaged by this Conference, and to make the effort required of us I must now ask for more staff; and more authority to co-ordinate the efforts of everyone engaged in the work of food production is essential if every available man is to pull his weight with the greatest possible effect."[88] What one deduces from Mackie's missives is that he was a man who wanted more control and it is not surprising that he was having difficulties with the administrative officials at the provinces. They wanted to protect their own sphere of influence with the African leaders and saw Mackie as encroaching into their turf.

With his vision for the DFP position, Mackie was proposing to create some form of an amalgamation between the agriculture, veterinary, and forestry departments. The CO had also been moving in this direction by expanding the advisory committee on agriculture and animal health to include forestry and fisheries. Mackie's request made practical sense but it was politically toxic. These departments would have been more effective if they coordinated their work; however, more often than not, these departments were in conflict with each other. Mackie was essentially asking for the heads of those departments to now be under his own authority. Perhaps if a neutral DFP was appointed and the directors of all three departments were under his control, his proposal may have had a fighting chance, but to bring the other departments under Mackie's control was too risky a move that neither the CSG nor the governor were prepared to undertake. In reply, the CSG asked him to submit a list of functions he considered vital for the DFP.[89] On June 10, 1941 Mackie wrote the CSG a confidential letter with a description of the functions of the DFP. Mackie suggested six duties for the director of food production:

1. To be the sole channel through which all requirements for supplies would pass through.
2. To administer all funds meant for the development of production and allocate such funds to the department that would carry out the work.
3. To collaborate with the Food Controller on schemes that increased production and to authorize such schemes without subject to any other authority as long as those schemes conformed to the policy of Government.
4. To co-ordinate the work of food production to make sure there was no waste or overlapping.
5. To locate work where it was of most permanent value for the country.
6. To see to a smooth flow of supplies.[90]

Later in June the governor directed the CSG to circulate a document defining the duties of the DFP. Mackie's suggestions were accepted almost verbatim. Instead of the six duties that he had submitted, the circular from the CSG listed four duties. The sixth duty in Mackie's letter was combined with the fourth. What was conspicuously absent was the first duty that Mackie had stated in his letter. The governor did not grant him that authority because he wanted the respective departments to still maintain some level of independence and authority. This factor was very important to the governor and he made it clear at the end of the circular that the DFP was not going to interfere with the normal duties of the departments:

> His Excellency wishes it clearly to be understood that this definition of the Director of Food Production's duties in no way implies any interference with the normal functions of Departments but is directed solely to ensure that development should not be hampered by administrative delays and that the limited staff of qualified officers available may be employed to the greatest effect.[91]

The DFP had no authority to assign the different officers of the technical departments. That was the responsibility of the director of their department. If the DFP needed a technical officer for any specific purpose, he had to arrange it with that department's head and the CSG. The governor's approach was a middle way toward dealing with what could have been a potential disaster. In one way, Mackie got what he wanted, and in another way, the other department heads maintained authority over their respective departments. Looking closely at the defined duties that the governor gave Mackie as the DFP, the position was merely ceremonial. He was already carrying out most of these duties as the director of the agriculture department. The only function that would have truly given him additional authority was the one the governor decided not to grant him.

DEARTH OF AGRICULTURAL STAFF

Mackie was satisfied with his new position as DFP and felt he could make a difference in food production. What continued to be a major problem in the execution of his work was the dearth of staff. In order to increase production, he needed agricultural staff to help him in this work. This he believed was not only urgently needed during wartime but also for the postwar period. The agricultural staff were instrumental for the extension of services that were vital for improved production by African farmers. He argued that increased production could only be achieved through three principal means: stimulating the African farmer to put forth more efforts; using Europeans to develop more government estates; and allowing firms to develop estates.[92] In the case of Nigeria, the first option was the best. Historically, cultivation by the African small farm holder had been fundamental to the Nigerian economy. Mackie did not think that it was good policy to divert European staff to government estate development when African production had not reached its peak. There were vast areas that still needed an agricultural officer and there weren't any to provide. Allowing firms to develop estates was one option he did not want to consider because it was controversial. Unlike some other British colonies in Africa like Kenya, Nigeria did not have private estate production. In the early years of colonization, this option was resisted and part of the reason was because of the Nigerian system of land tenure.[93] When Lever Brothers, a British firm, wanted communal land to be appropriated to the company for plantation agriculture, Governor Hugh Clifford responded by addressing the Nigerian Council in 1920, telling them that

> agricultural industries in tropical countries which are mainly, or exclusively, in the hands of the native peasantry a) have a firmer root than similar enterprises when owned and managed by Europeans, because they are natural growths, not artificial creations, and are self-supporting, as regards labour, while European plantations can only be maintained by some system of organised immigration or by some form of compulsory labour; b) are incomparably the cheapest instruments for the production of agricultural produce on a large scale that have yet been devised; and c) are capable of a rapidity of expansion and a progressive increase of output that beggar every record of the past, and altogether unparalleled in all the long history of European enterprises in the tropics.[94]

Though Clifford claims that the reason for denying the introduction of plantation agriculture is the productive character of peasant agriculture, the ultimate reason was the controversy over land and labor that plantation agriculture was going to create and this was bound to wrestle the authority upon which the colonial state rested.[95] Mackie had not foreclosed on the idea of developing government estates in the future. His thinking around such estates was for the postwar period. He felt that such estates could be parceled out to some of the returning soldiers to cultivate under the supervision of a European agriculture official. He wrote, "I should like to see for several of these estates started before the war ends both in the N.Ps [Northern provinces] and the S.Ps [Southern provinces], for even if they are planted up with permanent crops which take several years to grow into bearing I am sure that there will be a demand for our produce for several years after the war ends."[96] Mackie was not thinking in terms of an empire that was ending anytime soon, but an empire that would endure many decades after the war. He was in effect planning for the second colonial occupation.

To execute his task of ramping up production, Mackie urgently needed to increase staff in his department. Even though he had made this demand to the CO, no staff was forthcoming. Mackie's assumption was that he was not getting these staff because the CO did not value the potential of Nigerian agriculture. This reflects Mackie's impatience and suspicions whenever his demands were not immediately met. This was a time of war and extraordinary difficulties for Britain. Most of the young men had entered the military service and other colonies were also vitally important to the empire in terms of production. It is true that Nigeria was a large colony with agricultural potential, but it did not have a monopoly of all production. The available officers had to be shared with other colonies as well. The problem of labor shortage was being experienced by other British colonies as well. This by itself is an indictment on the colonial system that failed to train African labor to fill such needs that could have been easily fulfilled by Africans. Herein lie the roots of the failure of the second colonial occupation that was symbolized in Nigeria by the enactment of the 1945 Nigerian Development Plan. Nevertheless, Mackie's passion for the development of agriculture in Nigeria and his desperate desire for the Nigerian colony to make significant contributions to the war through enhanced production cannot be overlooked. Mackie's work during this time formed the bedrock for the agriculture proposals that became part of the 1945 development plan.

REORGANIZING THE DEPARTMENTS

Before the war, Mackie had submitted a detailed plan of agricultural expansion to the CO. It was intended to help with wartime supplies and postwar recovery. He did not receive any response to this plan, which was submitted through the Nigerian secretariat. Mackie felt that the CO had ignored this plan but it is doubtful that the Nigerian secretariat submitted it to London. As the war was coming to an end and plans were in motion for postwar development, the CO requested a detailed agriculture plan from Nigeria in 1944. Governor Arthur Richards invited Mackie and the other two directors of the departments of forestry and veterinary services to a meeting at the Government House in Lagos. The goal of the meeting was to coordinate development policy and to facilitate teamwork where their departments overlapped. All three heads of departments accepted the invitation and had a meeting with the governor, the chief commissioners of the eastern, northern, and western provinces, the development secretary, and the acting deputy chief secretary. At the meeting, the governor announced a new structure that he felt would enable the three departments to function collaboratively. The governor was attempting to balance centralization with regionalization in order to respond to the ethnic and political realities that Nigeria was facing. Before the arrival of Arthur Richards in Nigeria from Jamaica where he was governor, Bernard Bourdillon, the Nigerian governor had already divided Nigeria into three regions: northern, eastern, and western. Bourdillon had become doubtful of his own decision because he believed that under the new structure, the northern region would be insulated from the rest of Nigeria, a concern that Hugh Clifford had earlier raised against Lord Lugard's indirect rule policy. Before his retirement in 1943, there were proposals of a new constitution that would govern the regions but these reforms had not been enacted. When Richards came to Nigeria, he rushed through constitutional reforms and instituted the three regions.[97] This constitution was novel due to its regionalism, although it had a "quasi-federal" structure to it. As Samuel Coleman has noted, "Sir

Arthur Richards argued that this embryonic, quasi-federal structure was a practical means of obtaining two of his major objectives: it would promote Nigerian unity and at the same time would provide within that unity for the country's diverse elements."[98]

The political changes occurring with regionalization meant that the structure of the colonial state also had to be reorganized. In this vein, the governor wanted the offices of the heads of the three departments moved from their respective locations to Lagos and their new responsibility was that of serving as advisers to the Nigerian central government. New deputies were appointed for these departments and were given offices at the locations where the directors previously had their main offices. The deputy for the northern provinces had an office in Kaduna, the deputy for the eastern provinces had an office in Enugu, and the deputy for the western provinces had an office in Ibadan. The governor also considered appointing a fourth deputy for each of the departments with offices in Lagos. The governor said the goal of the changes was to free the directors of the departments to travel around the country more. The deputies who were assigned to the different provinces were to be advisers to the chief commissioners. The governor argued that these deputies had to be in a position in which they could give authoritative advice to the chief commissioners without reference to the department heads. The deputies were to be "subject to the orders of the Chief Commissioners in all Administrative matters relating to their Departments, but Chief Commissioners would not of course, be in a position to give directions on technical matters. On such matters the Deputies should seek directions from their Head of Department in Lagos."[99] The authority to post officers to these departments was also to emanate from the secretariat. By giving control of staff appointments to the secretariat, as well as subjecting the deputies to the control of the chief commissioners, it is reasonable to argue that the governor was attempting to weaken the technical departments, while at the same time strengthening the political wing of the colonial state. Nevertheless, the governor believed that the overlapping and frictions between the three departments were a result of the three heads of departments working in locations isolated from each other and from the secretariat in Lagos. His position was that by putting them in one location, this problem was going to be solved. The authority to discipline departmental officers was now bestowed on the chief commissioners and if necessary, referred to the secretariat in Lagos.[100] This reorganization was intended to resolve the perennial conflicts between the technical and administrative officials. Development was now vested in the hands of the administrative and not the technical officials. This was antithetical to development during the second colonial occupation when the technical "experts" had more sway in development policy directions and implementation in the colonies.

Be that as it may, Richards' reforms helped to address the tensions between the technical and administrative staff in the provinces and districts. Part of the conflict was that the administrative officials felt that the staff of the technical departments worked under them. Conversely, the staff of the technical departments wanted to have more autonomy from the administrative officials in other departments to carry out their work without interference. With these structural changes, the governor clearly defined the boundaries of authority. Not only were the technical staff to take their orders in the provinces from the chief commissioners, but they were also to be disciplined by them. While Mackie spent several years pushing for more authority and independence, now he was even stripped of the authority he previously had. He could no longer assign his officers and the governor imposed deputies on the department heads who reported not to the director, but to the chief commissioners. The deputies conferred with the director solely on technical matters. It is not surprising that this did not go well with Mackie. While the other two heads of departments accepted what the governor said, Mackie protested. He said that he did not like the idea of surrendering to the secretariat his personal authority to make staff assignments. The governor simply responded that "while the views of the head of any Department would be taken, the final exercising of authority would of necessity have to be done centrally, and in some cases there was clearly need for the exercising of some control over the postings made by the Heads of Departments."[101] This was a big change for the heads of departments who exercised authority in assigning their staff. Mackie insisted that he would "resist interference with his executive control over the officers of his Department."[102] The governor responded that neither Mackie nor any head of department could be regarded as having complete command. They would have to rely on his directions.[103] By shifting the authority from the technical officials to the administrative officials, the governor was in danger of bureaucratizing the development process. The effect of such a policy was that the development process would be slow and less responsive to the needs and problems of the local people.

For decades, the different technical departments had accumulated power and gained a considerable level of independence in their affairs. They had also wrestled with each other to expand their own spheres of authority. The administrative officials had always wanted to rein in the powers of the department heads and bring them under their own control. One of the reasons some of the Residents were not giving access to the technical staff was because they believed that the departments were running their own schemes and projects irrespective of the traditional administrations. Yet, the Residents did not want the technical staff to have direct access to the local authorities. Such access must always come through the Resident or the provincial commissioners. Governor Richards's way of resolving these tensions was to bring the heads of the technical departments under the central secretariat and strip them of their executive authorities, leaving them with limited powers. Their powers were so limited that they were deprived of directly advising the chief commissioners who were powerful in shaping the policy direction at the regional levels. The role of department directors was now merely to be advisers to the central government. Most schemes and projects took place at the provincial and district levels and not at the central level. The governor had effectively chosen sides in the conflict and it was obvious from Mackie's responses that his days in Nigeria were numbered.

While the new structure that the governor announced consumed a substantial part of the meeting, that policy was a prelude to the hard work that lay ahead in crafting development plans for the postwar period. At the meeting, the development secretary asked that something definite should be said about the ongoing preparations for the development proposals that the CO requested and asked that "the Governor might rule the latest date at which these proposals should be furnished, as well as a statement of suggested policy for each of the three Departments represented at the meeting."[104] Mackie and the other two technical department heads said they would have their statements of policy and proposals ready no later than the end of January 1945, and the governor agreed to this deadline.[105]

THE AGRICULTURAL PLAN

On January 30, 1945, as promised, Mackie submitted his proposals for agriculture development. The task of drawing up these plans wasn't a challenge for him as he had already presented such a plan to the CO four years' prior. This was the plan that he believed was ignored and forgotten about by the CO. In submitting this new revised proposal, Mackie requested that one of the six copies be sent directly to the S of S as it stood. This request reveals the distrust he had of the Nigerian secretariat. He saw the proposals as a plan that would "expand the Agricultural Department sufficiently to provide Nigeria with Agricultural services which are adequate for the needs of the country, bearing in mind that Nigeria is and will always remain an Agricultural country."[106] This view by Mackie that the Nigerian productive force would always be agricultural reflects the agrarian bias of the colonial state. Nigeria did not remain an agricultural country. The oil booms of the 1970s pushed Nigeria away from being a food producer to a food importer. However, Mackie was right that Nigeria at the time was an agricultural country and to an extent would remain one, even though its food imports have risen substantially. A substantial majority of the people in Nigeria still rely on agriculture for sustenance. Though Nigeria's economy is now based on the export of crude oil, Nigerian-farmed agricultural products remain a staple of internal trade. Apart from poultry, rice is the only staple that is imported into the country at a commercial rate. A good quantity of rice consumed in the country is also locally grown. The maize, yams, cassava, plantains, etc. that are staples on Nigerian dining tables are grown locally. These are not usually cultivated by big industrial farms but by small holding farmers. Despite the oil revenues, agriculture remains the sector that provides the most economic empowerment to the majority of Nigerians. A majority of Nigerians live in rural areas and depend on subsistence farming. From what they produce, they feed their families and sell the rest to gain purchasing power. But the increase in food production did not come easily in the postcolonial period. It took several government programs such as Operation Feed the Nation to reverse the food crisis that Nigeria was experiencing in the period during the oil boom and thereafter. In a sense, Mackie's vision of a strong agricultural service that would be adequate to the needs of Nigeria in the present and in the future was correct. Nigeria today, as in the colonial times, has been to a large extent self-sufficient in food production. What has plagued Nigeria is its inability to produce enough for exports.

The plan for agriculture submitted by Mackie was divided into five sections: general agriculture including agricultural research; marketing and produce inspection; agricultural training; irrigation; and oil palm research. The estimated cost of the plan was £12,184,000 over the ten-year period. Mackie's view was that because they wouldn't have the staff necessary to implement the whole plan within the ten-year period, it should for all practical purposes be considered a fifteen-year plan. Based on this, the estimated amount that would be spent in the ten-year period of the plan was £8,000,000.[107] In estimating his plan, Mackie was afraid that the financial demands being made for agriculture were too large. He indicated that his plan might be criticized for being too excessive. He was being overly cautious and conservative when he indicated that £8 million might be enough for the ten-year period. The Nigerian development plan was estimated at about £55 million: the estimates given by Mackie were only about 20 percent of this. Given the importance of agriculture for the economic empowerment of the country and its potential to better the standards of living of the people, agriculture should have received more investments.

The first section of the plan was on agricultural policy in Nigeria. This section begins with the definition of agricultural development. It stated: "Agricultural Development is not a series of schemes it is a question of continuous research and sound extension work. There is nothing else to it."[108] This apt definition of agricultural development laid the foundation for the plan. For many years, the view of agriculture development was a proliferation of many schemes. The provincial and district officials carried a series of such schemes, often without making use of all the technical resources available through the agriculture department because of the tensions that existed. For this reason they had a high failure rate. The proposed plan envisaged a more coordinated effort that would bring together research and extension work. Mackie and his department were strong proponents of agricultural research. Mackie thought the department should spend several years studying any crop or system of farming before the African farmer was asked to adopt it.

Mackie's insistence on research and field trials was to reduce or eliminate instances of failed local schemes. Such failures were detrimental to the colonial state as the farmers' confidence in the state declined when schemes failed. Failed crops had severe consequences for the peasant farmer also due to their challenges in getting labor. If a farmer who had been cultivating maize adopted the cultivation of rice because he was asked to do so by the state, he invariably had to significantly reduce the amount of maize he cultivated or eliminate cultivating maize altogether because of the problem of labor. If rice had not been carefully researched and studied over time to be sure that it would be successful, and it failed, the consequences of this failure to the farmer were severe because he had neither capital nor reserves to rely on. Most farmers were always one step away from "bankruptcy." There was always the problem of risk aversion for the farmer. Farmers underwent such difficult circumstances during droughts and were reluctant to invite such circumstances upon themselves with the introduction of new crops. Careful research was necessary in order to gain the farmers' confidence. Mackie wrote, "From the time when an Agricultural Officer is first posted to a new area it is usually at least 10 years before he can make any appreciable progress with extension work, but after that steady progress can usually be recorded."[109] It took that much time because the officer had to gain the farmer's confidence through his own demonstration farms. Mackie insisted that for the agriculture policy of his department to be carried out well, every member of the department "must himself be a farmer, and he must be able to farm as well as or better than the people of the district in which he is working." He continued, "It cannot be too strongly stressed that the main and perhaps only function of an Agricultural Department is to teach the people how to farm better than they do at present. It is therefore essential that the Department should actually farm a considerable area of land, and that our farms in addition to being research stations should also be used for the training in farming of both European and African staff."[110]

Mackie challenged the assumption that if you were an agriculture officer, you knew how to farm. From his years of experience in the department, he knew that this was not always the case. Some of the agriculture officers were "arm chair" farmers. They knew the theory of farming without having hands-on practical experience of farming. Rather than standing and telling people what to do, Mackie wanted the officials to be involved in the job. They needed to know how to farm; not only how to farm, but also how to be better farmers than the people they were working with. The only way the African farmers would adopt their methods was if they proved to them through practice that they were better farmers. Mackie wanted to be absolutely sure that before the indigenous form of cultivation was changed, the methods proposed by the department had been thoroughly tested and found to be superior to the methods used by the locals. He wrote, "We are therefore learning to farm under all possible conditions and the more we study the question the more we become convinced that it is extremely unwise to try and change native systems of Agriculture until we are sure that the change is sound from the point of view of the native farmer under his own local conditions."[111] What Mackie was proposing was not always the attitude of officials in Nigeria or in most British dependencies in Africa. The African farmer was frequently looked upon as inferior and without any sound knowledge of cultivation. The colonial officer imposed a new method of cultivation on them without taking into consideration the local conditions and this often led to disaster, causing the colonial official to lose credibility. For Mackie, the credibility of colonial officials in the eyes of African farmers was very important. Mackie wrote, "The African farmer is generally a capable Agriculturalist within the limits of his own environment and tools and if we try to force him to do something which he knows is unsound we merely lose both his confidence and respect."[112] Most African agrarian societies accorded respect to good farmers. One's wealth was measured by how successful a farmer he was. Mackie was advocating for colonial agriculture officials to show excellence in farming so that the people would be willing to adopt the new methods that they used.

Another important aspect of Mackiean agricultural policy was the training of African staff. This policy placed high priority on using more African staff in the department. One of the failures of the colonial state was the exclusion of Africans in the higher cadre of service. The labor shortages of the war and postwar period would have been avoided if Africans had been integrated in the service. Mackie recognized the failure and wanted African staff to become a core labor force of the department. The departmental school in Ibadan had been training African staff since 1921 and the one in Samaru since 1928, and this staff was considered crucial to the success of the department's work. However, these schools trained Africans for the lower level positions. Mackie's proposal was that the school in Ibadan should be expanded to award degrees in agriculture to African staff. He also looked forward to a time when women would be trained as agricultural assistants. He wrote:

> It is now generally agreed in the Department that to enable a European Officer to be of maximum value to the country he should have an African staff of up to

> 20 trained people working under him. The fully trained African Assistant has undoubtedly been a success and I am now quite satisfied that there is scope for African Agricultural Officers.[113]

What he meant was that Africans were capable of being district officers and should be trained as such and not limited to the subpar positions of assistants to European agricultural officers. He was proposing that African staff should also be trained to the level to which they could be agricultural officers in their own rights. If this plan was implemented, it would bring about two important benefits: it would help resolve the perennial problem of Nigerian agriculture, which was the dearth of agricultural officers, and it would reap financial benefits, since it was more economical to have African staff in these positions than European staff. For Mackie, African staff trained with degrees in Ibadan could go to Trinidad for advanced training in tropical agriculture.[114] This Mackiean policy, though late in coming, was progressive for a colonial state that was ever doubtful of the capabilities of Africans to manage their own affairs.

Another important aspect of Mackiean policy was the reorganization of the agriculture department. Mackie's proposal took into consideration the decision of the governor to move the director of the department to Lagos and also to appoint deputies for each of the provinces. The director would also have a senior deputy director, a secretary, and a statistician working with him at the secretariat. The idea of having these additional staff was to enable the director to travel more freely in order to give sound advice to the governor. Mackie's organization of the department was intended to adequately cover each part of the country with agricultural services. He recognized that his goal of providing each agriculture officer with twenty trained Africans was not possible in the ten-year period of the plan. He insisted that no positions in the agriculture department be reserved for Europeans and each position should be opened for whoever is qualified, be it an African or a European. Part of the reasoning for this policy was to make sure that the Africans whom he intended to train as officers would have positions available to them. More forward thinking than most of his peers, Mackie was making efforts to break down the racial prejudices of the colonial state. He believed that Africans would be able to assume the same positions in the department that were being held by Europeans. The African staff recognized and appreciated this attitude, as shown in their farewell speech to Mackie when he retired from the Nigerian service. Their words that no one else in the department had worked harder than Mackie to advance the welfare of the African staff were borne out of their experiences working with him.[115]

Mackie's proposal called for each deputy director to have a team of specialist staff, experimental farms, a stock farm, a school where assistant officers would eventually be trained, and each province was also to have a team of agricultural officers.[116] This was in line with the plan to have new methods well researched before the African farmers were asked to adopt them. Nigeria was a place with varied climatic conditions and topography. The expert team working with the deputy director would help research and investigate crops and methods that were suitable for the area. In the case of Nigeria, the approach was not going to be "one size fits all." The team of experts working with the deputy director was to include botanists, a pasture research chemist, entomologists, an engineer, an economist, experts in dairy, poultry, and pasture research, a geneticist, a mycologist, and a horticulturist. Mackie did not include soil conservation officers despite criticism from Dr. Tempany. Mackie's argument was that he did not like the term because he felt that "every Agricultural Officer and Forestry Officer is a soil conservation Officer and they should never be allowed to forget it. To apply this title to special officers is to give the impression to the others that soil conservation is not their business."[117] While the other experts included in his list were all directly related in some way to plants cultivation, he also included an economist in his list. One may wonder about Mackie's choice of an economist as part of the local agriculture team. If there was a need for an economist, shouldn't they be working at the central secretariat? Mackie's plan called for a statistician working with the director of agriculture in the central secretariat to help him with crunching data. At the provincial level, what he felt was needed was an economist. The role of the economist was to closely study the economics of peasant farming. He wrote, "Farming after all is economics—and the Nigerian farmer is an economist."[118] Having economists at the local level was important for collecting data on the economics of peasant farming and also to be able to assess the contribution that women made in peasant farming. It was very easy to see what contributions the men made because they were the ones who were regarded as the farmers. Women made enormous contributions through their labor. They cooked meals for those who worked in the farms, they helped with watering crops where irrigation was not present, and they did the weeding after the crops had been planted. The peasant farmer, in choosing what crop to plant and what quantity to cultivate, had to make an economic decision. This deserved study if local agriculture was to be successfully expanded to improve the economy of the colony and that of the people.

Mackie's definition of agricultural development as being research and extension influenced his agricultural proposal. Rather than focusing on developing big agricultural schemes, he focused on research/investigation and extension work. His idea was to have a strong research and investigation center in each of the provinces and then extend the success of that labor to the local farmers. Some officials in this late colonial period were tempted to engage in schemes that would guarantee quick returns. The next chapter will look at one such scheme in Nigeria. Mackie understood that solid agricultural development projects needed time and he saw no need to rush through the process. He wanted to institute a solid foundation in research and investigation and his plan encapsulates this principle. In the western provinces, there was already the main research station at Moor Plantation. This station was equipped for both laboratory and field investigations. The area also had a stock farm that was established in 1932 at Illorin and was researching the breeding of cattle that would be resistant to trypanosomiasis.[119] He proposed that a breeding farm be established to produce animals for distribution. At the time of drafting the proposal, there was a farm school in Oyo that was still operating on an experimental basis. If this farm became successful, he proposed that many other farm schools be established. While Mackie's proposal is commendable in its emphasis on studying and researching the problem, this had a weakness of not doing much in terms of practice. At a time when the country needed immediate relief, his plan's insistence on research meant things would be going slowly.

Significantly, his plan did not call for the mechanization of agriculture, in contrast to most postwar agricultural development schemes. He believed such initiatives would never be successful in southern Nigeria; in fact, he felt that they would spell disaster. They could only be successful, he argued, if they were "accompanied by a sound system of manuring and soil conservation, for their use involves the complete stumping of large areas."[120] He was very weary of using tractors because he believed they caused erosion. Beyond the problem of erosion, there was also the cost and availability of spare parts. The Mokwa agricultural development experiment that we will analyze in the next chapter demonstrates the fears Mackie had with mechanization. Mackie's plan called for the trial of one large-scale government plantation in the western provinces based on cocoa, citrus, and white kola. His plan did not provide details on the cost and size of such a plantation.

Mackie acknowledged that, unlike in the western provinces, the organization of agriculture in the eastern provinces was not as advanced. The main agricultural product from the eastern provinces was the palm fruit. These grew wildly in the forests, unlike in the western provinces where farmers had adopted the planting of cocoa or in the northern provinces were nuts and seeds were planted by the farmers. In the eastern provinces, there were no specialist officers and no testing laboratories. The department had some experimental stations in Umuahia, Nkwale, Bamenda, Yandev, and in Esosong. It is important to note that Esosong and Bamenda are today in Southern Cameroons but were originally part of the eastern provinces of Nigeria. In the east, Mackie felt that the first essential thing to do toward agricultural development was to focus on research and experimentation. He wanted to establish a central research station along the lines of Moor Plantation in this region.

This station was to be provided with laboratories, housing accommodations, buildings, water supply, etc. The plan did not identify the location of a station as a decision had not been made. His next proposal for the region was a stock farm that would deal with "the improvement and management of all kinds of stock including poultry."[121] Serious research in the eastern provinces was important because one of the fundamental problems in the region was that of soil fertility.

In his reorganization proposal, Mackie divided the northern provinces into the western area and the eastern area. Samaru was the headquarters of the agriculture department in the northern region. Like the western provinces, it had a research station and several studies had been carried out there on soil fertility and mixed farming. He proposed the establishment of new school buildings in Samaru and also to increase office, laboratory, and housing accommodations. He also proposed to develop irrigation, establish farm schools in the provinces, and have a settlement scheme for ex-soldiers. Mackie's research proposal for this area was the testing of agricultural machinery and artificial manures. While he did not support machinery in the western provinces, he was in support of the use of machinery in the northern provinces. The northern provinces did not have as many rains as the western provinces and thus erosion and the problem of the soil losing nitrogen was not a serious concern in this region like it was in the eastern and western provinces. The eastern part of the northern provinces also suffered the same problems that the eastern provinces of Nigeria faced. There were few agricultural officials in this area, and there were no facilities for research. Mackie's plan called for the establishment of a headquarters for the assistant director of agriculture and his specialist staff. He also wanted to build a central research station, along the lines of the one proposed for the eastern provinces. Such a center was estimated to cost £100,000. He proposed the establishment of an experimental farm in Maiduguri and also the establishment of a school for the training of local administration and other junior staff.

A careful analysis of Mackie's plan for agricultural development shows that it is skewed toward research. His plan also devoted a whole section to oil palm research and he made a strong case for it. There are no big agricultural schemes like those we would see in the postwar period. Mackie was biased toward research and extension work, which he saw as key to agricultural development in a "peasant" economy. He believed that if this was done in Nigeria, then Nigeria will have a strong economic footing. It is worth emphasizing that this plan was a revision of his 1940 plan and he retained much of the language of the old plan. As you read the plan, you gain the impression that Mackie had all the intentions to carefully nurture this plan to full implementation.

MACKIE'S RETIREMENT

While Mackie's plan may give the reader the impression that he had the intentions of remaining in Nigeria to see to its implementation, a few days after submitting the plan on January 30, 1945, he resigned from his service in Nigeria and moved back to Britain. His personal correspondences upon the occasion of his retirement showed that he was frustrated with his service in Nigeria and he believed that he would not have the freedom to implement this plan. In one personal handwritten letter to a friend, he stated his reasons for resigning. He said that the governor had made it quite clear that he would welcome his departure from Nigeria.[122] His second reason was that he did not think systematic agricultural development was possible under the present circumstances, in which the technical department had been weakened by being stripped of authority and subjected to the political officials. He couldn't accept that the director of agriculture should lose his executive authority and that his agricultural officers should be taking instructions from administrative officers rather than from him.[123] He felt like the agriculture department was a subordinate service and that the Nigerian government was running a kind of dictatorship. The technical advisers were no longer consulted and they were not allowed to make their plans public. Another reason Mackie gave were the attempts to make him a subordinate to the director of supplies the previous year, and the sense that he was currently a subordinate to a second rate member of his own service. He said all the main proposals of his predecessor, Faulkner, and his own proposals of the past twenty years had been restructured by the administration. At the end of his letter, he wrote, "I and my staff have reached the conclusion that the chief concern of the Govt is to make Nigeria safe for Admin Dept. and Agric. Development is merely a sideline. Naaja Lagos is rapidly becoming a public scandal and a job hunter's paradise. This is fully realised by the Africans."[124] He saw the colonial state's marginalization of the agriculture department as being detrimental to development. This is a contradiction because the CO had already set in motion a plan for development that the Nigerian colonial state took seriously and were working toward. Agriculture was an important facet of that plan. In fact, Lagos wanted the CO to make substantial investments in agricultural development. The question of whether the governor supported agricultural development and expansion, was not at issue, rather it was the question of power and the vision of development. The political administration wanted more control and centralization but Mackie wanted the department to have more control. As Joseph Hodge has rightly noted, "Mackie suggested that achieving agricultural development in a country with the size and population of Nigeria was not a question of miracles but of continuous research and sound extension work, which he felt had been compromised by the subordination of the department to the rest of the administration."[125]

Though Mackie's proposal became the agricultural plan of Nigeria in the 1945 Development Plan, he never received any public credit or acknowledgment for it. So on April 17, 1946 he wrote to the S of S protesting that his contribution to the plan was not acknowledged.[126] The S of S made enquiries with Governor Richards. In his response, the governor acknowledged that Mackie's contributions to the plan were considerable. Nevertheless, as the governor he had to take full responsibility for the plan. He wrote, "The recognition that the various sections of the Plan had been prepared by the officers named in no way implied that those Heads of Departments were solely responsible for formulating the plans outlined therein."[127] The governor also argued that it was only possible for the heads of departments to quickly prepare the Ten Year Plan of Development because of the work that had been done to a large extent by the previous heads of departments. He concluded, "Mr. Mackie is by no means the only former Head of Department who has contributed to the proposals made in the Sessional Paper, a great many both past and present officers have made valuable contributions. It was not, however, considered fitting that acknowledgment of these contributions should be included in a document of this nature."[128]

With or without any public acknowledgment, Mackie was by far the most influential person in Nigerian agriculture in the late colonial period and the CO was aware of his contributions. When Mackie's plan was up for discussion in the CO after his resignation, Dr. Tempany said:

> I would like to say that Capt. Mackie's plan represents the outcome of an enormous amount of work spread over 5 years. When I was in Nigeria I had the opportunity of discussing in great detail the earlier forms of the plan. . . . I have nothing but praise for this memorandum. I think that in its preparation Capt. Mackie has rendered a signal service to Nigeria, and after studying it with care I can find no points in it with which I am in serious disagreement.[129]

CONCLUSION

By looking at agricultural planning and policy in Nigeria through the lens of the director of agriculture, James Mackie, this chapter reveals the conflicts and contradictions, as well as the racial biases, of the colonial state. The conflicts between the technical and administrative departments were detrimental to the development efforts. It was these conflicts that led to the resignation of one of the best agricultural officers in the British colonial service. His resignation was monumental to the direction that agriculture policy in Nigeria took in the postwar period, as we will see in the next chapter. The fractious relationship between the technical and administrative departments was resolved by subordinating the technical departments to the administrative authority. While this was a short-term victory to the administrative arm of the colonial state, it was a long-term loss for Nigeria because the people could have benefited from some of the progressive policies of Mackie such as training Africans and women as senior agriculture officers.

Apart from the conflicts, there were also contradictions in the Mackiean policy. The three main pillars of his policy were research, experimentation, and extension. He insisted that crops and systems had to be thoroughly investigated before they were implemented. While this tripartite approach to agricultural development led to some successes such as green manuring in the western provinces of Nigeria and mixed farming in the northern provinces, it was too slow, overly cautious, and very conservative. He was pushing this policy at a time when there was heightened need for increased production to meet the war and the postwar needs. These two conflicting impulses of his policies were ill-aligned. The policy was also unable to restructure traditional agriculture in ways that it would meet the immediate needs of the colonial state.

Mackie's policies were not immune to the racial prejudices of the colonial state. While he advocated for the training of African staff and he acknowledged some good in African agricultural practices, he was also advocating change through his policies. This change was not going to happen through the instrumentality of Africans and their locally produced knowledge but through European investigations and experimentations. By doing this, Mackie was excluding the African farmers from the knowledge production process. A better approach to knowledge production would have been collaborative research between the African farmers and the Europeans.

Though Mackie's agricultural policies were those adopted as part of Nigeria's 1945 development plan, most of these policies did not survive the wind of change that reverberated throughout the British colonial world during the second colonial occupation. By 1947, during the height of the Sterling Crisis and with the new Labour government in power, there was a shift in agricultural policy. The policy of careful research and field trials that was reflective of most agriculture departments of the British colonies was abandoned in favor of large mechanized schemes that promised quick returns. This new shift in agriculture policy also brought with it significant failures. One such catastrophic failure was the Niger Agriculture Development Scheme, Mokwa (NAP), discussed in the next chapter. NAP, like many of its peers, such as the East Africa Groundnut Scheme and the Gambia Egg Scheme, did not go through careful research and investigations. For this reason, this project became a very expensive social experiment in modern agriculture.

NOTES

1. *The Second Colonial Occupation* calls this policy the Mackiean policy.

2. In the archival sources, these words are used interchangeably. Both words will be used throughout the book.

3. One agriculture official described them as people with a pass level certificate in History. This was meant to be an insult.

4. Throughout this work, the following terms will be used interchangeably to refer to the African rulers such as the emirs, chiefs, and warrant chiefs: African authorities, local authorities, or local administration. These are used to replace the colonial terminology of native administration, native rulers, or native authority.

5. John W. Cell, "Colonial Rule" in *The Oxford History of the British Empire: The Twentieth Century*, Edited by Judith M. Brown and WM. Roger Louis (Oxford: Oxford University Press, 1999), 232.

6. Hodge, *Triumph of the Expert*, 85.

7. Toyin Falola, *The History of Nigeria* (Westport, Ct: Greenwood Press, 1999), 16.

8. Ibid., 68–69.

9. A Valedictory Address Presented by the Entire Staff, Agriculture Department, Nigeria, on the retirement of James Mackie, February 16, 1945, Mackie Papers, Rhodes House (Hereafter, RH): MSS. Afr. S. 823.

10. Hodge, *Triumphant of the Expert*, 149.

11. Sven Speek "Ecological Concepts of Development? The Case of Colonial Zambia" in *Developing Africa: Concepts and Practices in Twentieth-Century Colonialism*, edited by Hodge, Hodl & Kopf, 144.

12. See Suzanne Moon, *Technological and Ethical Idealism: A History of Development in the Netherlands East Indies* (Leiden: CNWS Publications, 2007).

13. Mackie, Proposals for the Closer Collaboration with Native Administration for the promotion of Agricultural Development, August 2, 1930, Mackie Papers, RH: MSS. Afr. S. 823 (4).

14. Ibid.

15. Harry A. Gailey, *The Road to ABA: A study of British Administrative Policy in Eastern Nigeria* (New York: New York University Press, 1970), 5.

16. Suzanne Moon, "The Emergence of Technological Development and the Question of Native Identity in the Netherlands East Indies," *Journal of Southeast Asian Studies* 36 (2005): 201.

17. Ibid.

18. See Steven Pierce, *Farmers and the State in Colonial Kano: Land Tenure and the Legal Imagination* (Bloomington: Indiana University Press, 2005) and Robert Shenton, *The Development of Capitalism in Northern Nigeria* (London: James Currey, 1986).

19. Mackie, Proposals for the Closer Collaboration with Native Administration for the promotion of Agricultural Development, August 2, 1930, Mackie Papers, RH: MSS. Afr. S. 823 (4).

20. Ibid.

21. See Juhani Koponen, "From Dead End to New Lease of Life: Development in South-Eastern Tanganyika from the Late 1930s to the 1950s" in Joseph Hodge, et.al. *Developing Africa*, 47

22. Annual Colonial Report, Sierra Leone, 1904, 19.

23. William Buhler, Stephen Morse, Eddie Arthur, et al., *Science, Agriculture and Research: A Compromised Participation?* (London: Earthscan Publications Ltd., 2002), 44.

24. Paul Richards, *Indigenous Agricultural Revolution: Ecology and Food Production in West Africa* (London: Hutchinson, 1985), 43.

25. Paul Tiymabe Zeleza, *A Modern Economic History of Africa: The Nineteenth Century* (Nairobi: East African Educational Publishers, 1993), 87.

26. George Howard Jones, *The Earth Goddess: A Study of Native Farming on the West African Coast* (London: Longmans, Green and Co, 1936), 35.

27. Ibid., 35–36

28. Zeleza, *A modern Economic History of Africa*, 88.

29. Goran Hyden, "The Resilience of the Peasant Mode of Production: The Case of Tanzania" in, *Agricultural Development in Africa: Issues of Public Policy*, edited by Robert H. Bates and Michael F. Lofchie (New York: Praeger, 1980), 221.

30. Toyin Falola, *Culture and Customs of Nigeria* (Westport: Greenwood Press, 2001), 139.

31. O. T. Faulkner and J. R. Mackie, *West African Agriculture* (Cambridge: Cambridge University Press, 1933), 11.

32. Richards, *Indigenous Agricultural Revolution*, 50.

33. Ibid. 51.

34. Major E. S. Grogan, cited in Kianne Rocheleau, Philip Steinberg and Patricia Benjamin, "Environment, Development, Crisis, and Crusade: Ukambani, Kenya, 1890-1990," *World Development* 23.6, (1995):1042.

35. Recent scholarship has challenged the notion that Africans have been ineffective in managing their environments thereby causing environmental degradation. See Melissa Leach and Robin Mearns, eds. *The Lie of the Land: Challenging Received Wisdom on the African Environment* (Oxford: James Currey, 1996).

36. Helen Tilley, *Africa as a Living Laboratory,* 157.

37. Mary Tiffen, Michael Mortimore, et.al, *More People, Less Erosion: Environmental Recovery in Kenya* (Nairobi: Acts Press, 1994), 13.

38. Ibid., 118.

39. For some examples of this historiography that is critical of European science or that sees it as a tool of control and hegemony in Africa, see: Francis B. Nyamnjoh, "Potted Plants in Greenhouses: A Critical Reflection on the Resilience of Colonial Education in Africa," *Journal of Asian and African Studies* 47/2 (2012): 129–154; Megan Vaughan, *Curing their Ills: Colonial Power and African Illness* (Stanford: Stanford University Press, 1991); Jonathan Sadowsky, *Imperial Bedlam: Institutions of Madness in Colonial Southwest* Nigeria (Berkeley: University of California Press, 1991).

40. Helen Tilley, *Africa as a Living Laboratory: Empire, Development, and the Problem of Scientific Knowledge, 1870–1950,* (Chicago: The University of Chicago Press, 2011), 158.

41. Speek, "Ecological Concepts of Development," 141–42.

42. William Beinart, Karen Brown, et al, "Experts and Expertise in Colonial Africa Reconsidered: Science and the Interpenetration of Knowledge," *African Affairs* 108/432 (2009):420–421.

43. Ibid., 433.

44. Faulkner and Mackie state this intention in the preface of their book. They wrote, "This book is written especially for the candidates of Government service in West Africa in the Administrative and Agricultural Departments; but we hope it may prove useful or interesting to those who intend to come out as missionaries." Faulkner & Mackie, *West African Agriculture*, vii.

45. Helen Tilley, "African Environments & Environmental Sciences: The African Research Survey, Ecological Paradigms & British Colonial Development 1920–1940," in *Social History & African Environments,* William Beinart and JoAnn McGregor, eds. (Athens: Ohio University Press, 2003), 118.

46. Faulkner and Mackie, *West African Agriculture*, 6.

47. Mackie Papers, Mackie to CSG, January 4, 1939, Mackie Papers, RH: MSS. Afr. S. 823.

48. Mackie to CSG, February 22, 1939, Mackie Papers RH: MSS. Afr. S. 823.

49. CSG to Mackie, March 16, 1939, Mackie Papers, RH: MSS. Afr. S. 823.

50. Mackie to CSG, April 11, 1939, Mackie Papers, RH: MSS. Afr. S. 823.

51. David Anderson and David Throup, "Africans and Agricultural Production in Colonial Kenya: The Myth of the War as the Watershed," *The Journal of African History* 26,4 (1985): 334.

52. Mackie to CSG, April 11, 1939, Mackie Papers, RH: MSS. Afr. S. 823.

53. Anderson and Throup, *Africans and Agricultural Production in Colonial Kenya*, 335.

54. Ibid.

55. Ibid.

56. CSG to Mackie, July 17, 1939, Mackie Papers, RH: MSS. Afr. S. 823.

57. Mixed farming is a method of farming in which there is a mixture of arable farming with the raising of livestock.

58. Confidential Memorandum by Mackie, October 26, 1939, Mackie Papers, RH: MSS. Afr. S. 823.

59. Faulkner and Mackie, *West African Agriculture*, 64–65.

60. See Robert L. Tignor, *Colonial Transformation of Kenya: The Kamba, Kikuyu, and Maasai from 1900 to 1939* (Princeton, NJ: Princeton University Press, 2015), 342–44.

61. See Richards, *Indigenous Agricultural Revolution*, 128.

62. B. W. Hodder, *Economic Development in the Tropics* (London: Methuen, 1968), 113-114.

63. Faulkner and Mackie, *West African Agriculture*, 66.

64. Ibid., 67.

65. Ibid., 52.

66. Ibid., 58.

67. Marc Milner, "The Battle of the Atlantic" in John Gooch, ed. *Decisive Campaigns of the Second World War* (Routledge, 1990), 51–52.

68. Confidential Memorandum by Mackie, October 26, 1939, Mackie Papers, RH: MSS. Afr. S. 823.

69. Ibid.

70. Mackie to CSG, December 29, 1939, Mackie Papers, RH: MSS. Afr. S. 823.

71. Glanville was a senior agricultural officer in Sierra Leone and seconded to Nigeria as a principal agricultural officer. He was an expert on rice production.

72. Mackie to CSG, April 10, 1940, Mackie Papers, RH: MSS. Afr. S. 823.

73. Ibid.

74. Ibid.

75. Mackie to Abrahall, May 21, 1940, Mackie Papers, RH: MSS. Afr. S. 823.

76. Ibid.

77. He was the commissioner of the Northern province from 1936 to 1943. Sir Theodore died in 1961. Other private letters from colonial officials in the agriculture department affirm the conflicts between the department and the administrative officials. By presenting Mackie's own version of events, the goal is not to indict Sir Theodore Adams or other administrative officials. The goal here is to show that there were conflicts between the agriculture department and the administrative department and these were detrimental to development.

78. Mackie to Abrahall, May 21, 1940, Mackie Papers, RH: MSS. Afr. S. 823.

79. Ibid.

80. They may be other reasons for what Mackie is perceiving as obstructions. Without accessing Sir. Theodore's papers, it is difficult to litigate this conflict. Sir Theodore perhaps could have his reasons for delaying or blocking Mackie's proposals. There is some merit to Mackie's allegations because his correspondence was directed to the CSG and the governor was referenced to have intervened at different occasions to move things along.

81. Mackie to Abrahall, May 21, 1940, Mackie Papers, RH: MSS. Afr. S. 823.

82. The minutes of this meeting referenced by Mackie were not in the archival files consulted.

83. Memorandum on the Policy of the Agricultural Department, June 18, 1940, Mackie Papers, RH: MSS. Afr. S. 823.

84. Ibid.

85. Ibid.

86. Mackie to CSG, May 28, 1941, Mackie Papers, RH: MSS. Afr. S. 823.

87. Ibid.

88. Ibid.

89. Mackie references these instructions from the CSG in his letter to the CSG on June 10, 1941 outlining the duties of the DFP.

90. Mackie to CSG, June10, 1941, Mackie Papers, RH: MSS. Afr. S. 823.

91. Circular by CSG, June 21, 1941, Mackie Papers, RH: MSS. Afr. S. 823.

92. Mackie to CSG, April 18, 1942, Mackie Papers, RH: MSS. Afr. S. 823.

93. See Philips, *The Enigma of Colonialism*, 59–79.

94. Hugh Clifford, *Address to the Nigerian Council*, December 29, 1920 (Lagos: Government Printer, 1920), 186.

95. See Dan Mou, *State Power, Agrarian Policies and Peasant Welfare: Politics of Agricultural Marketing and Commodity Boards in Nigeria* (Bloomington: Author-House, 2014), 168.

96. Mackie to CSG, April 18, 1942, Mackie Papers, RH: MSS. Afr. S. 823.

97. For more on the Richard's constitution, see Kalu Ezera, *Constitutional Developments in Nigeria: An Analytical Study of Nigeria's Constitution-Making Developments and the Historical and Political Factors that affected Constitutional Change* (Cambridge: Cambridge University Press, 1960), 64–81; Eme O. Awa, *Federal Government in Nigeria* (Berkeley: University of California Press, 1964).

98. James S. Coleman, *Nigeria: Background to Nationalism* (Berkeley: University of California Press, 1958), 276.

99. Minutes of a Meeting held at Government House, January 8, 1945, Mackie Papers, RH: MSS. Afr. S. 823.

100. Ibid.

101. Ibid.

102. Ibid.

103. Ibid.

104. Ibid.

105. Ibid.

106. Mackie to CSG, Proposals for the expansion of Nigerian Agriculture, January 30, 1945, Mackie Papers, RH: MSS. Afr. S. 823.

107. Ibid.

108. Ibid.

109. Ibid.

110. Ibid.

111. Ibid.

112. Ibid.

113. Ibid.

114. The Imperial College of Tropical Agriculture in Trinidad was founded in 1921 to provide postgraduate training in tropical agriculture for the agricultural services of the colonial empire. Most of the graduates of the school were appointed to different agriculture departments. Upon leaving Nigeria, Faulkner was appointed principal of the school in 1938.

115. A Valedictory Address Presented by the Entire Staff, Agriculture Department, Nigeria, on the retirement of James Mackie, February 16, 1945, Mackie Papers, RH: MSS. Afr. S. 823.

116. Mackie to CSG, Proposals for the expansion of Nigerian Agriculture, January 30, 1945, Mackie Papers, RH: MSS. Afr. S. 823.

117. Ibid.

118. Ibid.

119. This was a disease transmitted by tsetse flies. It is also called nagana and when cattle were infected with it, it could be fatal because it caused weakness, fever, anemia, and lethargy. If mixed farming was going to be successful, it was important that cattle used should be resistant to the parasite that caused this disease.

120. Mackie to CSG, Proposals for the expansion of Nigerian Agriculture, January 30, 1945, Mackie Papers, RH: MSS. Afr. S. 823.

121. Ibid.

122. No archival records consulted directly confirmed Mackie's assertion that the governor welcomed his departure.

123. The first page of the letter, together with the receiver's name and date of the letter, is missing. Mackie Papers, RH: MSS. Afr. S. 823.

124. Ibid.

125. Joseph Hodge, *Triumph of the Expert*, 228 .

126. Mackie to Hall, April 17, 1946, Mackie Papers, RH: MSS. Afr. S. 823.

127. Richards to Hall, September 4, 1946, Mackie Papers, RH: Afr. S. 823.

128. Ibid.

129. Planning and Reorganization of Agriculture, Minute by Dr. Tempany, June 30, 1946, TNA: CO583/272/3.

Chapter 4

Late Colonial Agricultural Development

The Mokwa Scheme

The shift in British development policy after the Great Depression reached its peak in the period after World War II. This period marked the height of the second colonial occupation. The different colonial governments in Africa increased metropolitan investments in the development of the colonies. Development was no longer simply the economic exploitation of African resources; there was now a strong social welfare component. In 1945, Britain expanded the 1940 Colonial Development and Welfare Act and infused it with millions of pounds. France created *Fonds d'Investissement et de Developpement Economique et Social des Territoires d'Outre-mer* (FIDES) in April of 1946 to help build public infrastructure and provide social services such as housing, sanitation, and schools. In fact, over the course of the next ten years, France invested about $542 million in today's value.[1] During this period, the colonial administrations in Africa also introduced multiyear development plans. Even the Portuguese, who saw their colonial mission in Africa as more spiritual than material, had to change course during this period. They introduced a series of development plans in their African "overseas provinces": four six-year plans between 1953 and 1979 that invested in social progress.[2]

This chapter looks at the shift in colonial agricultural development policy during the height of the second colonial occupation. This is done through the lens of one development scheme, the Niger Agricultural Development Scheme, Mokwa.[3] British agricultural policy, which before World War II was known to be very cautious and conservative, assumed a more progressive posture after the war. Colonial agricultural departments were now embarking on large-scale projects that ended up becoming an embarrassment to British science and the development mission as a whole. In Nigeria, for example, the Mackiean policy of careful investigations, experimentation, and extension was abandoned in favor of large-scale mechanization schemes that did not go through this process. Four reasons accounted for this shift: the Sterling Crisis in London; the change of government in London; the need to extend the life of the empire; and the influx of new agriculture officers. The war had left a severe economic impact on Britain; at the end of the war, it was the most indebted nation in the world. It owed more than £3 billion, most of which was owed to territories and dominions in the Sterling area, such as India and Egypt. Britain also had a balance of payment deficit of about £1,250 million.[4] Britain sought a loan of $5 billion from the U.S. to deal with its immediate economic problems.

The U.S. agreed to provide Britain a loan of $3.75 billion but the conditions were harsh. Britain had to make the pound convertible within twelve months and also remove trade protectionist policies in the metropole and colonies. This led to a run in the dollar reserves of the Bank of England, leading to the beginning of the Sterling crisis, which intensified Britain's postwar economic problems.[5] In light of these problems, African colonies became, in the eyes of Britain, a mythical El Dorado where revenues could be generated for its balance of payment and postwar reconstruction. In these territories, the development of agriculture was most seductive in terms of generating the kinds of revenues London needed. Clement Richard Attlee's new Labour government impressed on "individual administrations the need to intensify the exploitation of imperial resources in an effort to use the colonies to earn dollars by exporting to the United States, and save dollars through substitution of imports from the dollar area to Britain."[6] The directives emerging from colonial officials in London encouraged colonial officials and technical experts to think boldly as they drew up plans that would aid rapid production. As Joseph Hodge notes that, the newly hired agriculture officers in the postwar period did not embrace the cautious and conservative approach of the older agricultural officers. Indeed, they were bold in their approaches as they advocated rapid mechanization of agriculture.[7] With London's blessing, colonial governments embarked upon big and bold agricultural development schemes. Some of these schemes included the East Africa Groundnut Scheme, the Gambia Poultry Scheme, and the Tobacco Scheme at Kasungu, Nyasaland. In Nigeria, the scheme that would best symbolize development during the second colonial occupation was the Niger Agricultural Development Project, Mokwa. This scheme defied the Mackiean policy that insisted on careful investigations and experimentations. Poor planning was responsible for the failure of the Mokwa scheme and several other postwar development projects. This scheme represents an excellent example of the practice of development and its consequences. This developmentalist agenda and the related planning failures, which were aimed at renewing Britain's imperial hold on Africa and giving it a new lease of life, ended up shortening the life of empire.

THE CDC AND ECONOMIC DEVELOPMENT AFTER 1945

Earlier in 1945, Parliament enhanced and expanded the 1940 CD&W Act to help develop the resources of the colonies for the betterment of the colonial people. This was followed by the passage of the Overseas Resources Development Act in 1948 to develop the economic resources of the colonies. The goal of this Act was to supplement what private enterprises were already doing in the colonies. There were areas where private enterprises were not equipped or able to develop the economic resources immediately, and the Act envisioned the British taxpayers helping to fund development in such cases. This Act created two corporations: the Overseas Food Corporation (OFC) and the Colonial Development Corporation (CDC). The OFC was tasked with increasing world food production at a time of heightened fear of world food shortages as a result of population growth. One of the schemes that this corporation operated and is most remembered for is the East Africa Groundnut Scheme, Tanganyika.[8] The colossal failure of this scheme was a big disappointment to those who had pinned their hopes on the ability of British science and technology to master and control nature, and to use it to Britain's economic advantage. The OFC operated several schemes throughout the British colonies and many of these suffered the same fate as the groundnut scheme.

Like its OFC twin, the CDC was not very successful in its mission. The corporation was charged with the duty of "securing the investigation, formulation and carrying out of projects for developing resources of colonial territories with a view to the expansion of production therein of foodstuffs and raw materials, or for other agricultural, industrial or trade development therein."[9] The CD&W Act of 1945 made available £110 million for the CDC to borrow for its work in the development of the colonies' economic resources. E. R. Wicker notes that the 1945 Act made an implicit distinction between the "commercially remunerative" and the "commercially non-remunerative" aspects of economic development. Whereas the CO disbursed grants to the colonial governments for their commercially non-remunerative work of development, a public corporation (the CDC) disbursed the funds for the "commercially remunerative" ventures of the British government. As a public corporation, the CDC was independent of the British Parliament in its daily administration.[10] The belief was that the CDC would play a vital role in helping Britain with its balance of payments crisis. Arthur Creech Jones, the S of S, told Prime Minister Clement Attlee that the CDC was going to increase colonial production "on an economic and self-supporting basis with an eye to the production of foodstuffs, raw materials and manufactures whose supply to the UK . . . will assist our balance of payments."[11] The expectations in London were that the CDC would be successful in its mission and the power to control the direction of the CDC rested on the S of S. He could give a general direction to the CDC board on matters that affected the public interest. The CDC also relied on the S of S and the Treasury to approve loans for every scheme that was carried out, since the CDC had no funds of its own.

Although the CDC could operate projects solely on its own, its preference was to operate in partnership with commercial enterprises. When such an arrangement was entered into, there had to be a separate company founded, in which equity was shared, with the CDC directly controlling the company's operations. When the CDC entered into such partnerships, it was expected that it would have controlling interests.[12] In its early years, the CDC tended to be the sole owner of the projects or schemes that it carried out. This was in stark contrast to the idea of a public corporation in Britain where such bodies solely owned and controlled the scheme. Only eight of the fifty projects that were in existence by the end of 1950 were in partnership with private enterprises. After 1950, the CDC changed its model and was more engaged with private enterprises for its schemes and projects. Having suffered many losses in its early years, "by the end of 1953 the Corporation had reduced the number of projects for which it was solely responsible to sixteen, and in five of these the C.D.C. was negotiating for association with private enterprise or colonial government authorities."[13] In order for the CDC to show "vigorous and even spectacular activity" in its work of developing the colonies, the CDC engaged in some schemes that were not economically and commercially sound.[14] The Conservatives' return to power in 1951 was instrumental to changes in the direction of the two corporations. They wanted to reign in the reckless and unprofitable spending of these corporations and so decided to disband the OFC and subject the CDC to stringent regulations, making it much more like a development bank.

THE OILSEED MISSION TO NIGERIA

The CDC's involvement in development projects in Nigeria came by way of the oilseed mission that visited West Africa in 1947. This mission was to explore the possibilities for large-scale production of groundnuts and other oilseeds in Ghana and Nigeria, in order to meet the great demand for oilseeds in Europe. This group reported that the area around Mokwa, close to the Niger River, showed possibilities for large-scale mechanized production of groundnuts. The team that visited Nigeria envisioned this new project as having three goals:

1. To increase cereal and oilseed production for the local market and for exports.

2. To settle an unpopulated area with new village communities in which there would be a combination of collective mechanized farming and local agricultural skills and experience.
3. To formulate a new pattern of farming that could be extended to cover all the cultivable land in the area and could be applied to other parts of the country.[15]

The Nigerian colonial government was skeptical of introducing large-scale mechanized farming, because this had not been its pattern of agricultural development previously. Before the introduction of the wooden plows in the late 1930s, attempts at introducing small-scale mechanized farming had failed mainly due to the cost of plows and their maintenance. London persuaded Nigeria to participate, convincing its officials that Nigeria would be able to replicate the successes of the Gezira scheme[16] in the Sudan where there was a successful partnership between commercial corporations and tenant cultivators. In April of 1948, two colonial officials from Nigeria were dispatched to Gezira on a fact-finding mission. These officers visited Gezira and the Mechanized Crop Production Scheme at Ghadambaliya.[17] The report they presented upon their return influenced the future direction of the Mokwa scheme, shifting the original thinking about what it would entail. There was a change "in emphasis from the increase in the production of groundnuts, sought by the Oilseeds Mission, to mechanized farming to give genuine independent settlers more corn to eat and larger share of crops to sell."[18] The production of food that the farmers could themselves consume was important and this was in line with the policy that Mackie had laid down in the early 1940s. He had insisted that farmers who cultivated cash crops must also be self-supporting by cultivating enough food to feed their own families.

EARLY SETTLEMENTS AND CULTIVATION AT NAP

The CO asked the CDC in 1949 to join the Nigerian colonial government in establishing the Niger Agricultural Development Scheme, Mokwa.[19] In establishing the scheme, it was agreed that the CDC would make the finances for the scheme available, while Nigeria would be responsible for losses up to £31,793 incurred in the first seven years of the scheme. Also, Nigeria guaranteed the CDC a 3 percent annual return in the first ten years of the scheme. Based on this agreement, work began in June of 1949. The initial staffers at the work site were eight expatriates and a project manager. No Nigerian staff was employed at the professional level. This initial team of expatriate staff established a training farm and an engineering training school for the local boys. The involvement of Nigerians at this initial stage of the scheme was by way of a local advisory committee. The Resident of the Niger Province appointed the chairman of this committee. Members were drawn from the traditional authorities and also included the provincial heads of development departments. Though this committee had the title of an advisory committee, their advice did not involve the technical operations of the scheme. Their main responsibility was the recruitment of settlers and dealing with their welfare and complaints.[20]

As executed, the scheme had three partners, the principal ones being the Nigerian colonial government and the management company, NAP. The settlers were the third partners in the scheme and had no administrative representation or say in the decision making. These were the responsibilities of the respective partners:

1. The Nigerian colonial government. Through the traditional authorities, it provided the land that was needed, the main roads, and the supply of water.
2. The Niger Agricultural Development Project Ltd.[21] This was the managing company. This company was set up to clearly define who had control over the scheme. It was responsible for administering the settlement area; providing the farm roads, fertilizers, tractors and agricultural equipment; supplying the technical and mechanical staff; and clearing and preparing the land for the initial sowing of seeds.
3. The settlers. They were responsible for the sowing of seeds, weeding, hoeing, and in some cases, harvesting.[22]

Though the Mokwa scheme was modeled after Gezira, the schemes only shared some similarities. Like Gezira, the land was parceled out to the different settlers. The settlers at Gezira each received about ten acres of land. In the Mokwa scheme, the idea was to create ten settlements and each settlement was to have eighty farmers with their families. Each farmer was awarded 48 acres to cultivate, half of which would be fallow. Apart from the acreage awarded to the farmers, another 576 acres was to be used as a demonstration farm to conduct trials on crops and rotations. The goal was to have about 65,000 acres of usage when the project was in its full maturation.[23] While the Gezira farmers had ownership of the land, the settlers at Mokwa did not own the land; they were only granted use of it. Gezira, like Mokwa, had a tripartite partnership structure: the cultivators, the government, and the Sudan Plantation Company. Though these structures look similar, in the case of Mokwa, the cultivators did not have an ownership stake in the scheme. The farmers were tenants of the company, and the Nigerian colonial government had the responsibility of providing the farmers to the company. In both schemes, the management company provided technical supervision.

There were two main areas where Gezira and Mokwa differed significantly. First was in the area of mechanization. Unlike Gezira, the key innovation in Mokwa was mechanization. Mechanization was to showcase the power of modern technology in transforming rural agriculture. Meanwhile, at Gezira, the tenants were responsible for their own labor force to weed, pick the cotton, clean the fields, and maintain their irrigation ditches.[24] The second important difference between the two schemes was in the area of research. It took several years of experimentation and field trials through pilot schemes before settlers were brought into the Gezira settlement. This was not the case with the Mokwa scheme. The scheme was put together quickly without field trials and experimentation. Postwar colonial development was a challenge to the Mackiean approach of field trials and experimentation that was considered too cautious and conservative. In the opinion of the new policy makers, such an approach was unable to respond to the high production needs of the period.

Despite the lack of field trials and experimentations, the first group of farmers moved into the first settlement called Ndayako in 1951. Following this was the Pannini settlement established in 1952. The original plan was to have eighty farmers in each settlement. Three years into the project, only 135 farmers had been settled. The Ndayako settlement had 78 farmers instead of the 80 farmers that were needed and the second settlement at Pannini only had 57 settlers. The Pannini settlement was comprised of people from outside of the Mokwa area, while the first settlement had people from within the area. This scheme, like the groundnut scheme that was managed by the OFC, was doomed from the very beginning. The progress of land clearance was slow and the cost was high. In March of 1952 about 7,754 acres of land had been cleared. The average cost of clearance per acre in November of 1951 was £12.8; by February of 1952, it was £12.13.[25] This continuously rising cost was associated with removing the tree stumps from the land that had already been cleared. Since the project was intended to showcase the power of mechanized agriculture, the land was initially plowed with Fordson Major diesel tractors and Ransomes Dragoon disc plows. The clearing was done in a hurry and no one considered stumping the trees. These concealed roots ended up creating problems for the equipment and slowed the progress of the work. More than 5,000 acres of land cleared had to be stumped and rooted manually by hand. To demonstrate how deep the roots were and to corroborate the extent of the problem, the manager of the scheme kept a 54-feet long stumped lateral root in the verandah of his office.[26] It cost about £13 per acre to remove the stumps and to root the land. By the end, clearing was no longer done by machines but by hand because it was considered by the management of NAP to be cheaper than any other method. Mechanized clearing was considered to be extremely expensive in equipment, maintenance, and staff and so it was abandoned.[27] This was also the case with the East Africa Groundnut Scheme that had started only a few years earlier. One would have thought that the British government would have learned from those mistakes, but the bureaucratization and fragmentation of the colonial system meant that lessons were learned slowly. The groundnut scheme experienced some of the problems that Mokwa faced. A year after the project commenced, only 5 percent of the scheduled land had been cleared and the cost of the project for the year had doubled. As Stefan Esselborn has noted, "In the second year, when 600,000 acres of peanuts should have been planted according to the original plan, not even 50,000 acres were cleared, and perhaps as little as 13,000 acres of this actually represented properly cleared and rooted former bush."[28] The delays were caused by the high breakdown rates of the machines used, most of which were not suitable for the Kongwa environment. It took several weeks to get spare parts for these machines.[29]

Beyond the problems of mechanized clearing that plagued the Mokwa scheme, management was becoming doubtful of the capabilities of the African farmer. Having observed the settlers for a year, the management was not certain whether the African farmer would be capable of cultivating the 48 acres of land that had been allocated to him. Though half of the land was to remain fallow, there was no certainty that even after the company had plowed the land and prepared it, the farmer would be able to plant and maintain 24 acres of land. This doubt raised serious questions about the economics of the scheme. O. E. Mercer, the regional manager of the CDC in West Africa, believed that the economic viability of the project depended on how much of the land the individual settler could cultivate. Given that the company had already spent half of its capital on a project that had not reached 25 percent completion, the question was whether the scheme should continue to build out the rest of the settlements or whether it should be downsized? If the company made the decision to continue with the full implementation of the scheme, more capital infusion was required.[30] The decision was made that the company should await the end-of-the-year report in order to determine the way forward. However, the company at this time was short of working capital and a suggestion was made that the CDC should advance a loan to the company if the Nigerian colonial government was unable to make arrangements for further capital in 1952.[31] The June 1952 report on the Mokwa scheme, while not as bad as the March report, still showed a bleak future. The general outlook in terms of production looked poor. The cost of production greatly exceeded the value of output. The total acreage cleared by this time was only 8,225. There was a delay in overhauling the tractors because spare parts had to be imported. The cost of using the tractors was much higher than had been anticipated because maintenance and running costs were 100 percent over the estimates.[32]

The increased cost of removing roots meant that the company was expending significantly more capital than was budgeted. By the second quarter of

1952, it became obvious that the work could not continue without some additional capital infusion. To alleviate the issue of capital, the CDC and the Nigerian colonial government equally subscribed to an additional share capital of £60,000 to further finance the scheme. For the quarter that ended in September of 1952, however, the scheme continued to fall outside of its estimates. For example, it cost £11,258 to run the tractors. This figure represented more than 100 percent of the budgeted amount. The estimates for seeds and fertilizers were £5,000, but the company ended up spending only £1,500. The reason less money was spent than estimated was because they could not find enough people for the settlements. For the first nine months of the year, the company had already lost £22,763 and estimates were that the losses might increase to about £30,000 by the end of the year. The outlook for 1953 looked poor, as a preliminary study showed that the scheme would continue to operate at a significant loss.[33]

At the end of 1952, the company's losses stood at £29,599, a figure close to the projected loss of £30,000 given in the September report. This amounted to a loss of about £250 per settler. The total amount of land that was cleared by the end of the year was only 8,684 acres. For the whole of 1952, only 1,704 acres of land was cleared. It became obvious that in order for the scheme to become financially viable, the revenue per acre had to increase dramatically and that possibility was nowhere near in sight. The crops were underperforming and dry weather during the planting season led to the failure of the groundnuts. Though the bambarra nuts had performed a little better, maize and millets failed. The only crop that performed well was the guinea corn.[34]

The failure of the groundnut scheme was in no way a surprise to the settlers. They had shown reluctance to plant the seeds at the time of the year that the company officials told them to. Groundnuts were usually planted in May, but farmers were asked to plant them in July. They were planting them this late because of delays in clearing and stumping the land. The experts that ran the scheme believed that the seeds would still perform well even though they were planted late. The crop ended up failing. This failure was bad for the settlers who had to rely on one-third of the yield for their own subsistence. Many of the settlers were unsatisfied and wanted to leave the settlement after the failure. The colonial officials were discredited in the eyes of the farmers. By the end of the year, discussions were already opened between the CDC and the Nigerian colonial government as to the future of the scheme.[35]

NAP AS A SOCIAL EXPERIMENT

K. D. S. Baldwin argued in his book, *The Niger Agricultural Project: An Experiment in African Development* that the Mokwa scheme was never expected by the CDC to be very profitable. He writes, "The Corporation pointed out to the Government that a wide-scale social experiment of this sort brought great development advantages to the country concerned, but was an abnormal risk with small return for any party unless the Government took a large share in the undertaking."[36] This scheme is a good example of what James Scott calls "high modernism." He argues that high modernism "was a supreme self-confidence about continued linear progress, the development of scientific and technological knowledge, the expansion of production, the rational design of social order, the growing satisfaction of human needs, and, not least, an increasing control over nature (including human nature) commensurate with scientific understanding of natural laws."[37] Britain was attempting to socially reorder the society and use the power of science to bring about progress and a change in the human conditions of the people. Christophe Bonneuil has observed that the language of experimentation was one that was deliberately used in development narratives beginning from the 1930s. Late colonial development schemes were viewed as experiments that were both scientific and social. He argues that these schemes had two things in common: they put experts in power, and the physical and social space of the schemes was designed according to plans produced by scientists.[38] Before this time, political officials relegated technical staff and the scientists who worked in the African colonies to second-class status. Nigeria was no exception. The previous chapter showed how district officers treated the agriculture department staff poorly. Mackie resigned his service in Nigeria as a result of this second-class treatment of the technical staff by the administrative officials. In this late colonial period when massive agricultural schemes were favored, the scientists and the technical staff assumed more influential status in the colonial state. They designed these schemes that were supposed to showcase the power of science in the development of rural and backward regions. African colonies saw an upsurge of new scientists and technical officers who pontificated over development schemes. These had the kind of authority and prestige that those who had worked in Africa before them could have only dreamed of. Bonneuil notes that these experts:

> were mobilized by the colonial state to help appropriate and master African environments, pathologies, and societies. In British Africa, the 1930s saw increasing concern with soil erosion and deforestation as well as with malnutrition and public health. These brought to power a flood of experts. The gospel of soil conservation legitimized scientific measures (including confinement of people in settlement schemes, where access to land and grazing were restrained) against "irresponsible" Africans who had to be prevented from destroying their environment.[39]

The value placed on experts thus changed during this late colonial period. In the early years of colonial rule "the administrative officers were more powerful, more conspicuous and relatively more numerous."[40] However, in the late colonial period, the technical officers "considerably outnumbered the Administration in the field and progressively exerted more influence at all levels of government."[41] Mokwa witnessed the presence of many foreign experts who were unaware of the local conditions, unlike the previous agricultural department staff who had spent several years working in the area and understanding the culture. As Baldwin rightly states, "Undue haste at Mokwa gave the farmers no time to satisfy themselves that the new methods were better than their own. Furthermore, none of the senior staff had worked in Nigeria before. None spoke Nupe or even Hausa, hence all their dealings with the farmers had to be through interpreters. Finally there was a serious break in the continuity of staff at the end of 1950. It is difficult to see how this could have been avoided. If no senior staff were available in Nigeria, they had to be recruited from somewhere else."[42] The resignation of Mackie in 1945 and the changes in the agriculture department had created shifts in policy direction. The officials at Mokwa did not have to follow Mackie's policy of painstakingly attempting to understand African agricultural practices and testing of new methods before they made the farmers change their practices.

The second common feature of development in the late colonial period was that the physical and social space of the various schemes were in accordance with plans produced by what James Scott calls "the scientific bureaucracy." Members of this bureaucracy included "engineers, planners, technocrats, high-level administrators, architects, scientists, and visionaries."[43] They believed that the human condition could be improved through social engineering. Thus, "Agricultural and social activities were construed in terms of uniform fields and villages, with rigid schedules. Farmers were told what to plant and what cropping system to use. The timing of each farming operation was centrally controlled."[44] Mokwa was a social experiment in which a traditional society was to be completely reorganized with the goal of expanding agricultural production. This social experiment was created because of the circumstances that the Europeans found in Africa. The places where these settlement schemes were going to be located had sparse populations and it was difficult to bring the people under their control and to make them do what they wanted. Locating the settlements in sparsely populated places provided at least two advantages: they had the land that they needed without undue pressure from the locals and they could exercise more power. By creating these new settlement schemes, the Europeans were attempting to shift the balance of power from the agrarian community to the company.[45] Settlement schemes "were the laboratories where the developmentalist state attempted to shape agrarian societies and environments so as to render them compliant to 'development': more productive, more commensurable to expert knowledge, and more amenable to state intervention."[46] This primarily explains why the

Nigerian colonial government was willing to invest in NAP even though it knew that it might not be profitable. It saw value in this experiment of social engineering as these people were brought within the control of the colonial state.

The Gezira Scheme in the Sudan is a good example of how the Europeans engineered a new social order. The area where the scheme was established was treated as if nothing had existed there prior to its establishment. The British did not take into consideration the social organizations that had existed and the patterns in which land was used. The goal was to bring the people under British control and create a new social order. This scheme, as Victoria Bernal notes, "represented an attempt not simply to remake or reform rural Sudanese society, but to *create* a (colonial) Sudanese society: a homogenous society of hardworking and disciplined peasants. The British did not try to transform local practices so much as obliterate them, starting literally from the ground up, with new systems of production and productive relations of their own design."[47] The area in Mokwa was treated as such and if NAP was successful, this would have been replicated in other parts of Nigeria. Unlike Mokwa, Gezira was to a large measure successful. There are two important reasons for this. First, the farmers in Gezira clamored to be part of the scheme, while those in Mokwa were not interested in being a part of the scheme. In Gezira there was demand for land, in Mokwa there was no pressure on land at all. The second important reason was that the Gezira scheme was preceded by decades of experimentation on a small scale, while Mokwa did not undergo such experimentations.

The scientists and technical experts who created Mokwa saw it as a showcase of the power of planned mechanized agriculture. The poor results and the near bankruptcy of the scheme just two years after the settlements had been established created doubts as to its successful future. It is important to note that when the oilseeds mission conceived this scheme, it was never intended to be a social experiment but a profitable venture whose outcome would quickly help alleviate postwar shortages. It was the CDC that considered it a social experiment and marketed it as such to the Nigerian colonial government. As the scheme began, neither the settlers nor the staff saw themselves as part of a social experiment. Between the settlements of the first farmers up until 1952, the scheme was never described as an experiment. The staff that was managing the scheme believed that it was going to be successful economically. A major shift occurred in 1953 when the language of experimentation was now commonly used to describe the scheme. As was the case in the East Africa Groundnut Scheme, the rhetoric of experimentation "helped to justify the huge amounts of money lost in such schemes and to excuse in advance all errors."[48] In 1953, it was obvious that the scheme was failing but describing it as an experiment allowed the scheme to avoid the public embarrassment that its failure would cause both the CDC and the Nigerian colonial government, the two major investors in the scheme.

The major shift in the rhetoric of experimentation occurred when Elspeth Huxley, a British/Kenyan writer and journalist contacted the CO requesting information on the progress in Mokwa. Earlier, she had visited Nigeria and experienced at first hand the high hopes that the people had about the scheme. In February of 1953 she was writing a piece that touched on NAP and wanted certain facts about the scheme's progress. She wrote in her letter to the CO that

> One has to be a bit careful with these things—one may write that it is the blue-eyed pet of the Government and full of bright promise, and then find that it has fallen under a cloud and is about to be closed as uneconomic.[49]

The CO's proposed reply to her was sent to the CDC for review. In this reply, the CO wrote: "I think that it would be preferable not to treat the scheme as a 'blue-eyed pet of Government' but as a serious and rather expensive experiment which would ultimately break even financially and point to a possible way of mechanising African, peasant agricultural production."[50] The CDC responded to the CO requesting a modification to the letter. They wanted the CO to expunge from the reply to Huxley any suggestions that the scheme can be made to pay for itself.[51] The CDC understood that the scheme was not economically viable. They were more comfortable with the language of experimentation as that gave them a cover. In the end, the response that was sent to Elspeth Huxley read: "I think that it would not be preferable to treat the scheme as a 'blue-eyed pet of Government' but as a serious and rather expensive experiment. It might also be desirable to point out that it will probably be necessary to wait for some years before the value of the scheme can be assessed."[52] It was carefully worded and did not include any language of future financial solvency. The scheme was an expensive experiment, they argued, but it was going to take some years to assess its actual value. What was the actual value of the scheme? The CO would later argue that the value of the scheme was not economic but social. By saying the scheme was an experiment the emphasis was no longer on profitability but on knowledge gained. Huxley's response to the information received showed that she was not convinced of the CO's argument and was critical of this and many other schemes that were being undertaken in Africa. She wrote, "All that you say is interesting and confirms the general experience that none of these big mechanized schemes is really economic and the same goes for land settlement. I quite agree they have a value as experiments even if they only prove negatives. Unfortunately (perhaps) a great many Africans now feel that mechanization will solve all problems and get round the food shortage everyone warns them about."[53] Huxley's own experience spending three months traveling in Kenya and seeing the agricultural schemes that were carried out there left her convinced that there was value in these agricultural schemes. Her book, *A New Earth,* tells of many success stories despite the problems of agricultural development in Africa. She devotes a chapter of her book to discussing the Meru settlement schemes, which she claims everyone was proud of "because of their success and above all of their economy."[54]

DETERMINING THE FUTURE OF NAP

With the shift toward the language of experimentation, the important question the partners in the scheme had to answer was: What should be its future? The insistence that NAP was an experimental scheme was in preparation for the CDC's withdrawal as it had a fiduciary duty to British taxpayers. By 1953 it was obvious the CDC wanted to discontinue its support for the scheme and vigorous debates took place on what might the future of NAP be. Within the northern region where the scheme was located, the officials disagreed over whether it should be continued or discontinued. J. D. Brown, the director of agriculture in the northern region believed that the scheme was a failure and it should be ended immediately, but local Resident of the Niger Province, M. V. Rackhouse, made a strong case for continuing the scheme. Brown's argument was that the scheme was uneconomic and the knowledge that would be gained from the scheme was not worth spending £50,000 a year. At the end of 1952, the approximate cost of producing an acre of groundnuts or guinea corn was £7.9 and the calculations showed that the cost of producing an acre would not fall below £6.2 even at the targeted size of six settlements. The company's revenues were dependent on the value and yield of the crop, as well as the output of the settlers. The annual yield of groundnuts was estimated at 560 lbs. per acre and guinea corn at 1120 lbs. per acre. The price of groundnuts in 1953 was £36 a ton and that of guinea corn varied. A reasonable and fair market price of guinea corn for the sake of estimates was £15 a ton. The company based future prospects on a price of £28 for a ton of groundnuts and £12 for a ton of guinea corn. If the annual yield of groundnuts was 560 lbs. per acre, then the company's revenue would be two-thirds of that. At £28 a ton, that would be about £4.13. The annual yield of guinea corn was 1120 lbs. per acre of which the company was entitled to two-thirds. At £12 a ton, that would be about £3. Brown's argument was that if six settlements were operating at full capacity, the cost of cultivating an acre would still be £6.2 per acre, while the revenue per acre for groundnuts would be £4.13 and that of guinea corn £3. Based on these calculations, the company would still lose £2.07 per acre in the cultivation of groundnuts and £3.2 per acre in the cultivation of guinea corn. He argued that there was nothing to suggest that "this revenue can be bridged by increased efficiency in the use of machines, and on the basis of six settlements the price of groundnuts would need to rise to £40 a ton before ends could be met. Even on a basis of ten settlements maturing in twelve years the estimated cost of cultivation shows little or no margin of profit from this revenue."[55]

Brown also believed that the existing structure of remunerating the settlers did not encourage them to cultivate more. Settlers were required to cultivate 24 acres while allowing 24 acres to fallow. The settlers, he argued, were capable of cultivating the 24 acres but were unwilling to do so because they were required to do too much for too little pay. He wrote: "It is possible that they may ask themselves whether they would not be happier cultivating even less than 8 acres in the bush in complete freedom rather than enjoying the products of 8 acres cultivated under the direction and management of the N.A.P."[56] The problem here was not the backwardness or conservatism of African farmers, it was the project design. The amount of work the Africans were required to do was too onerous and the return was too little.

One of the reasons advanced in the reports for the poor yield of crops in 1952 was weather. The argument from the management of the scheme was that the low yield resulted from the complete drought in August. Brown rightly argued that "Mokwa is in a rain belt which more often than not has a 'small dry' period in July and August (unlike the northern groundnut areas) and this factor is one of the many peculiarities of the belt and only one of the problems that have to be met at Mokwa."[57] That the technical experts were not aware of this fact shows how much they ignored the locally produced knowledge. Nigerian agriculture had a rich history of experimental trials and research. That NAP did not go through such trials was a result of the urgency in getting the scheme started to respond to the oilseeds crisis. Most people familiar with the geography of this region of Nigeria are aware of the "August Break," a period marked by lack of rainfalls. This was the primary reason that the farmers were reluctant to plant the seeds when they were asked to do so. Brown's conclusion was that there are no prospects that will ever make the scheme return any financial profits for its shareholders, that it was ahead of its time, and the mechanization of agriculture in the northern region "will not be economically feasible until prices of export crops on the one hand and local wage rates on the other, rise very much higher than they are at present."[58]

Brown's argument notwithstanding, Rackhouse saw the scheme as having future positive prospects. He argued that the scheme should not be abandoned because it served a purpose beyond the immediate economic benefits. He noted that the success of the scheme could not be measured based on the total yields or finance "but only through visual contact with the scheme by those who have seen the improved tilt after ploughing and the solid expanses of miles of growing corn in 1952 and of growing groundnut in 1951."[59] The idea of visual contact was to show what was new and modern. This was to distinguish what was now being done at NAP with the traditional system of cultivation. The idea of visualization was important for colonial and postcolonial development officials. For example, IR-8 was widely used in Southeast Asia in the 1960s to distinguish tradition and modernity and also as a "symbolic divider marking the onset of a new political and economic dispensation."[60] The impact of this scheme for Rackhouse was more than the economic bottom line but a complex endeavor that would take time to sort out. It wasn't simply an agricultural scheme but one that cut across different sectors of the colonial state. For this reason, it was not only plagued by technical problems but also by "economic, administrative, political and sociological problems which must also be solved. Even on a small scheme, a solution to such a variety of problems cannot be obtained over a short term."[61] Rackhouse noted that the duration for which the scheme was in operation was too short to condemn it to failure. Schemes of this nature took time to mature and so should start small and build up slowly. He argued that NAP was based on the Gezira Cotton Scheme in the Sudan, which took fifty years to reach its fruition of a million acres. He noted that at the initial stages of the Gezira project, "moderate targets were often being reduced in scope."[62] The Gezira scheme started with a pilot project of only about 1.038 acres irrigated by pumps in 1910. It was only after the successful production of cotton that work started on the construction of a dam in Sennar in 1913. World War I interrupted the construction of the dam and it was finished in 1925. Between those years of constructions, additional pumps were installed to help with irrigation.[63] In terms of planning and execution, the Gezira scheme had a long view in mind. It is important to note that although Gezira has often been hailed as one of the major successes of agricultural development planning in Africa, some have argued that in broader historical terms it is not. It is "stagnant, holds little hope of continually rising living standards for its inhabitants, and, as a major component of the Sudanese economy, it exposes that economy, and thus the society, to considerable potential and actual instability."[64] Rackhouse wanted NAP to be looked upon as Gezira and granted several years for it to mature. His reasoning was that NAP had the potentials to help in the development of peasant farming across Nigeria.

The question is, though, how long did NAP need to be in operation before its success or failure could be determined? Should it be fifty years like the Gezira project or seven years as was originally planned? These are questions that Rackhouse left unanswered. He was not absolutely sure that NAP would ever be successful but he believed that if it failed, this would help prevent repetition elsewhere. For him, it was an experiment worth continuing. He wrote:

> The experiment is only beginning. On the agricultural side, this season is the first when the ploughs have had comparatively rootless land to operate

> in. . . . A curtailment of the scheme now would be a great disappointment and set-back to the Native Authorities and the people of this Province and to all those from outside who have followed its progress with the greatest interest. . . . This experiment is being closely watched at home and in other colonies and should not be abandoned before failure is clearly demonstrated.[65]

Rackhouse's defense of the scheme was a question of prestige. It wasn't unreasonable for him to make a case for the continuation of the scheme. He was the colonial administrator who had direct authority over this province and the failure of the project reflected poorly on him and British science. For this reason, even at this late stage, he was still arguing that the scheme should be expanded to six settlements and then later to the ten settlements that were originally envisaged and he wanted the colonial government to provide the capital for these efforts. For him, this scheme was meritorious in serving as a model for other African colonies that had land development problems. He wrote, "This scheme must be regarded as an experiment which is to some considerable extent aimed at solving land development problems which also occur in other African colonies."[66] The Nigerian inspector general of agriculture agreed with Rackhouse, writing that "the Resident, Niger Province, quite rightly states that the project is an experiment, and is only just beginning. There should be no consideration of abandonment as too much is at stake, not solely from the consideration of invested capital, or from the requirements of the local area, but from an all-Nigerian development aspect."[67] The chief concern for them was the embarrassment this would be for the colonial state and invariably Britain, and the doubts this would raise about the ability of British colonialism to deliver the goods promised.

In arguing that the scheme was an experiment it was implied that lessons were going to be learned from the scheme whether good or bad. If we agree that this project was purely an experimental scheme as has been argued by the major stakeholders, then it was a very expensive experiment. It was expensive not only in terms of the financial resources poured into it but also in terms of the human resources. Apart from the Europeans who managed the scheme, many African farmers and their families had invested their time and labor into an endeavor that was not sold to them as an experiment but as a project that could potentially change their lives economically and socially. The farmers who were recruited as settlers were not told they were entering living laboratories. They had hoped for better yields in the scheme. The community at large was affected as the scheme attempted to create a new social order in which the people were no longer directly responsible to their chiefs but to the company. A never before present social organization and relations had been created by this scheme. In a way, NAP disrupted both the economic lives of the people and their social relations completely. Continuing the scheme in the same pattern for the unforeseeable future meant furthering the destruction of the fabric of this African society.

NEGOTIATING THE END OF NAP

The Colonial Development Corporation was not assuaged by the arguments that Rackhouse had advanced. It was determined to withdraw from the scheme because it believed that it had a fiduciary responsibility to British taxpayers and should not continue to lose money for what it considered an experiment. By the early part of 1953, the financial stakeholders of NAP felt that they had three possible options on what to do with the scheme: abandon the project, continue it at its present level, or expand it to five or six settlements and then perhaps later to ten. Each of these courses of action posed a problem. If the project was discontinued, it meant that the stakeholders had to acknowledge that the project had failed. Here, the stakeholders had varying interests. If the CDC was the only shareholder of the company, this would be the course of action it would take because as a corporation it had a responsibility to its shareholders and profit was part of that responsibility. The CDC would have easily received the support of the Conservative government, which was very skeptical of these "white elephant" projects in the colonies. In assessing whether to wind down the scheme, the Nigerian colonial government had different considerations from those of the CDC. It had to take into consideration "sociological and political factors, and economic considerations besides the single one of profit."[68] This project was located in the northern region and had strong backing from some of the officials from the region. The transformative merits of the scheme had also been sold to the local authority of the region and discontinuing it would raise social and political problems for the colonial state. These officials in the northern region needed the cooperation of the African authorities. Ending the scheme meant that they were reneging on their word to the African authorities whom they had assured would bring economic transformation through improved agriculture.

To continue the scheme at the present level meant that it had to be on an experimental basis, a model that the CDC was not interested in participating in as its mission was not to conduct experiments. If the CDC withdrew its financial support, the colonial government would be forced to assume full financial responsibility and administrative control of the scheme. That meant that the company established to run the scheme would now be solely owned by the Nigerian colonial government. There was no doubt that the CDC wanted Nigeria to take over the CDC's investment at face value. The implication of this was that Nigerian taxpayers would have to assume the losses of the corporation given that, as part of the agreement for the CDC to be involved, Nigeria was going to cover the losses for the first seven years. Expanding the scheme to five or six settlements required a further infusion of capital. Where would this capital come from? The CDC estimated that the total capital required for expansion to five schemes was £560,000 and to six schemes was £580,000. The conditions under which the CDC was willing to provide more capital were unfavorable to the Nigerian colonial government as it could only provide funds through debenture.[69] Given the three actions that could be taken, it was obvious the CDC would withdraw from the scheme.

A discussion had already been opened between the Nigerian Central Government (NCG) and the Northern Regional Government (NRG) on the future of the scheme. While the CDC was awaiting the response from the NCG, it took steps to officially withdraw its support for the scheme. In a November 1953 letter to the CO, the director of the CDC wrote, "We still await the Central Government's definite proposals but I am now writing you formally to seek approval for the Corporation's intention to abandon participation in this scheme and to ask that it shall qualify for waiver of interest."[70] The CO did not provide the immediate waiver sought, as it was reluctant to let the CDC abandon the project without negotiating an exit from the scheme with the appropriate authorities. The CO responded:

> Definite approval, however, would have to await such a satisfactory agreement and the Secretary of State will wish to be given the opportunity to consider the terms of the agreement before it is finally accepted by the corporation. He will wish in this connection to be given a full report on the reasons which have induced the corporation to abandon its participation and to be satisfied that adequate arrangements are made under the agreement for an appropriate valuation of any assets belonging to the corporation which are transferred to other authorities.[71]

Even before the CDC had the opportunity to respond to the CO letter, the S of S, Oliver Lyttleton, wrote the Nigerian government. He seemed not to have been aware of the debates that had been going on about the future of NAP.[72] His letter referenced the positive report that had been given by G. W. Nye, his deputy agricultural adviser, after his visit to Mokwa in November of 1952. The tone of his letter was very positive and even hoped that other regions of Nigeria may be interested in the Mokwa scheme. He offered to send one of his advisers to Nigeria to help with determining a future for the project should there be a need for such assistance.[73] The information the S of S had about NAP was old, as the project continued to experience severe losses in 1953. He was basing his comments on the assessment Nye had given in his 1952 report in which he concluded that if the project was allowed to proceed without being pressured to be profitable, it would be successful under the present management.[74] Most of the stakeholders in the scheme understood that the scheme had failed. In 1954, it was hard to find anyone, including ardent supporters such as Rackhouse, who believed that the scheme was going to be successful within three to five years. Some of the supporters were looking at it as an experiment that may take several years for success in terms of knowledge gathered. Financial success at NAP was not a remote consideration. This goes to show the disconnect that existed between the career civil servants, the politicians, the experts, and the colonial governments. When these colonial development schemes are seen from a distance, one may be tempted to see a heavily coordinated attempt by the different elements of the British bureaucracy to carry them out and to exploit the colonies. At a closer range, one sees a disjointed colonial system that had different competing interests. The colonial system's bureaucratic rigmarole was partially responsible for the failure of the second colonial occupation.

Be that as it may, the governor of Nigeria, Sir John Macpherson, responded to the S of S updating him on the different proposals that were being considered as a result of the CDC's decision to withdraw from the project. The Nigerian council of ministers considered four alternative solutions. The first option was that the NCG should take over the CDC's interests in the scheme; the second was to invite the NRG to assume full control of the scheme; the third was for the NCG to take over the interests of the CDC at valuation and then invite the NRG to provide the funds that were needed to cover the recurrent expenditures of the scheme for another five years; and the final option was for the NRG to take over the interests of the CDC and assume all the costs required to continue the scheme for the next five years.[75] The decision of the council of ministers was that the NCG could not assume any future financial responsibility for the scheme and had no interest in operating the scheme or taking over the interests of the CDC in the scheme. The NCG was willing to transfer its shares in the scheme free of charge to the NRG. The decision was passed by the NCG to the NRG to determine either to operate the scheme with or without the CDC or to wind it down.[76] The NCG's offer to transfer its shares in the scheme to the NRG was not a gift but a liability. Regionalization had already taken place and it was unfair to use money that belonged to the central government to prop up a failing project in the northern region. It was obvious to the NCG that the scheme was a failure and continuous participation meant investing in a project that couldn't generate any profits. This shows that the council of ministers was not persuaded by the arguments of Rackhouse and the inspector general of agriculture. Their papers advancing the continuance of the scheme were made available to the council of ministers for their full consideration. By April of 1954, when a parliamentary question was asked in London on the future of the scheme, the CO responded clearly that both the NCG and the CDC had withdrawn from the scheme and it was now under consideration by the NRG. The NCG continued to fund the scheme, awaiting the decision of the NRG. The reason they did this was to make sure that there was no break in continuity should the NRG choose to continue the scheme.[77]

The governor reported in May of 1954 that the NRG was interested in continuing the scheme and that it made a bid of £60,000 for all the assets of NAP. The NCG and the CDC accepted the bid. This proposal was subject to the approval of the executive council of the NRG.[78] The NRG was overly generous and optimistic in putting up the said bid amount. Both the NCG and the CDC would have gladly let go of all the assets at £1 because they wanted to be immediately relieved of any burden of association with the project. They were bound to lose more money should they continue to participate in the scheme. By taking over this scheme, the NRG was assuming responsibility for the management of the scheme and its employees who were to become staff of the NRG. The executive council did not immediately approve the transfer of the company to the NRG. While the NRG saw great value in the continuation of the scheme as an experiment, it had problems with the cost involved. Their plan was to modify the settlement scheme and reduce it to a compact area of about 4,000 acres. A prerequisite for the scheme was "some further clearing against tsetse fly, re-alignment of holdings and protection against erosion ."[79] The modified scheme was going to investigate mechanical cultivation and cropping and the size of holdings. They were also going to examine the possibility of introducing cattle to the scheme. The scheme needed to solve many technical issues and they felt that an experimental farm would be essential to its success.[80] With the modification of the scheme, the cost was also substantially reduced. The capital cost was going to be £91,500 and the annual recurrent cost was estimated at £21,000. The NRG planned to approach the S of S to provide £51,000 grants from the CD&W funds. This was over and above what was already allocated to the NRG. The NRG had proposed in their request the provision of the remaining £40,000 that was needed to execute the new project. Should the S of S refuse to grant them the £51,0000 request, their alternate plan was to find savings under the agricultural section of their development plan. For the annual expenditures of the scheme, the NRG was confident that it could provide £10,000 annually and was requesting that the S of S provide the remaining £11,000 as an additional grant. The annual revenue accruing from the scheme in the first year was estimated at £4,000 and this was expected to cover the cost of plowing.[81]

In the negotiations with the NRG, both the NCG and the CDC agreed that June 1, 1954 would be the date for the transfer of full responsibility to the NRG. The long awaited response from the NRG was received on the eve of this official transfer of ownership. The response received was not the anticipated approval of the executive council but a request for money from the CD&W fund to help cover the £106,500 that the scheme was estimated to cost over the next five years. The basis for such a request was that the cost of running this scheme was an unexpected commitment and it was important that the scheme should be continued. They cited the secretary's own letter to the governor in which he agreed with his agricultural adviser that the scheme was important and its value was not only good for Northern Nigeria but would make a valuable contribution to the agricultural development of Nigeria.[82] Their argument here was that the imperial government had some responsibility to help aid the project with the CD&W funds. Was the letter sent at the last minute as an attempt to force the hand of the CO to provide funding for the scheme? It may have been perceived that way. The NRG acknowledged the possibility for such a perception. The letter noted: "I am to emphasize that this request is in no sense an attempt to take advantage of the present situation and public interest in this country and in the United Kingdom in Mokwa."[83] Obviously, it was taking advantage of the situation. This request could have been sent earlier when the negotiations were ongoing. Though the NCG and the CDC had decided to withdraw from the project, they understood the challenges for the NRG not to want to continue the project. The NRG felt obligated to keep the scheme alive for two reasons. The first reason was that the settlers were subjects of the NRG and the government had a moral obligation to these settlers. The second reason was that the NRG seemed convinced of the experimental value of the scheme even when its director of agriculture had argued against the continuance of the scheme. Given that the NRG had raised the hopes of its people as to the value of the scheme, it felt that abandoning the scheme would be a public embarrassment to both the prestige of the colonial government and Western science. Although the abandonment of this project was bound to create public relations problems for the CO which had become accustomed to media reports of such failures, it was palatable for them to accept the failure of this scheme because the Conservative Party, which was now in government, was opposed to public sector investments in colonial development. For them, this was the domain of the private sector.

The official transfer of the scheme occurred as scheduled despite the late request by the NRG. A day later, the NRG wrote a letter to the CO requesting for a grant to cover the cost of continuing the modified project. Dick Gresswell, a Nigerian official who was back in Britain on holiday, met with officials at the CO to discuss the letter. At this meeting, three main conclusions emerged. He was told that it was contrary to the existing policy for CD&W funds to be used to rescue CDC projects. He was also informed that there was no parliamentary authority that permitted the Treasury or the CO to give CD&W funds after the end of 1955/56. This is because the 1945 Act was enacted for a ten-year period and funding through the Act had to terminate in 1955. Therefore there was no need to ask for grants for the recurrent expenditures for the next five years, which would have been 1955 to 1960. The final point was: "Provided that H.M. Treasury agree that the new Mokwa project is eligible for C.D. & W. assistance, the probable ruling by the Colonial Office will be that costs, over and above the Regional contribution to the end of 1955/56, must be met from balances in Nigeria's current territorial allocation."[84] While the CO did say they had not heard anything from Nigeria regarding the proposed grant that the NRG was requesting, they agreed to approach the Treasury and to inform them that Nigeria would be making an application for assistance for the NAP scheme effective June 1, 1954. Gresswell's takeaway from the meeting was that the CO was expecting a new plan that would lay out what the NRG intended to do at Mokwa and how that fitted into the ten-year plan and why it was not included before.[85] Given that the CO was expecting the NCG to communicate with them in reference to grants for the Mokwa scheme, the Nigerian administration sent a letter to the S of S on June 29, 1954 making a strong case for assistance to the NRG for the continuance of NAP. In conclusion the letter said:

> I shall therefore be grateful if you will give consideration to the possibility of making available assistance from Colonial Development and Welfare Funds to the Northern Regional Government bearing in mind the fact which your Agricultural Adviser has pointed out and which was contained in your saving No. 111 of the 14th of January, 1954, that the scheme stands a chance of success and should make invaluable contribution to the Agricultural development of Nigeria provided it is not expected or required to show a profit in the nearest future.[86]

This letter used the secretary's own words to convince him to provide support for the scheme. In response, the S of S agreed to consider an application for assistance from the CD&W funds without making any commitments. However, he informed the Nigerian administration that should the application be approved, the money had to be found from within the allocation that had been made to the Nigerian territory and that money would not be sourced from other areas of the CD&W fund.[87] The problem the NRG faced was that the CD&W fund was coming to the end of its ten-year period and the NCG was also reluctant to use funds that were awarded for the whole of Nigeria on a project that was now solely the responsibility of the NRG.[88]

NAP UNDER THE NRG

After the NRG took over the scheme, the scope of operations was reduced from what had been planned prior to the transfer. The agricultural engineer of the project was asked to list all equipment available and to indicate that which was required to run the project for the meantime. Other equipment was sold or transferred to other stations.[89] The NRG was also prepared to sell some of the buildings in Mokwa that they felt were not useful to the project. Unlike the old grandiose plan to establish a big settlement scheme, the project under the control of the NRG was much reduced and was truly an experimental scheme. This was what should have happened in 1949 when the scheme was first conceived. In a meeting held in June of 1954 by some of the senior staff of the agriculture department,[90] it was agreed that only minimum experimental work should be carried out at the initial stage in order to assess the "possibility of extending the working season." It was also decided that parts of the demonstration farm should be used for experimental purposes. For the next planting season, they were preparing to cultivate not more than 3,000 acres and not less than 1,500 acres.[91] This figure was a far cry from the project's initial goal of cultivating 65,000 acres. The acres that they were projecting to cultivate were even smaller than the 8,684 acres that they had cleared and were planting at the end of 1952. Capping cultivation at 3,000 acres was truly a step toward cutting costs and using the project purely for field trials and experimentation. After the NRG took control of the project, the emphasis was on planting guinea corn, soya beans, groundnuts, and cotton. The new scheme also had fewer settlers. In 1955, there were only ninety settlers in the scheme. In August of 1955, the farmers were debited with the cost of cultivations, cash advances, and the value of guinea corn that was supplied to them as food. This amounted to about £11,546.10. Farmers then sold their produce to the NRG. The NRG did not expect it to be profitable anytime soon. On the eve of Nigeria's independence in 1960, this scheme remained an experimental project. In the postcolonial period, a college of agriculture was built in the Mokwa area and the area remains a strong agricultural region. NAP never became a huge success in mechanized rural agriculture as was envisioned, but it was successful as an experimental station and that area has continued to emphasize agricultural production as its primary economic output.

PROBLEMS WITH NAP

Residents of Manchester, United Kingdom woke up on the morning of July 8, 1954 to the following headline in their local paper: "ANOTHER GROUNDNUTS SCHEME Failure in Northern Nigeria." The article went on to report that the Niger agricultural project, Mokwa, which was initiated in 1949 with colonial development and welfare funds, sought to develop an area of over 2,000 square miles, but had to be wound up after only developing a little more than 8,000 acres. The story concluded by making references to the failure of the Tanganyika groundnut scheme.[92] The failure of this project was a source of embarrassment for the British as they were still living in the shadow of another failed development scheme, the East Africa Groundnut Scheme. The important question that needs to be answered is: Why did NAP fail?

The problems with this scheme started in its initial planning. It began without any extended field trials and investigations. There weren't even any field trials to determine if the location was good for oilseeds. The only consideration given was that there was good water supply, high rainfall, and easier evacuation routes.[93] Like the East Africa Groundnut Scheme, the CDC and the colonial state skipped field trials because they needed to produce primary products quickly for export. The scheme was rushed from the beginning because Britain needed foreign exchange to deal with its balance of payments and to generate revenue for postwar reconstruction. Also, this scheme and many others like it started when the second colonial occupation was intended to deal with world food shortages and the impending "Malthusian crisis." The demonstration farm that was established carried out very limited experiments on the "the use of fertilizers and variety trials."[94] No thorough scientific investigations had been carried out to determine which seeds were going to be more productive on project site. The rush to begin the scheme is evident in the fact that it was started before the management company and board was even formed.[95]

One of the contradictions of this scheme is the language of experimentation that was repeatedly used to describe it. On the one hand, the scheme was said to be a social experiment, and, on the other hand, its development was clearly rushed in order to generate quick revenues. My argument is that there was a founding hope that NAP might be successful. Rackhouse revealed in his confidential memo that

> a decision was taken about the lay-out of the scheme during a five minute ride over it in an aeroplane and grave mistakes resulted. An aerial survey was undertaken at great expense of the whole of Kontagora Emirate whereas a close contoured plan of the pilot area was required. . . . Insufficient attention was paid to the question of water supply, it being assumed that the provision of water at the bottom of a well was adequate for settlers who had never pulled a skin of water from a well in their lives.[96]

Rackhouse was very critical of the scheme. Though he was the Resident of the area, the scheme was neither his idea nor that of other local officials. It was a project that came from the outside, in this case the metropolitan government, and it went completely against the local practice of careful research and incremental change. Not only was the scheme an outside project but it was also micromanaged by the central organization of the CDC in London. Rackhouse argued that the central organization tried to micromanage the project in order to get quicker returns. They insisted on clearance and cropping targets and wanted immediate returns for the money invested in the scheme. He wrote:

> By insisting on clearance and cropping targets and immediate returns for their money they [CDC] caused a loss of some £20,000 to £30,000 over stumping, breakages of machinery and waste of manpower. These stumps are still being removed at great expense and there is still a large area to do. They were responsible for sowing up by direct labour the newly cleared land with guinea corn, thus incurring a great loss both in money and prestige when it failed.[97]

The management of the scheme was pressured for quicker returns meaning that they could not have long-term planning and execution in view but instead would have to resort to options that would raise money immediately.[98] Since the scheme was established, Rackhouse wanted it to stay open.

Another major problem this scheme faced was the settler problem. This problem plagued the scheme from the outset. A political decision was made that the settlers in the first settlement should only be drawn from the Mokwa area. The reason behind this was the fear that the local people would oppose settlers being brought in from other regions of the country, creating problems for the execution of the scheme. Many migrants, such as the Igbo people of Eastern Nigeria who were residents in the northern region and had provided the first labor for the scheme, were prevented from being settlers. For the rest of the settlements, the decision was made that settlers should only be drawn from the northern region. The reason was because of the contempt that northerners had toward the southerners and settling them there would be perceived as a land takeover. However, the North was not able to supply enough labor for the efficient execution of the scheme. For a scheme that involved the resources of the whole of Nigeria, there shouldn't have been ethnic restrictions in the allocation of settlements. People who were willing to work the allotted acres should have been recruited from the different parts of the country. Such a policy was not possible because of the land tenure system that the colonial system had failed to change because it needed the cooperation of the local authorities. NAP found itself besieged by the same problems that plagued a similar agricultural development scheme in French West Africa, Office du Niger. Like Office du Niger, Mokwa was a sparsely populated area. The initial settlers were from the local area but as the project expanded, recruitment of settlers became a major problem that preoccupied the French and they started using coercive recruitment techniques[99]

By the middle of 1952, NAP had serious issues attracting settlers and those who had been recruited to the first settlement had performed abysmally. The Ndayako settlement was a great failure from the onset. There was no mechanism to ensure that these settlers were qualified to be awarded land. Most of them were attracted by the desire to get land for free. It was later discovered that a large number of these settlers were not good farmers and were not interested in doing their share of the work. After the failure of the groundnut crop in 1952 and the aggressive collection of the two-thirds proceeds by the managing company, most of them decided to leave by the end of the year.[100] At this point, only one settlement had been fully established and there were hopes that the second settlement would be fully set up by the end of 1952, followed by the third settlement in 1953. By March of 1952, only one and a half settlements had been achieved. In discussing the quality of settlers, Baldwin writes that the Department of Labor in Kaduna was asked to send all available men of northern provinces or adjacent French territory who were seeking work. The 225 men who arrived were unimpressive:

> Some were ex-Servicemen, who appeared never to have wanted work, let alone agricultural work. Others were obviously thoroughly unfitted for hard manual work—one had a withered leg and could not walk without the help of a stick, another had advanced syphilis, two had been discharged unfit from the Army and four or five were aged about 80. Within three weeks, desertions had been so heavy that only eighty-seven remained. Shortly afterwards most of the others left, some of them being sentenced to imprisonment by native courts as rogues and vagabonds for idling round railway stations.[101]

By the end of June of 1952, 24 of the original 78 settlers in the Ndayako settlement had been replaced and in order to achieve the standard of cultivation desired, 24 more settlers needed to be replaced. Four more settlers were dismissed from the settlement by September of 1952 and some of the farmers were resistant to hoe areas for the cultivation of groundnuts and Bambara nuts. As a result of this, the company was forced to take over the direct cultivation of 260 acres of land.[102] Losing more than half of the settlers in the first year of the settlement meant a great waste of time and resources. The settlers were not familiar with the type of farming they were being introduced to. They had to learn, and it was hoped that they could get better in time, thereby leading to more positive outcomes. Continually replacing the farmers meant that no significant experience was gained and scarce resources were expended on the training of new settlers. The settler problem plagued the scheme throughout its existence. Attracting volunteer settlers was a problem because the people in the region were not starving for land and they considered their farm lands to be fertile. They did not see any reason to abandon those lands to embrace a new form of farming that had not been tested and proven to be more beneficial to them than their own ways. Finding good settlers became a perennial problem and the company was unable to fill the settlements according to schedule. Before the end of 1952, the company was forced to replace ten unsatisfactory settlers and nine more had surrendered their holdings.[103]

Another problem that the scheme faced was mechanical. The tractors that were used in the scheme were not suitable for the land. Based on the experiences acquired by the engineering department of CDC from the East African Groundnut Scheme, they decided against the mechanized clearing of Mokwa using the 80 horsepower bulldozers. Their understanding was that only 130 horsepower bulldozers would be suitable. These were not readily available in Nigeria. They needed to be shipped from the U.S. and that was going to take several months, which meant further delays to the project. This was also going to significantly increase the budget of the project.[104] They resorted to the use of equipment that was readily available: the Fordson Major diesel tractors and the Ransomes Dragoon disc plows. These machines suffered mechanical problems and there were occasions when the farmers had to wait for months for spare parts to arrive from overseas. Baldwin writes that:

> delays in the arrival of machinery and parts was, throughout the period of operation of the scheme, a great administrative problem. In April 1952 two senior officers had to travel personally from Mokwa to Lagos to search for cases of spares which had been mislaid somewhere on Apapa wharf. . . . Matters were not helped by the inefficiency of the postal system. The delivery of letters and packets, and even the supply of stamps was irregular. Parcels clearly marked Mokwa were sent to Minna, 140 miles away.[105]

The mechanization aspect of the project created myriad problems, so they had to resort to hand tools. At the end, mechanization failed and the traditional African methods triumphed.

The designers and implementers of this scheme also rejected locally produced knowledge. Local farmers were not consulted in the design and implementation of the project. The contributions of the local emir or leaders were very marginal. They served in the advisory board but their role was limited to recruiting settlers and disciplining them. For example, if they had consulted the local people, the construction of the settlers' residential quarters would have been done differently. As it was, the houses were built facing the roads, a style of building that was alien to the local people. They built their houses facing each other, creating compounds as this style of construction reflected traditional African communal living and social bonding. The settlements never felt like home to the settlers and thus many of them ended up not living in houses that they were provided at the settlement. They lived in Mokwa city and came from there to their farms each morning and returned home in the evening, thereby defeating the purpose of establishing the settlements. This travel took away time and energy that would have been better expended in cultivating the allotted acres. The locals also understood the weather patterns and the appropriate times in which to plant their seeds. The technical officers never sought this knowledge from the locals.

The incentive scheme designed for the project represented yet another problem. The settlers received one-third of their produce, while the company kept two-thirds. The settlers did not see any incentive to cultivate more because they felt that the company was exploiting them. Local farmers who did not live in the settlement and were not part of the scheme cultivated about four acres of land a year and earned an average annual income of £25. They did this while having the choice to cultivate whatever they wanted to. A settler who was forced to cultivate about 24 acres of land still made about the same income. As Baldwin argues, "It is clear that in the first two years the average incomes actually earned by the settlers were only a half to three-quarters of what the average local farmers were obtaining on their much smaller plots without the aid of mechanical equipment."[106] This was also a vital reason many of the settlers chose to desert the settlement. Given that they could make as much money cultivating a smaller portion of land without the strict orders of the Europeans, they chose freedom over living in the settlement with all the restrictions and controls that it brought. The morale in the settlement was very low and the settlers did not believe in the scheme. For a scheme of this nature to work, the settlers must be committed to it. Gezira was successful because the farmers wanted to be part of the settlement. A substantial number of the settlers in the Mokwa scheme did not want to be there and so they brought a lackadaisical attitude to their work. The Company could not force the settlers to work because there was no proportional punishment. Expelling them from the settlement had little or no negative impact on them as they simply returned to their normal lives in their villages.

The problems that plagued NAP were similar to those faced by many other large-scale agricultural settlement schemes initiated in this late colonial period: lack of local knowledge, the failure of mechanical equipment, and settler unrests or high turnover. All of these problems could be explained with one phrase, "poor planning." The desire to produce quickly blinded the planners to these pitfalls. Even the Gezira scheme, which was hailed as a success story and upon which NAP was fashioned, took several years of incremental trials and expansion. NAP ignored thirty years of wisdom that had been accumulated by the agriculture department in Nigeria. As B. W. Hodder has noted, what we learn from the failure of this scheme is that

> any successful agricultural extension scheme based on large-scale, highly capitalized methods, depends initially on adequate knowledge about the characteristics and significance of tropical conditions, about the theory of this kind of development, and about the complex conditions existing in the actual area in which the development is contemplated. Secondly, any kind of agricultural innovation should proceed slowly and carefully, for the object of rural development should be simply to graft on to indigenous life the things that it lacks.[107]

CONCLUSION

The postwar development agenda of the British colonial state came to a screeching halt as most of the ambitious schemes embarked upon began to fail. These schemes failed because of imperial ideologies and contradictions of colonial rule. In the postwar period, there was a renewed sense of empire as Britain struggled with its economic recovery. As in the first colonial occupation, Britain had to give the appearance that its mission was to improve the conditions of the colonial people. Joseph Chamberlain had advocated "constructive exploitation" as a means through which Britain would achieve its imperial goals. The reluctance of Britain to invest metropolitan funds in the colonies meant that colonial rule was reduced to the plunder, extraction, and draining of colonial resources.[108] This led to the crises of poverty and underdevelopment in the colonies that became more glaring and received worldwide attention in the interwar years. Colonialism could no longer hide beneath its mask of a "civilizing mission." The development agenda enacted during the second colonial occupation was an attempt to recover the ideology of Chamberlain which had often been frustrated by the Treasury and those who insisted on the colonies being financially self-sufficient. While the practices had changed, the goal remained the same. The scheme at Mokwa offered an excellent example. The CD&W Act of 1945 was intended to respond to colonial poverty. No sooner had the development agenda begun than Britain passed a new act, the Overseas Resource Development Act, that created both the CDC and the OFC. These two corporations that were responsible for these failed development schemes had undercut the practices that had been enshrined in the colonial states. The goal to exploit African resources quickly meant that these new schemes were not subjected to the careful planning, research, and experimentation that were the hallmark of the technical departments. The results of the conflicts between the technical departments and the administrative department had fully manifested in the failure of this scheme. By subordinating the technical departments to the administrative department as Governor Richards had done in 1945, it was now easier to bypass the gradualism and conservatism these departments were often accused of. Such a cautious approach could have potentially prevented these failures.

The cautious and conservative approaches of the technical departments were lessons learned. Having worked with African farmers, these officials had accumulated knowledge that gave them better insights into agriculture planning and development among African communities. Mackie had insisted that through demonstration, the agricultural official has to convince the African farmer that he was a better farmer. It was only in doing so that their extension work would be successful. In the Mokwa scheme, the planners had no knowledge or ignored that wisdom of the agriculture department. This was detrimental to the whole development process as many of the settlers abandoned the settlements as a result of poor yields. They were not convinced that the European agricultural practices were better than African ones. The architects of the scheme also failed to involve the local people in the planning process. The assumptions were that the local practices are timid and backward. Unlike the Mackiean policy of the agriculture department, the planners made no effort to learn the traditional practices and to see how these could be integrated in the scheme. Some of the problems that the scheme encountered such as the designs of the housing could have been easily dealt with if the architects and implementers of the scheme had engaged the local people in the planning process. It was a missed opportunity for the planners to have failed to utilize the knowledge that had been produced by the African people and the agriculture department of Faulkner and Mackie.

The failure of the Mokwa scheme and others during the second colonial occupation was not a requiem to such large-scale mechanized agricultural schemes in Africa, South of the Sahara. In the postcolonial period, many African nationalists and educated elites who had witnessed the failure of these mechanized schemes in the colonial period were buoyed by American foreign aid to renew their commitment to mechanization as the pathway to economic prosperity for their nations. Rather than allowing these schemes to die or to replan them from the scratch, many of the emerging African leaders expanded these schemes or created new ones. They believed that food security and economic development required a massive takeover of agriculture by the government. They accomplished this by pouring more financial resources (often money borrowed from international financial organizations) into these "white elephant" projects. Some of the European expatriates who had managed these colonial failed schemes, together with American social scientists who were ministers of the "gospel of modernization," continued to provide ideological and technical assistance to these projects. The Mokwa scheme is an excellent example of this late colonial malaise that continues to afflict postcolonial governments. Though both the CDC and the Nigerian government had condemned this scheme to failure in 1953, they found a new trustee in the Northern Regional Government. The scheme would continue into the postindependence period with modifications. However it never became the miracle of modern agriculture that had been anticipated. Nevertheless, international organizations and African leaders continue to insist that agricultural development is the pathway to Africa's economic prosperity. As we shall see in the next chapter, this policy prescription is part of the legacies of the agrarian bias of the colonial state.

NOTES

1. James Eskdridge Genova, *Colonial Ambivalence, Cultural Authenticity, and the Limitations of Mimicry in French-Ruled West Africa, 1914–1956* (Peter Lang, 2004), 228.

2. Claudia Castelo, "Developing 'Portuguese Africa' in Late Colonialism: Confronting Discourses," in Joseph Hodge, et al. *Developing Africa*, 69–72.

3. Hereafter, NAP or the Mokwa scheme. This scheme has been mentioned in articles and books without receiving detailed studies and analysis. To date, there is only one detailed published study on the scheme. It is a book by K. D. S. Baldwin published in 1957, not long after the scheme failed. Baldwin had published the book on the suggestion of the Colonial Development Corporation. A long time has passed since Baldwin's book, and this project deserves a new analysis.

4. C. C. S. Newton, "The Sterling Crisis of 1947 and the British Response to the Marshall Plan," *The Economic History Review*, 37, 3, (1984): 392.

5. Niall Ferguson, *Empire: The Rise and Demise of the British World Order and the Lessons for the Global Power* (New York: Basic Books, 2004), 300.

6. Hodge, *Triumph of the Expert*, 208

7. Ibid., 234.

8. This scheme was created in 1947 was taken over by the Overseas Food Corporation in April of 1948. The project was estimated at £24 million. The scheme was in trouble by the end of 1948. The scheme was abandoned in January of 1951. Hodge, *Triumph of the Expert*, 210–211.

9. HMSO, *Overseas Resources Development Act*, 1948, Section 1.

10. E. R. Wicker, "The Colonial Development Corporation (1948–54)," *The Review of Economic Studies* 23, 3, (1955–1956): 213–214.

11. John Kent, *British Imperial Strategy and the Origins of the Cold War, 1944–49* (Leicester: Leicester University Press, 1993), 132.

12. HMSO, *Colonial Development Corporation*, 1948, 5. The booklet was prepared as a guide to the objects and methods of operation of the corporation.

13. Wicker, "The Colonial Development Corporation, 1948–1954," 216.

14. H. Nutcombe Hume, "The Work of the Colonial Development Corporation," *Journal of the Royal Society of Arts*, 104, 4984, (1956): 785.

15. A CDC Scheme for the Agricultural Development of an area near Mokwa, Nigeria (Niger Agricultural Project, Ltd), May 20, 1953, TNA: CO 554/458.

16. More on the Gezira scheme later.

17. The two officers were Mr. T. Weatherhead, who was a senior district officer, and Mr. D. W. H. Baker, who was the principal of schools at the agriculture department. K. D. S. Baldwin, *The Niger Agricultural Project: An Experiment in African Development* (Oxford: Basil Blackwell, 1957), 12–14.

18. Baldwin, *The Niger Agricultural Project*, 12–13.

19. Ibid., xiii.

20. Notes on Some Agricultural Development Schemes in Africa, October 16, 1951, TNA: CO 554/458.

21. This company was incorporated on March 1, 1950, to manage the scheme. It had an initial capital of £450,000 subscribed by both the Nigerian colonial

government and the CDC equally. Though each share was £1, the first share that was issued to the CDC carried two votes. This was to ensure that the CDC had control of the company.

22. The Niger Agricultural Project, May 20, 1953, TNA: CO 554/458.

23. Ibid.

24. Peter F. M. McLoughlin, "The Sudan's Gezira Scheme: An Economic Profile," *Social and Economic Studies* 12, 2 (June, 1963): 181.

25. Colonial Development Quarterly Report on Schemes in Operations for quarter ended June 16, 1952, TNA: CO 7304/52.

26. Report of G.W. Nye, OBE secretary of state's deputy agricultural adviser's visit to Mokwa, December 29, 1952, TNA: CO 554/458.

27. Notes on Some Agricultural Development Schemes in Africa, October 16, 1951, TNA: CO 554/458,

28. Stefan Esselborn, "Environment, Memory, and the Groundnut Scheme: Britain's Colonial Agricultural Development Project and Its Global Legacy" *Global Environment* 11 (2013): 67.

29. Hodge, *Triumph of the Expert*, 211.

30. Notes of a meeting at the CDC, June 29, 1952, TNA: CO 554/458.

31. Colonial Development Quarterly Report on schemes in operation for quarter ended June 16, 1952, TNA: CO 7304/52.

32. Ibid.

33. Ibid.

34. CDC Annual Report for 1952, TNA: CO 554/458.

35. Ibid.

36. Baldwin, *The Niger Agricultural Project*, 21.

37. James Scott, *Seeing Like A State: How Certain Schemes to Improve the Human Condition have Failed* (New Haven: Yale University Press, 1998), 89.

38. Bonneuil, "Development as Experiment," 265–267.

39. Ibid., 265.

40. Robert Chambers, *Settlement Schemes in Tropical Africa* (Abingdon: Routledge, 1969), 17.

41. Ibid.

42. Baldwin, *The Niger Agricultural Project*, 194.

43. Scott, *Seeing Like A State*, 88.

44. Bonneuil, "Development as Experiment," 267.

45. Ibid., 268.

46. Ibid., 269.

47. Victoria Bernal, "Colonial Moral Economy and the Discipline of Development: The Gezira Scheme and 'Modern' Sudan," *Cultural Anthropology* 12, 4, (1997): 453.

48. Bonneuil, "Development as Experiment," 268.

49. Huxley to Evans, February 25, 1953, TNA: CO 554/458.

50. Willis to Dumpleton, March 11, 1953, TNA: CO 554/458.

51. Dumpleton to Willis, March 13, 1953, TNA: CO 554/458.

52. Evans to Huxley, March 16, 1953, TNA: CO 554/458.

53. Huxley to Evans, March 17, 1953, TNA: CO 554/458.

54. Elspeth Huxley, *A New Earth: An Experiment in Colonialism* (London: Chatto & Windus, 1960), 217.

55. Brown to permanent secretary of the Ministry of Agriculture and Natural Resources, Lagos, March 26, 1953, TNA: CO 554/458.

56. Ibid.

57. Ibid.

58. Ibid.

59. Memorandum by Rackhouse on the Niger Agricultural Project, April 2, 1953, TNA: CO 554/458.

60. Nick Cullather, "Miracles of Modernization: The Green Revolution and the Apotheosis of Technology," *Diplomatic History* 28, 2 (April, 2004): 229.

61. Memorandum by Rackhouse on the Niger Agricultural Project, April 2, 1953, TNA: CO 554/458.

62. Ibid.

63. *The Gezira Scheme Past and Present.* A pamphlet issued by the information and publication section of the Sudanese government, 1977, 7.

64. Tony Barnett, *The Gezira Scheme: An Illusion of Development* (London: Frank Cass, 1977), 15.

65. Memorandum by Rackhouse on the Niger Agricultural Project, April 2, 1953, TNA: CO 554/458.

66. Ibid.

67. Memorandum to the permanent secretary of the Ministry of Natural Resources, May 9, 1953, TNA: CO 554/458.

68. Memorandum by the Ministry of Mineral Resources, Lagos, May 20, 1953, TNA: CO 554/458.

69. Ibid.

70. Dumpleton to Willis, November 30, 1953, TNA: CO 554/458.

71. Willis to Dumpleton, December 23, 1953, TNA: CO 554/458.

72. It was often the case that the career staff carried out these negotiations. The politicians were usually brought in at the end.

73. S of S to the officer administering the government of Nigeria, telegram, January 14, 1954, TNA: CO 554/458.

74. Report by G.W. Nye on Niger Agricultural Project, November 29, 1952, TNA: CO 554/458.

75. Macpherson to Lyttleton, February 10, 1954, TNA: CO 554/1269.

76. Ibid.

77. Macpherson to Lyttleton, April 3, 1954, TNA: CO 554/1269.

78. Macpherson to Lyttleton, May 13, 1954, TNA: CO 554/1269.

79. Niger Agricultural Project, Mokwa—Taking Over, Memorandum by the minister of Natural Resources, May 27, 1954, Nigerian National Archives, Kaduna (Hereafter NNAK): 151D.

80. Ibid.

81. Ibid.

82. P. H. G. Scott to F. E. V. Smith, May 31, 1954, TNA: CO 554/1269.

83. Ibid.

84. Dick Greswell to Peter Gibbs, June 18, 1954, NNAK: 151D.

85. Ibid.

86. Acting governor of Nigeria to Lyttleton, June 29, 1954, TNA: CO 554/1269.

87. S of S to acting governor, August 4, 1954, TNA: CO 554/1269.

88. The archival materials I have been able to access do not say if the NRG received the grant.

89. W. Matthewson (AG, principal agricultural engineer) to director of agriculture, Northern region, June 15, 1954, NNA: K151D.

90. Present at the meeting were the acting assistant director of agriculture, the acting principal agriculture engineer, the production officer, and the agriculture engineer. The managers of the project remained European but now working for the NRG.

91. Minutes of meeting held at Mokwa, June 7, 1954, NNAK: 151D.

92. "Another Groundnuts Scheme Failure in Northern Nigeria," *Manchester Guardian.*

93. *A CDC Scheme for the Agricultural Development of an Area near Mokwa, Nigeria (Niger Agricultural Project, Ltd)*, Report from NCG to Lyttleton, June 29, 1954, TNA: CO 554/1269.

94. Susannah Bolton, Eddie Arthur, William Buhler, et al., *Science Agriculture Research: A Compromised Participation* (London: Earthscan Publications, 2002), 55.

95. Memorandum by D.H Parkinson, March 14, 1945, TNA: CO 583/271/4.

96. Memorandum by M. V. Rackhouse, April 2, 1953, TNA: CO 554/458.

97. Ibid.

98. Ibid.

99. Monica van Beusekom, *Negotiating Development: African Farmers and Colonial Experts at the Office du Niger, 1929–1960* (Oxford: James Currey, 2002), 57.

100. Memorandum by M. V. Rackhouse, April 2, 1953, TNA: CO 554/458.

101. Baldwin, *The Niger Agricultural Project,* 39.

102. Colonial Development Quarterly Report on schemes in operation for quarter ended September 30, 1952, TNA: CO 7304/52.

103. TNA: CO 146/71/52.

104. Baldwin, *The Niger Agricultural Project,* 105.

105. Ibid., 114–15

106. Ibid., 79.

107. B. W. Hodder, *Economic Development in the Tropics* (London: Methuen & Co. Ltd., 1968), 139.

108. Dadabhai Naoroji, an Indian intellectual and MP in the United Kingdom House of Commons, articulated a theory on this that has come to be known as the "Drain Theory." This theory posits that British colonialism was a system that transferred Indian wealth and financial resources to Britain. This was not unique to India, but was the case in African colonies as well. See Dadabhai Naoroji, *Poverty and Un-British Rule in India* (Nabu Press, 2010).

Chapter 5

The Legacies of British Rule in Nigeria

After six decades of Britain's formal colonization of Nigeria, colonial rule came to an end on October 1, 1960. Independence did not bring a rupture to the relationship between Britain and Nigeria but a shift in the political structures of the country. Constitutional developments in Nigeria, starting with the Richards Constitution of 1946 through the Macpherson Constitution of 1951 and the Lyttleton Constitution of 1954, had gradually expanded the representation of Nigerians in the legislative councils and franchised many Nigerians, though the power to govern the colony was still reserved to the London-appointed governor general of Nigeria. Independence meant that Nigerians could now take political control of their own affairs. However, the political system comprises only half of a country's core structure. The economic system that constitutes the other half is so important that whoever controls it invariably controls the politics too. Postcolonial African leaders were conscious of the impact of political independence without economic power. In the Arusha Declaration, the Tanganyika African National Union reflected on this problem when they declared:

> Independence means self reliance. Independence cannot be real if a nation depends upon gifts and loans from another for its development. . . . How can we depend upon foreign countries and foreign companies without endangering our independence? The English people have a proverb which says, "He who pays the piper calls the tune." How can we depend upon foreign governments and companies for the major part of our development without giving to those governments and countries a great part of our freedom to act as we please? The truth is that we cannot.[1]

In Tanganyika, Julius Nyerere recognized that if he maintained the same economic relationship with the metropole that endured during colonial rule, his government was going to be unable to deliver the dividends that independence promised. His resolve was to try a new approach, Ujamaa, an experiment in African socioeconomic development. The emphasis was on rural agricultural development, economic self-reliance, and the nationalization of some sectors of the economy. Other postcolonial African nations charted different courses as they tried to deal with their newly founded independence and attempted to fulfill the promises that they had made to the people. In the early years of independence, postcolonial Nigerian nationalists continued to maintain close economic ties with Britain. For example, the governor of the Central Bank of Nigeria, Roy-Pentelow Fenton, who was first appointed in 1958, continued to serve as governor even after the independence of Nigeria. He was only replaced by a Nigerian, Aliyu Mai-Bornu, in July of 1963. In the same way, the higher echelons of the Nigerian civil service continued to be dominated by British expatriates, provoking demands for the Nigerianization of the civil service.

Neither the Nigerianization project nor the efforts made by some nationalists after independence to sever economic ties with the former "colonial masters" erased the sociocultural artifacts that colonial rule had left behind. Nigerians continued to speak the "Queen's English" despite its inability to truly tell our African stories and history; and Nigeria adopted the political and economic systems of her colonizer. The Nigerianization project was bound to be a failure as the Nigerian entity itself was a creation of the British and was an unwilling coalition of many ethnic and regional groups with their respective differences. To Nigerianize, whose Nigeria was it going to be? Apart from the fact that a majority of Nigerians wanted their colonizers gone, was there anything else on which Nigerians agreed? The lack of a national unifying identity meant that the Nigerianization project was going to be a challenge. It was common for leaders to think in terms of their ethnic or regional affiliations rather than the nation-state. The whole idea of Nigeria, both in terms of the nomenclature and as a political unit, was alien. This was an imposition from the outside and not an organic growth or locally militaristic conquest. It neither grew as a result of ethnic groups forming alliances or one powerful group conquering another to rule over it. The lack thereof of a nation-state that evolved locally by a group that shared common sociocultural and political interests meant that independence from Britain was going to be fragile. With the colonizer chased away, the nationalists who had formed working collaborations quickly recluse to their own ethnic or regional interests. Political parties were also regionally and ethnically aligned and the idea of "Nigeria" became what could be taken from the center to support ethnic or regional interests. These developments ended up reinforcing the regional and ethnic differences that the British had delicately managed within the fractured Nigerian structure. The fractious differences between the regions resulted in the 1966 Nigerian civil war. Britain scrambled to save Nigeria from disintegration but the damage had already been done, first at the Berlin Conference in 1885 when Africa was partitioned, then in 1906 when the Lagos colony and the Southern protectorate were amalgamated, and finally in 1914 when the Northern and Southern protectorates were amalgamated. All of these decisions were made without Nigerians at the table to decide their fate. Though Nigeria emerged from the civil war as "One Nigeria," the rupture with Britain that had begun to emerge in the late colonial and early postcolonial period had been solidified. Politically, Nigeria moved from a parliamentary system of government to a presidential one, and Nigerian leaders began to gradually disentangle its economy from Britain.

While there were both political and economic shifts in the period after the war, the colonial mentalité remained constant. Colonialism did not simply restructure the political and economic systems to benefit the colonizer; its primary goal was the restructuring of the mind. It achieved this through what the French Marxist philosopher Louis Althusser calls "Ideological State Apparatuses."[2] These institutions, which seem to be independent of the state, actually serve the ideological mission or interests of the state. These included the school, religious, and legal systems. Through these institutions, which have either direct or indirect support of the colonial state, a higher purpose is served in which the colonized mode of thinking, beliefs, and values are reshaped to fit the colonizer's purposes. The Nigerianization or Africanization of the mentalité was going to be a challenge that would require several decades of re-education to overcome. Sekou Toure of Guinea warned in the postindependent period that it was easier to build railroads, ports, and hydroelectric stations than to change the minds of the colonized.[3] To free the African of this colonial mindset was not an easy task and no serious policies were attempted by postcolonial governments to do this. In fact, after the civil war, Nigeria's policy goals mirrored the traditions that had been left behind by the British. Such a return was shaped by the colonial mentalité, speaking to the enormous success of the colonial project that conditioned the colonized to see the world in a certain way and believe that any form of progress had to follow that trajectory. What emerged after independence was not the rejection of the colonial mindset that subjected Nigeria to a second-class status, but a continuation of the same policies and ideologies. The shift that occurred was simply from colonial to postcolonial mentalité. Postcolonial mentalité was no better than its predecessor. The difference is that the direct supervisors or operators were no longer Europeans but Africans. Nigerian leaders were now doing the bidding of their former colonial masters under whose tutelage they had emerged as leaders in the first place. Despite the rhetoric nationalist leaders asserted as they clamored for independence, they continued to draw from the same well of ideas that the European colonialists had rather than trying radical new approaches such as Nyerere's Ujamaa in Tanzania. It was not surprising that development continued along the lines that had been laid during colonial rule.

This chapter posits that there are three artifacts of development from the colonial period that remain central to African development planning today. These are multiyear planning, agrarian bias, and the reliance on international experts. These three legacies of British colonial rule exercise enormous implications for Africa's development. Practitioners of development need to pay close attention to these ideas, as they are partly responsible for the development failures of the postcolonial period.

MULTIYEAR PLANNING

In 1921 the Soviet government issued a decree establishing Gosplan. Gosplan was a centralized specialist group that played an economic advisory role. This was a move toward centralized planning in Russia. Gosplan started issuing five-year development plans in 1928 and remained in existence till the dissolution of the Soviet Union in 1991. Following the Great Depression, new policies of multiyear development planning were also introduced in many European colonies. This new approach to development was different from what was happening in the Soviet Union. In Russia, economic planning and the allocation of resources were centralized. That was not the case with colonial development. As this book has shown, colonial development evolved and shifted over time, but at no point was the goal to centralize the economy either in London or Paris. Colonial administrators exercised significant leverage in the planning and allocation of resources. While there were officials in the metropole who favored metropolitan-centered approaches or wanted the economies to be more integrated with metropole, none advocated the centralization of planning and allocation of resources of the colonies. Multiyear planning emerged not because the European colonial governments wanted to copy Soviet-style economic planning, but in response to colonial poverty and postwar economic challenges. Colonial administrators were endowed with the responsibility of drawing up plans that would utilize their resources to improve the lives of their subjects. London had no intention of running all the economies of the different colonies from the metropole. While the decision on the allocation of financial resources for development was made by the colonial office and the Treasury, the planning itself was done by the colonies. The colonial governors and their staff were better equipped to understand the needs of their colonies and what investments were needed. The British plans of this era emphasized social welfare over economic development, though the latter was not excluded. The 1940 and 1945 CD&W Acts had envisaged ten-year plans but the implementation of the plans was later broken into five-year periods because the officials realized ten-year periods were too difficult to plan.

The introduction of the 1945 development plan in Nigeria during the second colonial occupation was the starting point of a legacy of multiyear planning. While this plan had little input from Nigerians, the later plans had Nigerians actively involved and they wholeheartedly embraced the idea of progress through multiyear planning. As Nigeria advanced toward independence from Britain in 1960, it continued to design development plans. In September of 1953, at the request of the Nigerian colonial government and Britain, the International Bank for Reconstruction and Development[4] undertook an economic mission to Nigeria. The task of the mission "was to assess the resources available for future development, to study the possibilities for development in the major sectors of the economy and to make recommendations for practical steps to be taken, including the timing and co-ordination of developmental activities."[5] After the mission had spent three months in Nigeria, it prepared an integrated program of development for Nigeria. In its report, the mission identified the lack of "technical and managerial skills and knowledge of the country's resources to carry out an accelerated program of development."[6] To resolve this skills shortage problem, a recommendation was made that personnel be recruited from overseas while Nigerians were trained.[7]

Twenty days after the IBRD submitted its integrated plan of national development, on October 1, 1954, Nigeria became a federation. The implication of this was that the regional governments could either adopt or reject the recommendations that the IBRD made. Adebayo Adedeji has noted that "Although each government made references to the mission's work, the five development programmes of the governments were far from constituting an integrated, mutually consistent and coordinated development programme."[8] The five plans of development resulted from the half-hearted attempts of the different governments to create their own plans. The federalization of the government meant that there were now four different regional governments and the Federal Territory: the Northern Regional Government (NRG), the Western Regional Government (WRG), the Eastern Regional Government (ERG), the Southern Cameroons, and the Federal Territory of Lagos. All of these governments had their own development programs. The different programs from the different governments took different directions. Both the federal government and the WRG prepared complete plans for the five-year period beginning in 1955 and ending in 1960. The NRG only published a policy statement on the development program and then in 1958 revised it to extend to 1962. The ERG, which was experiencing financial difficulties, only published an outline of a development plan projected to cost £5.2 million. In

1958, the ERG extended its plan to 1962 and increased the capital expenditure to £20.7 million.[9]

In 1959, the National Economic Council wanted to bring some order to the uncoordinated plans that were in existence. It proposed that a national development plan be prepared for Nigeria "with the objective of the achievement and maintenance of the possible rate of increase in the standard of living and the creation of the necessary conditions to this end, including public support and awareness of both the potential that exists and the sacrifices that will be required."[10] As preparations were underway for a postindependent development plan, it turned to the local Ford Foundation office to help with recruitment of international experts to assist in these efforts. The Ford Foundation Office in New York contacted a Harvard economics professor, David Bell, who "had helped organize and provide Harvard advisory assistance, funded by Ford, to the planning commission in Pakistan. Bell learned of Wolfgang Stolper's interest and enlisted him to head the Nigerian team."[11] Other team members included Lyle Hansen, a Harvard economist who had worked in Pakistan, and Peter Clark, who had just completed his PhD in Economics from the Massachusetts Institute of Technology. None of these three economists were experts on Nigeria, or even African colonial economies for that matter. Stolper's area of research was the East German economy. His first experience with Africa was an eight-week visit to Nigeria organized by the Center for International Studies at the Massachusetts Institute of Technology in which he collected data on Nigeria and talked with some of the officials who worked there. With inputs from Nigerian politicians and British civil servants in Nigeria, the three economists helped design what became the Nigerian National Development Plan of 1962. The target of the plan was to achieve a growth rate of 4 percent per year, to be raised if necessary. The goal was to achieve this growth rate by investing 15 percent of GDP and raising per capita consumption by about 1 percent per year. It also wanted to raise the domestic saving ratio of 9.5 percent of GDP in 1960 to about 15 percent or higher by 1975. It was believed that this would lead to self-sustaining growth. The plan also proposed the rapid development of "opportunities in education, health and employment; and to improve access for all citizens to these opportunities."[12] While this plan put more money on the table, it did not introduce any fresh ideas. In terms of agricultural development, for example, the 1962 plan bore a strong resemblance to the 1945 agricultural plan. While the plan was mid-wived by modernization theorists who were determined to recreate Nigeria in the image of America, in reality, it continued some of the policies of colonial development. "Postcolonial" planners often drew from older colonial files for their development ideas. In some cases, the same buildings and offices that housed the colonial developers were used by "postcolonial" developers.[13]

The 1962 plan showed that the independence of Nigeria did not cause a rupture to the development policy that had been instituted during colonial rule. Even the three-year civil war that engulfed Nigeria from 1967 did not end this colonial legacy of multiyear planning. At the end of the war, the Nigerian government launched three more development plans: the 1970 plan, the 1975 plan, and the 1981 plan. The 1970 plan was a four-year plan intended to reconstruct the infrastructure that was destroyed during the war and also revive the postwar economy. In 1975, when Nigeria was flush with petrodollars as a result of the oil boom, President Yakubu Gowon who apparently quipped that "the problem of Nigeria was not money but how to spend it," launched the third Nigerian national plan. This plan was "the largest, most ambitious and imaginative development programme ever launched, not only in Nigeria but in the whole of black Africa."[14] It was intended to accelerate the growth of the economy and to increase standard of living.

Moreover, the civilian administration of Alhaji Shehu Shagari that came to power in October of 1979 continued the tradition of development planning. This administration launched the fourth development plan in 1981, billed as a four-year plan. Due to declining oil revenues, the plan could not be effectively implemented. By 1985, Nigeria was in a deep financial crisis and had to resort to IMF/World Bank loans. In doing so, Nigeria was forced to embrace neoliberal economic policies that promoted the free market and advocated the sale of government public enterprises. This temporarily ended the era of multiyear development plans that started in the colonial period. In recent years, Nigeria has returned to multiyear planning. In November of 2009, another development plan entitled "Nigeria Vision 20: 2020" was launched. Its goal is to stimulate economic growth and launch the "country on a path of sustained and rapid socio-economic development."[15] Unlike previous plans, this is an eleven year plan. The new government of President Muhammadu Buhari has yet to make any efforts to promote this plan. Nigeria is currently in an economic recession and the government has taken steps to borrow $30 billion to implement a new development agenda. It is too early to tell if and how this government will design its multiyear development plan.

If we return to our earlier definition of development as state interventions to order progress, it makes sense that multiyear development planning is popular in tropical Africa. The circumstances upon which colonial governments instituted development in the late colonial period have not changed much. Development was instituted by colonial states in response to colonial poverty and to mitigate social unrests that resulted from neglect. Postcolonial African governments inherited mass populations of poor people, many of them living in rural areas without many opportunities. As a result, many nations witnessed an upsurge of migrations from rural areas to urban areas. The urban areas did not have the infrastructure to absorb the influx of people leaving the countryside, creating social problems and unrest. Agricultural development became a tool for mitigating these migrations and stabilizing the state.

AGRARIAN BIAS

As previous evidence has made clear, the notion of agriculture as the pathway to Africa's development was not an innovation of the postcolonial period. Colonial administrations in Africa envisioned Africans to be perpetually dependent on agriculture. In a 1943 memo, the Colonial Advisory Council on Agriculture and Animal Health (CAC) wrote that agriculture "is by far the most important industry in the Colonial Empire, and upon it rests the material well-being of Colonial peoples."[16] For this reason, there needed to be coordination between the different technical departments in order "to establish agriculture as a way of life . . . to make the individual realize that he is a member of community, to encourage him to take part in community activities, and to discourage aimless drift from land into urban areas. This involves the encouragement not only of cooperatives in the narrow and technical sense of the term, but also of a cooperative spirit in the daily life of the farming community."[17] All throughout Africa, there was a proliferation of agricultural development programs. In Portuguese Africa, the settlement of white farmers in Angola and Mozambique was seen as means by which African agriculture could be improved. In French West Africa, a large irrigation project, Office du Niger, was intended to expand production. The development plans that emerged in the late colonial and early postcolonial period also assumed that Africa's future was dependent on agriculture. The longtime director of agriculture in Nigeria, James Mackie, stated boldly in his proposal for the expansion of agriculture that "Nigeria is and will always remain an Agricultural country."[18] As we have seen earlier in this book, this kind of thinking influenced the overall planning of development. The 1945 Nigerian plan made substantial investments in the development of agriculture and related services and it attempted to frontload resources by investing heavily in agriculture at the beginning of the plan and then relying on the revenues generated by agricultural to carry out the rest of the plan's implementation. There was faith in agriculture as the magic bullet that would end colonial poverty, reduce food shortages, stabilize the state, and mitigate rural-urban migrations.

Despite this focus on rural agriculture, the colonial state was unable to forestall the migrations from rural to urban areas. The failure of the state to revolutionize rural agriculture and deal with youth unemployment meant more migrations to cities. Between 1959 and 1965, Archibald Callaway, an economist affiliated with the African project at the CIS, conducted research in Nigeria looking at the problem of unemployment. There were many people in both rural and urban areas who had finished their primary education but were unable to find jobs. The colonial state and the missionaries had provided basic primary education and many who had graduated did not see agriculture as their best future prospect and thus they migrated to the urban areas in search of blue or white collar jobs. Callaway's research was necessitated by the presence of young people roaming the streets who had completed primary education but did not have the financial resources to go to secondary schools and had no jobs available for them. Callaway followed the lives of some of these young people from their villages through primary education and into their quest for jobs or higher education. His solution to the school-leaver problem was the creation of "modern agricultural experimental farms that will provide challenging employment for school-leavers who would otherwise swell the grown mass of urban unemployed."[19]

This "school leaver" problem was not new in the 1950s. Experts at the colonial office had identified it as early as the 1930s. As noted by Joseph Hodge, "The old problem of labor shortage was transformed by the Depression into a new crisis of labor surplus, in the form of growing unemployment and underemployment, low wages, and widespread urban and rural immigration."[20] Callaway's thinking was in no way a break from colonial thinking. Even the solution he proffered for this problem was one that was already advanced by the colonial developers in the 1930s and 1940s when they advocated a return to the land, again demonstrating an agrarian bias. Colonial officials also began to advance more extensive state-directed and social engineering development initiatives in the 1940s in response to the unemployment problem. They feared that, without such interventions, the problem of surplus labor might lead to a breakdown in colonial order.[21] By 1959, the western and eastern regional governments were already responding to this "school leaver" problem with farm settlement schemes that were aimed at providing rural employment and attempting to reduce migration to urban areas. These settlement schemes failed woefully.

Despite modernist visions of recreating Nigeria into an industrialized society, the 1962 Nigerian National Development Plan continued the colonial-era development policies that reflected an agrarian bias. The goals outlined by the 1962 plan and the specific projects associated with them did not diverge significantly from late colonial-era development. The 1962 plan summarized its goals as follows:

- the creation of more jobs and opportunities in non-agricultural occupations;
- the provision of advisory and training services to Nigerian businessmen to enable them to compete more effectively at home and abroad;

- the increase in the production of export crops through better seed distribution and more modern methods of cultivation, as well as through the increase in the area under cultivation;
- the introduction of more modern agricultural methods through farm settlements, cooperative (nucleus) plantations, improved farm implements such as hydraulic hand presses for the expression [sic, extraction] of palm oil, and a greatly expanded agricultural extension service;
- the expansion of the installed capacity of electricity generation to 643 MW by 1968;
- the expansion of railway mileage by the remaining 293 miles of the Bornu Extension; and an additional 14 Diesel Engines and 1485 wagons;
- the provision of 7 new docks in Lagos and Port Harcourt capable of handling an additional 3.6 million tons;
- the expansion of the system of tarred roads by about 3,000 miles; and completion of the new Niger River bridge at Onitsha and the Second Mainland Bridge at Lagos; and
- the expansion of cement capacity to not less than 980,000 tons per year.[22]

The 1970 plan that was launched after the Nigerian civil war continued to emphasize the importance of agriculture, allocating to it the third highest portion of the plan's investments. Transportation received 23.7 percent of capital allocation; the public sector as a whole received 13.5 percent; and agriculture received 10.5 percent. In actual expenditures, 23.1 percent was spent on transportation, 11 percent on education; and 7.7 percent on agriculture. Industry received 3.9 percent.[23] On face value, one may argue that if agriculture was that important to Nigeria, it should have received the highest investments in the plan. However, the focus of this plan was the reconstruction of infrastructure that had been destroyed by the war, revoking two decades of progress that colonial development had made. Given that Nigerian agriculture was still primarily based on peasant production, a 7.7 percent investment was significant for a plan that was aimed at rebuilding infrastructure. Halfway through the implementation of this plan, Nigeria experienced an economic boom. This boom was a result of the Arab oil embargo of 1973, which caused the price of oil to spike. Nigeria saw its foreign reserves rise from $222 million in 1970 to $5.203 billion in 1976. Nigerian oil revenues grew from 1.4 billion Naira in 1973 to 12.86 billion Naira by 1980.[24] An increase in public expenditure and a decline in the agricultural sector emerged during this period. There was evidence of the "Dutch disease."[25] Nigeria basically became a rentier state.

The Yakubu Gowon's plan of 1974 did not ignore the agricultural sector, even though Nigeria was flowing in oil revenues. Agriculture and mining were expected to contribute 55.5 percent of the GDP by the plan's end.

Agriculture and mining accounted for 68.9 percent of GDP in 1974. Agriculture received about 11 percent of total public capital investment. There was an urban bias underpinning this plan as industry received 11.5 percent, transportation 37.5 percent, and urban development 9.0 percent.[26] Massive road constructions were carried out in urban areas. Nevertheless, the Gowon administration introduced two major agricultural programs: the National Accelerated Food Production Programme (NAFPP) introduced in 1972 and the Agricultural Development Projects (ADP) established in 1974. Other agricultural schemes launched in the postcolonial period by the federal government included Operation Feed the Nation (OFN) and the River Basin Development Authorities (RBDAs) in 1976, the Green Revolution in 1980, the Directorate for Food Roads and Rural Infrastructure (DFFRI) in 1986, Better Life for Rural Women in 1987, National Agricultural Land Development Authority (NALDA) in 1992, Family Support Programme (FSP) in 1994, Family Economic Advancement Programme (FEAP) in 1996, National Fadama Development Project (NFDP) in the early 1990s, National Economic Empowerment and Development Strategy (NEEDS) in 1999, National Special Programme on Food Security (NSPFS) in 2002, and Root and Tuber Expansion Programme (RTEP) in 2003.[27] Several others schemes have been launched by state governments and nongovernmental organizations.

At the heart of these programs were the goals of increasing food production, conserving the environment to deal with population growth, and finally combating rural-urban migration. Though none of these programs have been very successful, agriculture is still the primary prescription for Africa's development by both African governments and international organizations and governments with interests in Africa. These organizations have embraced the notion that agriculture and not industrialization is the path toward Africa's economic growth. These new development policies in Africa as a whole and Nigeria in particular bear strong resemblance to the colonial doctrines of development. The practice of development has therefore come full circle in adopting the agrarian bias of the colonial state.

Agriculture occupies such an important place in African economies because of the oriental attitudes of the colonizers. African people were perceived as culturally backward, static, and without the intellectual prowess to advance beyond some basic skills. Such attitudes were reflected even in the forms of education that the colonial administrations offered Africans. The education was limited to teaching a few basic technical skills and rudimentary knowledge that would prepare them to be a cog in the wheel of the colonial state. In Nigeria, the colonial administration emphasized education along "native lines." The implication of this policy was that the education offered to Africans was not as sophisticated as that offered in Europe because Africans had no need for such an education nor the ability to absorb it. Uyilawa Usuanlele notes that Walter Egerton, the governor of Lagos, "introduced the defining issue in so-called 'Native education' which was compulsory manual and agricultural training to re-orientate African youths into taking to agricultural production rather than seeking clerical employment."[28] If the emphasis of colonial education and colonialism as a whole was on agriculture, it is small wonder that Africans have been conditioned to see agriculture as its pathway to prosperity. The danger with this thinking is that the solution to Africa's development problems is seen solely from the perspective of agriculture. The standard template for development in Africa today is "agriculture, agriculture, agriculture!" Pick up the development agenda of any African country, South of the Sahara, and the overarching agenda is based around agriculture. In his study of development in Lesotho, James Ferguson has shown how this agrarian bias colors the whole development enterprise. He notes that in the Thaba-Tseka project, there was an exaggeration of the importance of agriculture while understating the role of migrant labor which accounted for most of the economy.[29] Ferguson notes that for the planners, "the inhabitants of the project area were always 'farmers' and the centrality of agriculture in the local economy was the unquestioned premise of the whole project."[30] But was this true? Though the FAO/World Bank Report on the project claimed that farmers in the region generated their income principally through agriculture, this was not the case. The people obtained cash primarily through migrant labor, an important fact that the report ignored.[31] The report also claimed that 70 percent of the gross national product came from the sale of pastoral products, while actual estimates put it at about 2 or 3 percent.[32]

Despite the failure of agriculture to lift Africans out of poverty, African leaders have continued to embrace the essentialism of colonialism and the neocolonial world order. This has ended up handicapping African governments who are always at the doorsteps of Euro-American hegemonic powers and institutions begging for more aid to fuel these failed agricultural agendas promoted by the same Western institutions. Though Nigeria has invested billions of dollars in agricultural schemes and projects in the postcolonial period, it is still a major importer of finished food products and manufactured goods. Nigerian leaders have been stuck in the colonial mode of thinking that agricultural production is the answer to Nigeria's economic challenges. Today, agriculture accounts for less than 18 percent of GDP and crude oil as high as 75 percent. No serious efforts have been made at industrialization, thus continuing the colonial economic pattern of the colony being the producer of primary products for the industries of the metropole. African states will remain impoverished unless they break their economies from the colonial binds of concentrating on the production of primary products for industrialized economies. While agriculture has a role in Africa's development, it should never be the only lens through which development is conceived.

INTERNATIONAL EXPERTS

One of the enduring legacies of development planning is its outsourcing to international "experts." As discussed previously, Nigerians had little input in the planning that took place during the second colonial occupation. Colonial officials dominated the development committees and the few Africans who were privileged to serve in these committees were ex-officio members who did not have a vote. It was not the Nigerians who decided what projects needed to be adopted but the European officials. The local people were not integrated into the process and their voices were marginal. The international experts were both the producers and custodians of knowledge, isolating the indigenous people from this important process. In the last chapter NAP was presented as a case study of the practice of development that fails to harness local talent and adopt locally produced knowledge. This scheme, by far the largest agricultural development scheme in colonial Nigeria, was planned and executed without any input from the locals. The Oilseeds Mission that came to Nigeria conceived it; the CO supported it and convinced the CDC to partake in it; and it was planned and executed by the Nigerian government, the CDC, and the managing company, NAP. International experts ran NAP with no input from the locals. Had local knowledge been consulted, some of the problems that plagued the scheme could have been mitigated. NAP failed because of the experts' ignorance of the history, culture, topography, and farming practices of the locals and their refusal to consult them in the planning process.

Be that as it may, the postcolonial governments returned to these same international experts to help draft and implement later development plans. The 1962 Nigerian National Development Plan is an important example. Though the two committees (the National Executive Council and the Joint Planning Committee) that were responsible for the design of the plan were composed mainly of Nigerians, the planning was still controlled by international experts. Jeremiah Dibua argues that the entries in Wolfgang Stolper's diaries demonstrate that he played a "preeminent and dominant" role in drawing up the plan.[33] The chairman of the National Executive Council was the prime minister of Nigeria and his personal economic adviser was Narayan Prasad, who worked for the World Bank. The Joint Planning Committee had Wolfgang Stolper, an American economist, leading the planning. Both Prasad and Stolper jointly controlled this committee, a system that led to several conflicts between the two. It is also important to note that the initial chairman of this committee was the governor of the Central Bank who himself was a British colonial expert. Permanent secretaries who were British expatriates were also involved in this committee. It is hard to make an argument that this plan was a Nigerian plan. While Stolper stressed that the framework that was set up for development planning was geared toward forcing the formulation of the plan to start from the grassroots, he acknowledged that the roots did not go as deep as would have been desirable.[34] Though the regional plans were intended to be at the grassroots level incorporating local ideas, they too were not spared of these foreign influences. A good example was the eastern regional plan. Not only was Stolper directly influencing the course of events in the eastern region, in his diaries, he made reference to an African American, Daniels,[35] who had great influence in the region.[36] Daniels was the head of the industrial division of the Eastern Region Development Corporation. Stolper accused him of being an empire builder who wanted to "sink lots of money into crazy industrial undertakings, when it should go into palm grove rehabilitation and hydraulic palm oil presses."[37] These are all visible signs of foreign influence in the development of these plans. Be that as it may, it is ironic that Stolper, who was one of the secular missionaries of the gospel of modernization, was insisting on an agriculture path for Nigeria rather than industrialization. It is instructive that Daniels, an African American, was pushing an industrial path for the eastern region, a policy Stolper described as wasteful. Industrialization was precisely what African countries needed at this time if they had any chance of lifting the people from poverty and expanding the economy beyond the production of commodities for export. Arthur Lewis, a black development economist and an economic adviser to the newly independent Ghana, advocated industrialization as a pathway to growth and development. This perspective meant Lewis approached the problem of surplus labor in the rural areas differently. As noted earlier in this chapter, both the colonial and postcolonial governments attempted to solve this problem by promoting agricultural schemes. For Lewis, the solution lay in industrialization.[38] Unfortunately, expatriate economists like Lewis who wanted to chart an industrial future for tropical Africa were a rare minority in the early postcolonial period.

The use of expatriate economists came under criticism early on in the design of Nigeria's plan by a Nigerian economist Ojetunji Aboyade, whom Stolper speaks of highly in his diaries.[39] Aboyade noted that the Nigerian government took the view that "indigenous economists were either unavailable or incapable of carrying out the technical responsibility." Though he believed that the economists that were sent to Nigeria were able economists, he writes that "there is no doubt that they have not come from an economy with an image of strong planning tradition."[40] It is paradoxical that Stolper and his U.S. team would recommend central planning for Nigeria when the U.S. did not use strong central planning in the development of their own economy. Some have argued that using Nigerian economists as Aboyade has suggested wouldn't have made any difference in the plans that were designed because these economists were influenced by Western ideologies. Inderjeet

Parmar notes that Nigerian economists and elites were "developed and nurtured by British colonials and supported by American aid. Its nationalism was always skewed toward reliance on the West for defense, trade, ideology, and legitimacy."[41] Nevertheless, Western-trained Nigerian economics had a good understanding of the history, culture, and politics of Nigeria that placed them in a better position to advise and make judgments on the path the country should follow. Their absence from the development process was because their views did not necessarily match the views of the Western financiers of development. Parmer has shown that Nigerian economists and educated technocrats who did not hold onto the pro-Western viewpoints were branded as "communists" and legislated against for employment in the Nigerian civil service.[42]

Africa's reliance on "international experts" for development is an unwanted gift from colonialism. Several decades after independence, African governments continue to hold tenaciously to the belief that they need foreign economists and experts to help them with their development. James Ferguson accurately captured this problem when he wrote:

> In Zimbabwe, in 1981, I was struck to find local agricultural "development" officials eagerly awaiting the arrival and advice of a highly paid consultant who was to explain how agriculture in Zimbabwe was to be transformed. What, I asked, did this consultant know about Zimbabwe's agriculture, that they, the local agricultural officers, did not? To my surprise, I was told that the individual in question knew virtually nothing about Zimbabwe, and worked mostly in India. "But," I was assured, "he knows development."[43]

Such unbridled faith in international experts has suppressed indigenously produced ideas and has succeeded in setting Africa backward in terms of knowledge generation. It is small wonder that African governments invest so little in research and development.

Apart from the fact that international organizations insist on attaching their "experts" to the loans/ aid packages, African leaders have been conditioned by colonialism to believe that the expatriate is better equipped to handle and execute more technical and scientific tasks, even where the African is more qualified. It is not uncommon to have many African entrepreneurs rent "White men" to be CEOs of their companies. This gives them an advantage when bidding for government contracts. The Americans and the Europeans have understood this pervasive sense of colonial-era mentality in Africa and they have taken advantage of it. This has led to a crisis of development in Africa in which international financial and development institutions such as the World Bank and other European and American-sponsored development agencies share a substantial portion of the blame. As Thandika Mkandawire and Charles Soludo have rightly argued, "There has been hardly any development program in much of Africa without the tacit or explicit involvement/endorsement of the donors. In several important aspects, many of the policies/programs which have turned out to be 'bad' were at their insistence. With Africans adjudged 'incapable of thinking for themselves and implementing policies,' a deluge of over 100,000 foreign technical experts costing over $4 billion annually to maintain have literally taken over the process of policy/project design and sometimes implementation."[44] These so-called experts are often ignorant of the African situation or deliberately use Africa as a living laboratory for experimentation.

CONCLUSION

African leaders have to stop seeking solutions to development problems by looking toward the West. Four decades of experimenting with solutions proffered by the West have left many Africans poorer. Perhaps it is time for African governments to embrace self-reliance and seek solutions that are rooted in Africa's unique history and experience. This would mean tapping into the locally produced knowledge that was rejected during colonial rule and has been ignored in the postcolonial period. While Nyerere's socialist experiments in Tanzania failed for a variety of reasons, including the economic strangulation of his agenda by some Western institutions, his efforts have to be commended because he made attempts to design a development program that took into consideration not only the need to be self-reliant, but also the African core values of communal living and sharing. The challenge has been that many postcolonial African governments have failed to take such risks, clinging tightly to whatever economic policies have been dictated to them by their Western financiers. Colonialism conquered Africa militarily, economically, and intellectually but Africa must fight back.

NOTES

1. Tanganyika African National Union. *The Arusha Declaration and TANU's Policy on Socialism and Self-reliance*. Dar es Salaam: Public Section, TANU, 1967.

2. See Louis Althuser, "Lenin and Philosophy and Other Essays." Transcribed from French by Ben Brewster. Accessed November 30, 2016, https://www.marxists.org/reference/archive/althusser/1970/ideology.htm

3. Elliot P. Skinner, "Development in Africa: A Cultural Perspective," in Robert O. Collins, ed., *Problems in the History of Modern Africa* (Princeton: Markus Wiener Publishers, 2008), 173.

4. Hereafter, IBRD.

5. World Bank, *The Economic Development of Nigeria: Report of a Mission Organized by the International Bank for Reconstruction and Development at the Request of the Governments of Nigeria and the United Kingdom* (Baltimore: John Hopkins Press, 1955), vii.

6. Ibid. 3.

7. Ibid. 4.

8. Adebayo Adedeji, "Federalism and Development Planning in Nigeria" in A. A. Ayida and H. M. A. Onitiri, eds., *Reconstruction and Development in Nigeria: Proceedings of a National Conference* (Ibadan: Oxford University Press, 1971), 101.

9. Ibid., 100.

10. Federation of Nigeria, *National Development Plan, 1962–68* (Lagos: Government Printer, 1962), 46–47.

11. Clive S. Gray (ed.), *Inside Independent Nigeria: Diaries of Wolfgang Stolper, 1960–1962* (Burlington, VT: Ashgate Publishing Company, 2003), ix.

12. Federation of Nigeria, *National Development Plan, 1962–68* (Lagos: Federal Ministry of Economic Development, 1962), 23.

13. In analyzing the nation-building efforts of the Americans in the Plain of Reeds, Vietnam, David Biggs shows how this effort failed because the Americans "could not escape the landscape, webs of bureaucracy, and political movements that had been shaped by ninety years of colonial rule and ten years of anticolonial warfare." Some of the engineers moved back and forth among the French, the Vietnamese, and the American domains. Biggs notes that even today, the engineers and planners still occupy the same offices that were inhabited by the pre-1975 and 1954 agencies. See David Biggs, "Breaking from the Colonial Mold: Water Engineering and the Failure of Nation-Building in the Plain of Reeds, Vietnam," *Technology and Culture* 49, 3 (July 2008): 599–623. Also for more on this continuity, see Elizabeth Lunstrum, "State Rationality, Development, and the Making of State Territory: From colonial extraction to postcolonial conservation in Southern Mozambique," in Christine Folke Ax et al. (eds), *Cultivating the Colonies: Colonial States and their Environmental Legacies* (Ohio, Athens: Ohio University Press, 2011), pp. 239–274; Andrew Bowman, "Mass production or production by the masses? Tractors, Cooperatives, and the Politics of Rural Development in Post-Independence Zambia," *Journal of African History* 52, 2 (July 2011), 201–221.

14. Gordon Idang, "The History of Planning in Nigeria," *Administration for Development in Nigeria*, Paul Collins, (ed.) (Lagos, Nigeria: Africa Education Press, 1980), 24.

15. Abuja, *Nigeria Vision 20:2020 Economic Transformation Blueprint*. National Planning Commission, December, 2009.

16. CO 852/397/2, CAC, Papers and Minutes, 1943, "Principles of Agricultural Policy in the Colonial Empire" (CAC 639), March 31, 1943, in, Joseph M. Hodge, "Colonial Experts, Developmental and Environmental Doctrines, and the Legacies of Late British Colonialism." Edited by Christina Folke Ax, Niels Brimnes, et al. *Cultivating the Colonies: Colonial States and their Environmental Legacies* (Athens: Ohio University Press, 2011), 304.

17. Ibid.

18. Mackie to CSG, Proposals for the expansion of Nigerian agriculture, January 30, 1945, Mackie Papers, RH:MSS.Afr.S.823.

19. Final report to the Ford Foundation on Research on Government Policies Toward Surplus Labor resources in West Africa, 1962–1965, April 6, 1966, MIASC: AC236.

20. Hodge, *Triumph of the Expert*, 18.

21. Ibid.

22. Federation of Nigeria, *National Development Plan, 1962–68* (Lagos: Federal Ministry of Economic Development, 1962), 23–24.

23. *Daily Times*, May 8, 1973. Article written by V. P. Diejomach. It is entitled "Comparative Analysis of Second and Third Plans."

24. Ezekiel Ayodele Walker, "Structural Change, the Oil Boom and the Cocoa Economy of Southwestern Nigeria, 1973–1980s," *The Journal of Modern African Studies* 38, 1 (2000): 71.

25. The Dutch Disease is a concept used in economics to explain the relationship between the increase in the exploitation of natural resources and the decline in local manufacturing. When natural resources are exploited and exported, the currency of the nation becomes stronger and this causes the nation's exports to become too expensive. See Brian Pinto, "Nigeria During and After the Oil Boom: A Policy Comparison with Indonesia," *The World Bank Economic Review*, 1, 3 (May, 1987): 419.

26. Idang, "The History of Planning in Nigeria," 25.

27. There are scant primary and secondary resources available for these programs. For a good and precise overview of these schemes, see Iwuchukwu J. C. and Igbokwe, E. M. "Lessons from Agricultural Policies and Programmes in Nigeria" *Journal of Law, Policy and Globalization* 5, (2012):11–21.

28. Uyilawa Usuanlele, "Development and Education in British Colonial Nigeria, 1940–55," in Joseph Hodge, *Developing Africa*, 254.

29. James Ferguson, *The Anti-Politics Machine: "Development," Depoliticization, and the Bureaucratic Power in Lesotho* (Minneapolis: University of Minnesota Press, 1994), 82.

30. Ibid., 83.

31. Ibid., 82.

32. Ibid., 82–83.

33. Dibua, *Development and DIffusionism,* 76–77.

34. Stolper, *Planning without Facts*, 39.

35. No first name given in the diary.

36. In his diaries, Stolper mentions that he asked Pius Okigbo, who was in charge of economic planning in the eastern region, for a copy of the executive committee paper that was only seen by ministers. With reluctance, Okigbo gave it to him on the promise that the paper should not be shared with anyone. Stolper's reaction was this: "The information in it was pretty much what I had worked up with him when I was last in Enugu, but it was a courageous paper, laying down the law to the Prime Minister, pointing out that the ER financial situation was going to be desperate, that the Plan had to stress high and quick payoff projects, if the Region is not to bog down, and that more taxes would be needed." Gray, ed., *Diaries of Wolfgang Stolper*, 129.

37. Ibid., 129–30.

38. Robert L. Tignor, *W. Arthur Lewis and the Birth of Development Economics* (Princeton University Press), 83.

39. Ojetunji Aboyade was a professor at the University College, Ibadan. He later succeeded Stolper as adviser to the federal government for the second Five-Year Plan.

40. Aboyade, *Foundations of an African Economy: A Study of Investment and Growth in Nigeria* (New York: Frederick A. Praeger, 1966), 154.

41. Inderjeet Parmar, *Foundations of the American Century: The Ford, Carnegie, & Rockefeller Foundations in the Rise of American Power* (New York: Columbia University Press, 2012), 176.

42. Ibid., 173.

43. Ferguson, *The Anti-Politics Machine*, 258.

44. Thandika Mkandwire and Charles Soludo, eds., *African Voices on Structural Adjustment* (Trenton: Africa World Press, 2003), 2.

Conclusion

The postcolonial paralysis of African states is rooted in the European exploitation of the colonies. Colonial economies were set up as appendages to the metropole with the primary role of providing raw materials that fed the European industry. These products were in turn transformed into finished goods and sold back to the colonies at premium prices because of the value added to them. The colonial administrations were able to further their mission in Africa through excise taxes. The Great Depression almost led to the crumbling of this system as worldwide demand for products declined. Without resources to maintain the colonies and social unrest in the colonies themselves as a result of poverty and neglect, colonial administrations had to devise ways to maintain imperial control over the colonies. The developmentalist interventions that created the second colonial occupation were intended to reduce colonial poverty through the provision of basic welfare needs and economic development. Nevertheless, these policies did not attempt to change the structures that had impoverished colonial people. These structures endured in the late colonial period and were solidified in the postcolonial period. This was because colonial rule had created what Frederick Cooper called "the gatekeeper state."[1] Like their colonial predecessors, postcolonial African states have continued to depend on the extraction of resources for export. African leaders who have been privileged to be in control of the gate have used all sorts of maneuvering to maintain this system as it protects their power. However, such a system advantages only a few and creates instability in the polity as everyone wants to have control of the "national cake."

The poverty of African states is not only exacerbated by the fact that only a few people control the resources, it is also affected by the unequal structures through which the states find themselves linked to the world economy. As patronizing as it was, in the colonial system the metropole exercised some maternal role over the colonies. While the mission of the metropole was the exploitation of the colonized, nevertheless, it sometimes felt a sense of responsibility toward the colonies. In the postcolonial world-order, a sham system emerged that is a no-holds-barred capitalism that lacks both a soul and any sense of moral justice. This system has ensured that corrupt African governments are submerged in debt that they cannot repay; debts in which the interest payments have far outweighed the principal. A 2006 *New York Times* editorial called for international financial organizations to cancel debts owed by African countries. The editorial team noted that "African countries spend four times as much on paying back their debts than they do on health care. They are trapped into making ever-escalating interest payments that never touch the principal. Nigeria, for example, borrowed $5 billion, has paid $16 billion and still owes $32 billion."[2] In 2006 Nigeria was able to reach a debt deal with the Paris Club, heralded as historic. Hidden in the deal's details was the fact that even before the club was willing to negotiate debt relief, Nigeria had to pay $6 billion as arrears of the debt. In the final agreement, $18 billion was forgiven and Nigeria had to pay $12 billion to excise the debt.[3] Lost in this is the reality that money that could have potentially helped in alleviating poverty in Nigeria was transferred to Western governments and financial institutions. It's small wonder that the promises of independence have become a mirage. One may be tempted to ask if Africa's lot was better during colonial rule compared to the current state of affairs. In fact, it is not hard to find European apologists of colonial rule who have shamelessly made comparisons between colonial economies and postcolonial economies and concluded that Africans fared better during colonial rule than now. Writing in the *Los Angeles Times*, the British economic historian Niall Ferguson argues that "the economic consequences of independence gave the lie to the old leftist claim that Britain was exploiting its colonies. Between 1960 and today, the gap between Britain and Ghana has more than doubled, so that the average Briton is now 92 times richer than the average Ghanian. Today, according to the World Bank, aid accounts for 16% of Ghana's national income and covers fully 73% of government expenditures."[4] Ferguson goes on to note that Britain had left Ghana with "foundations for economic and political stability" such as "trade, balanced budgets, sound money, the rule of law and non-corrupt administration." He discounts the history of colonialism in Africa, which was the destruction of African societies in order to create a system in which Africans could be exploited. As the first chapter of this book shows, Joseph Chamberlain, the British secretary of state for the colonies, was unapologetic about this as he advanced his doctrine of constructive imperialism. African societies were broken for the benefit of the Europeans and they continue to be broken. For Ferguson, or anyone for that matter, to think that Africa was going to be successful in this corrupt and rigged system is to fail to acknowledge reality. Those foundations that Ferguson thinks the British bequeathed to Africa to ensure stability are part of Africa's postcolonial problems. Trade between metropole and colony was unbalanced because of the system of colonial economies. Many African countries were indebted at independence as a result of the failed developmentalist policies of the second colonial occupation. Many nations in the British Commonwealth suffered economically as a result of the Sterling Crisis of the 1960s. The rule of law during colonial rule was unjust and was more or less a dictatorship. Subjects who protested were brutalized and imprisoned by the colonial state. The colonial state was corrupt and it was this corruption that inspired the outward transfer of African resources for the economic benefit of the colonizers.

The development policies of colonial rule created an extractive system. The agrarian policies of the state pushed Africa toward producing cash crops for export. Postcolonial African governments have maintained this extractive system, placing them at the mercy of the bubbles and bursts of the global commodity markets. When there are bubbles in the system, the GDP of African countries rises and there is profligacy in government spending. When the bubbles burst, growth is stunted and many are left more impoverished without a state welfare system to support them. Thus, Africa has become a charity case where different Western organizations constantly concoct different programs to help "poor Africans." The perception is that Africans are suffering from a pervasive sense of hopelessness because of failed leadership. Each year, thousands of Americans and Europeans visit Africa to do "mission trips." Armed with a few DIY manuals, they want to build homes, schools, toilets, water wells, etc. for Africans. African hospitality is often misunderstood for invitations. At the end, these visits are often not about the Africans but the Westerners. Such visits to Africa on "mission trips" look good on resumes. The best help that the West can offer Africa is to dismantle the economic and neocolonial structures that continue to strangulate African economies and impoverish Africans. Neither colonialism nor postcolonial African states have been able to deliver the goods that were promised the people. Rather, the number of African poor is growing. Between 1996 and 2011, the number of people in Africa living on less than $1.25 a day has grown from 358 million to 415 million. Laurence Chandy of the Brookings Institute has attempted to respond to a common question about this reality: "Why is the number of poor people in Africa increasing when Africa's economies are growing?"[5] Chandy argues that there are five factors responsible for this: Africa's population growth of 2.6 percent a year, the extreme nature of Africa's poverty compared to other regions, the high levels of inequality, the "mismatch between where growth is occurring and where the poor are in the continent," and poor quality of data.[6] While these are important factors that help explain Africa's growing poverty, they fail to capture the historical nature of Africa's problems and how the structures that were erected continue to evolve in such a way that disadvantages Africa and leaves it poorer. The increasing globalized geopolitics and economy has succeeded in pushing Africa farther behind. To better understand this phenomenon, one may look at certain regions in the West such as the U.S. rustbelt. Though these places started far ahead of where Africa is today because they were industrialized, the nature of the new global economy has left them behind and many have become unemployed or underemployed and feel like they are drowning. Such sentiments led to the election of Donald Trump in the U.S. and the success of the Brexit vote in the United Kingdom. If these regions of the world that historically enjoyed enormous benefits from the rigged capital structures now feel the new economic structures are rigged against them, how much more disadvantaged do you think Africans have been and continue to be in this system? These regions are calling upon their governments to scale back on the level of their commitments to this global system because they think it works only for a few. That few does not include Africa. Nevertheless, many policies that are being pushed on Africa by international development agencies are simply more integration into the global economic system; Africans are called to liberalize their economies, cut taxes, retrench staff, privatize, etc., all the standard fare of neoliberal economics.

It was these policies that led to changes in my neighborhood. In the preface of this book I describe the changes that took place in Obudu. are described. These kinds of changes took places in several towns and cities in Africa, South of the Sahara. These did not happen suddenly but were several years in the making. Living through them did not allow me to see how dramatic they were. Stepping out of that environment for several years and returning there allowed me to appreciate how significant these were. Electricity had stopped being regular before 1995, as was the constant flow of public water. These problems kept getting worse over time because of neglect, and today are in a state of almost complete disrepair.

Though problems started cropping up beginning with the falling oil prices in the late 1970s and early 1980s, it was the imposition of IMF Structural Adjustment Programs (SAPs) in the late 1980s that was the death knell to social services in Nigeria. The Nigerian currency, which up until that point was stronger than the U.S. dollar, was significantly devalued and since then it has been almost in a free fall. The Nigerian government was advised to devalue its currency to make its exports more competitive. The problem is that Nigeria's primary export was oil and the price for oil was not determined by Nigeria. Since 1985, the Nigerian government has tried unsuccessfully to stabilize the value of the Naira. Despite using its foreign reserves to shore it up, it is still exchanging at N310 (Naira) to a dollar and far higher in the black market where most people get their foreign currency. The devaluation of the currency led to runaway inflation. Between 1986, when SAPs were introduced, and 1989, Nigeria's inflation rose from 5.4 percent to 40.9 percent. Inflation forced the interest rates to go up, which in turn discouraged investment. Simultaneously, the prices of domestic products went up relative to those of foreign products and these inhibited exports while at the same time stimulating imports, thus "depleting the nation's scarce foreign reserves and worsening the balance of payment position."[7] The rise in the prices of domestic products and the inability of producers to export these items meant a significant loss of income for local producers. Farmers were more reluctant to produce cash and food crops if their products were not able to compete with import prices. The decline in agricultural production affected the lives of the majority of Nigerians who continued to rely on agriculture for their livelihood. Nigeria in the late 1980s not only went through a food crisis, but also massive poverty. It was common to hear Nigerians quip, "SAP has sapped life out of us."

The economic situation of Nigeria exacerbated poverty in rural areas, as there was high unemployment. The resultant effect of this was a large number of people migrating to urban areas with hope of finding jobs. This migration created its own problems, as the urban areas did not have the resources and facilities to accommodate the growing population. The Nigerian government's solution to the problem of poverty in the rural areas was the introduction of two programs: the Directorate for Food, Roads and Rural Infrastructure (DFFRI) and the Better Life for Rural Women. DFFRI was established in 1987 and its target was "to provide water for 250 communities in each of the states of the federation, to construct 90,000km of feeder roads, and to promote rural housing, health and agriculture. . . . [And to] facilitate industrial growth, and improve the attractiveness of the rural environment."[8] This program was criticized for making false claims on the roads constructed, as well as receiving poor funding and not engaging in any direct food production.[9] As with most Nigerian programs during this time period, it was marred by corruption. With the financial backing of the Nigerian government, the wife of the military head of state, Maryam Babangida, established Better Life for Rural Women in 1987. Its focus was on empowering rural women toward economic growth and development. It helped women's organizations establish cooperative farms and cottage industries. The impact of these government interventionist programs was negligible as they were unable to stem the tide of rural poverty.

The Nigerian financial crisis, which had started from the early 1980s, reached its peak in 1992. The neoliberal economic policies that were introduced from 1986 did not help the economy to grow but actually saddled the country with more debt and a higher rate of unemployment. From 1986, the government started privatizing public enterprises and merging others. Many workers were retrenched from government services and even those who still had jobs did not show up to work because the government owed workers several months of salaries. The government became unable to invest in social services because it lacked the resources to do so. Forty-seven percent of the government's overall budget went into debt servicing and little was left for public investments. For example, prior to 1982, the government spent more than 6 percent of total expenditure on education, but by 1992, this was less than 1 percent. As Olumide Ekande argues, "This had severe repercussions for infrastructure, teaching, and research activities, and on the quality of students produced. It affected the morale of teachers who were owed arrears of salaries for several months and who had to abandon their duties out of necessity to seek other means of sustenance."[10]

The root of today's crumbling infrastructures has been in the making for decades because corrupt African leaders, in collaboration with Western institutions, mismanaged the economy. The international economic structures that were erected during colonial rule continue to have an impact on Africa's development today. For example, while the West keeps insisting that Africa needs free trade to be successful, its own policies undercut this argument. Africa is not able to compete in the free trade system that the West wants. It is estimated that the U.S. subsidizes its farmers by about $20 billion annually.[11] The U.S. shields its farmers from competition; African countries are not in a position to do this. Consider this fact to see how difficult it would be for Africa to compete in such an economy: the total 2016 budget of Nigeria, a country with close to 200 million people, is $30.6 billion.[12] African leaders have been aware of these unfair practices and the inequalities that have been created by the global system. In 1980, African leaders had an Extraordinary Session devoted to Africa's economic problems and they approved a groundbreaking continental economic policy called the "Lagos Plan of Action for the Economic Development of Africa, 1980–2000." Reflecting on Africa's problems, they wrote:

> The effect of unfulfilled promises of global development strategies has been more sharply felt in Africa than in the other continents of the world. Indeed, rather than result in improvement in the economic situation of the continent, successive strategies have made it stagnate and become more susceptible than other regions to the economic and social crises suffered by the industrialized countries. Thus, Africa is unable to point to any significant growth rate, or satisfactory index of general well-being, in the past 20 years. Faced with this situation, and determined to undertake measures for the basic restructuring of the economic base of our continent, we resolved to adopt a far-reaching regional approach based primarily on collective self-reliance.[13]

The goal of this policy was not to isolate Africa from the global economy, but to strengthen the economy of the continent and to position it to be competitive in the global sphere. This entails Africa making investments in its infrastructure and improving regional trade networks and communication facilities. It is not surprising that the *Lagos Plan* was met with fierce resistance from the international community and the IMF/ World Bank insisted that African countries adopt SAPs. African governments were left with no choice because they lacked the capital to implement these policies. Nigeria was reluctant to accept the SAPs. When Nigeria's head of state, Ibrahim Babangida presented the economic package and policies of the IMF to Nigerians for debate, they made their opposition known. Publicly, Babangida repudiated the IMF and said that Nigeria was going to seek local solutions to its economic problems. Despite this public stance, Babangida was actually not being transparent with Nigerians. As Bonny Ibhawoh has noted, the economic policies that Babangida unveiled thereafter included "deregulation of the exchange rate, higher agricultural prices, financial liberalization and partial privatization. . . . One year later, a full SAP was introduced, which elaborated and extended earlier adjustment reforms."[14] SAPs have remained very unpopular in Africa and yet African leaders have continued to resort to these neoliberal economic policies to grow Africa out of poverty. This was the idea behind the New Partnership for Africa's Development (NEPAD) that was championed by Thabo Mbeki of South Africa, Olusegun Obasanjo of Nigeria, and Abdoulaye Wade of Senegale. This development policy, adopted by African leaders in 2001, was praised by international organizations because it embraced the neoliberal economic policies championed by the IMF/ World Bank. Like the SAPs, this new policy has not led to the transformation that was envisioned for Africa. In 2007, Wade, who was one of the founders of NEPAD, accused it of simply being a talking shop that is spending millions of dollars but achieving nothing. He said, "Expenses adding up to hundreds of millions of dollars have been spent on trips, on hotels. But not a single classroom has been built, not a single health centre completed."[15] NEPAD has not been able to lift Africans out of poverty, though we continue to see slight upticks in the growth of African economies. The World Economic Forum says African economies are strong and they forecast a 3.7 percent growth in 2016.[16] Whether this growth will translate into concrete improvements in the lives of the people is a challenge many African people continue to face.

In April of 2014, Nigeria's economy was declared to be the largest in Africa after a rebasing calculation determined that its gross domestic product was more than $500 billion, with the economy said to be growing at over 6 percent a year. For the over 70 percent of Nigerians living in poverty, this meant nothing as they continued to experience poor social services such as failing schools, rationed electricity, potholes laden roads, and other crumbling public infrastructure. Most Nigerians who have the financial means do not educate their children in public schools but in private schools. Even families with very modest incomes have to purchase power generators because the National Electric Power Authority (NEPA) is now an acronym for Never Expect Power Always. Thirty years ago, there were no private elementary or secondary schools in Obudu, except the mission schools that had been taken over by the government and were being run as public schools. Today there are over twenty private schools and only the very poor bother to educate their children in the public schools. It is sad to say that despite the fact that all my siblings were educated in public schools, my nephews and nieces are in private schools today.

The 6 percent growth in the Nigerian economy has not translated into improvements in the social services. Nigeria today is experiencing economic growth without development. Perhaps it is time for Nigeria and other African countries to revisit their development agenda. The neoliberal approaches that have inspired development since independence have failed Africa; it is time for African countries to think of local approaches to development. For such a policy initiative to be successful, it must be self-reliant, not relying on Western loans or aid to be executed. Such external funding often ends up limiting Africa's efforts.

This book has shown that process matters as we try to understand Africa's development challenges. Africa's colonial history and its postcolonial relations in the global economic system have continued to impact Africa negatively. The second colonial occupation's promise of lifting African people out of poverty ended up being a smokescreen for more exploitation, leaving many of the countries with "development" debts at independence. The failure of this occupation was partly the result of the conflicts and contradictions of the colonial state. The state failed to make the key investments in both human and financial resources that were needed to effect the kind of positive changes that could have potentially lead to significant reduction in colonial poverty. In Nigeria, the ideological conflicts between metropolitan officials and the local administrators over who should control development and how it should proceed did not help the developmentalist agenda. Local conflicts in the Nigerian colonial state also had detrimental effects on the planning process and implementation of plans. This book has also revealed that the racial biases and prejudices of the colonial state excluded Africans from the development process and locally generated knowledge was rejected in favor of the knowledge of international "experts." Despite the rhetorical claims of modernization theorists, development in the postcolonial period has continued to mirror the practices of the colonial period. Blaming and shaming Africans and their leaders for the acute poverty in the continent fails to account for the fact that poor planning inspired by imperial ideologies and the material interests of the West are responsible for the failures of development in Africa.

NOTES

1. Cooper, *Africa Since 1940,* 5.
2. *New York Times*, September 24, 2005.
3. For more on this debt deal, see Center for Global Development, www.cgdev.org/initiative/nigerian-debt-relief
4. *Los Angeles Times*, March 11, 2007. Niall Ferguson. The Good Old Days of Colonialism.
5. See Laurence Chandy, https://www.google.com/amp/s/www.brookings.edu/blog/africa-in-focus/2015/05/04/why-is-the-number-of-poor-people-in-africa-increasing-when-africas-economies-are-growing/amp/
6. Ibid.
7. John C. Anyanwu, "President Babangida's Structural Adjustment Programme and Inflation in Nigeria," *Journal of Social Development in Africa* 7, 1 (1992): 14.
8. L. M. Olayiwola and O. A. Adeleye, "Rural Infrastructural Development in Nigeria: Between 1960 and 1990—Problems and Challenges," *Journal of Social Sciences* 11, 2 (2005): 94.
9. Anyanwu, "President Babangida's Structural Adjustment Programme and Inflation in Nigeria," 16.
10. Olumide Victor Ekanade, "The Dynamics of Forced Neoliberalism in Nigeria since the 1980s," *Journal of Retracing Africa* 1,1 (2014): 11.
11. *The Economist*, "Milking Taxpayers," February 14, 2015.
12. *Newsweek*, "Nigerian President Muhammadu Buhari Finally Passes 2016 Budget," May 6, 2016.
13. *Organization of African Unity*, Lagos Plan of Action for the Economic Development of Africa: 1980–2000, April 29, 1980.
14. Bonny Ibhawoh, "Structural Adjustment, Authoritarianism and Human Rights in Africa," in *Comparative Studies of South Asia, Africa and the Middle East*, XIX,1 (1999):162.
15. Didie Ba, "Senegal President Slams Nepad," June 14, 2007. Accessed November 24, 2016, www.iol.co.za/news/africa/senegal-president-slams-nepad-357495
16. John Mbu, "Despite Headwinds, Africa's Economy is still Strong," World Economic Forum, July 29, 2016. Accessed November 26, 2016, www.weforum.org/agenda/2016/07/african-economic-situation-the-fundamentals-still-remain-strong/.

Bibliography

PRIMARY SOURCES

Bodleian Library of Commonwealth and African Studies (BLCAS), Rhodes House, Oxford

Mss Brit. Emp. S. 332. Arthur Creech Jones Papers
Mss Afr. S. 2124. J. R. Mackie Papers
Mss Afr. S. 823. J. R. Mackie Papers
Mss Brit. Emp. S. 476 Oxford Development Records Project (ODRP) Food and Cash Crop Collection

The National Archives, Kew, London

Series CO 554. West Africa: Original Correspondence, 1944
Series CO 583. Nigeria: 1944–45
Series CO 847. Africa: Original Correspondence, 1937–1950
Series CO 852. Economic Department: Original Correspondence, 1935–1952
Series CO 879. Confidential Print: Africa 1895–1945

National Archives II, College Park, Maryland

Record Group 59, Records of the Department of State
Decimal Files. British Territories in Africa: British West Africa; Nigeria
Lot Files. Records of the Bureau of African Affairs. Bureau of African Affairs, West African Affairs. Country Files, 1951–1963

The Nigerian National Archive, Kaduna

File No. 2726. Irrigation Policy Northern Region
File No. 2705. Irrigation Schemes: Niger Province

File No. 26902/ S.1. Irrigation in N.R. (Northern Region)
File No. 26902/ Vol.II . Irrigation in the Northern Provinces
File No. 7823. Policy and Minutes of Discussions, Minna Division
File No. 7503. Policy and Minutes of Discussion, Kabba
File No. 11703. Agricultural Policy in Northern Region
EPD/E/168. Northern Region Agricultural Research Scheme: Financing of.

MIT Institute Archives, Massachusetts

A2236. Politics of Transition: Proposals, 1960.

GOVERNMENT PUBLICATIONS

Colonial Development Corporation. London: HMSO, 1948.

Nigeria. *A Ten-Year Plan of Development and Welfare for Nigeria 1946*. Sessional Paper No. 24 of 1945. Lagos: Government printer, 1946.
Nigeria. Federal Ministry of Economic Development. *First National Development Plan, 1962–1968*. Lagos: Federal Government Printer, 1962.
Nigeria. Ministry of Information. *Second National Development Plan, 1970–74*. Lagos: Federal Government Printer, 1970.
Nigeria. *Building the New Nigeria: National Development Plan, 1970–74*. Nigerian National Press, Apapa.
Nigeria. *Guidelines for the Third National Development Plan, 1975–80*. Lagos: The Government Printer, 1973.
Nigeria. Ministry of Economic Development. *Third National Development Plan, 1975–1980* (2 vols.) Lagos: Federal Government Printer, 1975.
Overseas Resource Development Act. London: HMSO, 1948.
Report and Proceedings of the Conference of Colonial Directors of Agriculture. Colonial no. 156. London: HMSO, 1938.

SECONDARY SOURCES

Aboyade, Ojetunji. *Foundations of an African Economy: A Study of Investment and Growth in Nigeria*. New York: Praeger, 1966.
Anderson, David. *Eroding the Commons: The Politics of Ecology in Baringo, Kenya 1890–1963*. Oxford: James Currey, 2002.
Anderson, David, and Richard Grove, eds. *Conservation in Africa: People, Policies and Practice*. Cambridge: Cambridge University Press, 1987.
Arnold, David. *Imperial Medicine and Indigenous Societies*. Manchester: Manchester University Press, 1989.
Arnold, M. H. ed. *Agricultural Research for Development: The Namulonge Contribution*. Cambridge: Cambridge University Press, 1976.

Ashton, S. R., and S. E. Stockwell, ed. *Imperial Policy and Colonial Practice, 1925–1945*. London: HMSO, 1996.

Ate, Bassey E. *Decolonization and Dependence: The Development of Nigeria—U.S. Relations, 1960–1984*. Boulder, CO: Westview Press, 1984.

Awa, Eme O. *Federal Government in Nigeria*. Berkeley: University of California Press, 1964.

Ax, Christian Folke; Brimnes, Niels; Jensen, Niklas, et.al. ed. *Cultivating the Colonies: Colonial States and their Environmental Legacies*. Athens: Ohio University Press, 2011.

Ayida, A. A., and Onitiri, H. M. A. (ed.). *Reconstruction and Development in Nigeria: Proceedings of a National Conference*. Ibadan: Oxford University Press, 1971.

Ayo, Edward Jide. *Development Planning in Nigeria*. Ibadan: University Press Limited, 1988.

Azikiwe, Nnamdi. *My Odyssey: An Autobiography*. London: Hurst, 1970.

Baldwin, K. D. S. *The Niger Agricultural Project: An Experiment in African Development*. Cambridge, MA: Harvard University Press, 1957.

Barbour, K. M. ed. *Planning For Nigeria: A Geographical Approach*. Ibadan: University Press, 1972.

Bardhan, Pranab, ed. *The Economic Theory of Agrarian Institutions*. Oxford: Clarendon Press, 1989.

Barnett, Tony. *The Gezira Scheme: An Illusion of Development*. London: Frank Cass, 1977.

Bates, Robert H. *Beyond the Miracle of the Market: The Political Economy of Agrarian Development in Kenya*. Cambridge: Cambridge University Press, 1989.

Bauman, Zygmunt. *Wasted Lives: Modernity and its Outcasts*. Oxford: Oxford University Press, 2003.

Bello, Ahamadu. *My Life: An Autobiography*. London, 1962.

Belmonte, Monica L. "Reining in Revolution: The US Response to British Decolonization in Nigeria in an Era of Civil Rights, 1953–1960." PhD dissertation, Georgetown University, 2003.

Berry, Sara, "Cocoa in Western Nigeria, 1890–1940: A Study of Innovation in a Developing Country." PhD dissertation, University of Michigan, 1967.

Berry, Sara. *No Condition is Permanent: The Social Dynamics of Agrarian Change in Sub-Saharan Africa*. Madison: University of Wisconsin Press, 1993.

Berman, Edward H. *The Influence of the Carnegie, Ford, and Rockefeller Foundations on American Foreign Policy: The Ideology of Philanthropy*. New York: State University of New York Press, 1984.

Beusekom, Monica M. van. *Negotiating Development: African Farmers and Colonial Experts at the Office du Niger, 1920–1960*. Oxford: James Currey, 2002.

Blackmer, Donald L. M. *The MIT Center for International Studies: The Founding Years, 1951–1969*. Cambridge, MA: MIT Press, 2002.

Bright, Rachel. *Chinese Labour in South Africa, 1902–10: Race, Violence and Global Spectacle*. Palgrave Macmillan, 2013.

Briggs, Asa. *Victorian Cities*. New York: Harper & Row, 1970.

Brockway, Lucile H. *Science and Colonial Expansion: The Role of the British Royal Botanic Gardens*. London: Academic Press, 1979.

Brown, Lester R. *Seeds of Change. The Green Revolution and Development in the 1970s*. New York: Praeger, 1970.

Brustein, William. *Roots of Hate: Anti-Semitism in Europe Before the Holocaust*. Cambridge: Cambridge University Press, 2003.

Buhler William, Morse Stephen, and Arthur Eddie, et al., *Science, Agriculture and Research: A Compromised Participation?* London: Earthscan Publications, 2002.

Butler, L. J. *Industrialisation and the British Colonial State: West Africa, 1939–1951*. London: Frank Cass, 1997.

Cain, P. J., and Hopkins, A. G. *British Imperialism: 1688–2000*. Routledge, 2011.

Campbell, Bonnie K. and John Loxley, ed. *Structural Adjustment in Africa*. New York: St. Martin's Press, 1989.

Carland, John M. *The Colonial Office and Nigeria, 1898–1914*. Stanford: Hoover Press Publication, 1985.

Chambers, Robert. *Rural Development: Putting the Last First*. New York: Longman, 1983.

Chandler, J. A. *Explaining Local Government: Local Government in Britain Since 1800*. Manchester: Manchester University Press, 2007.

Cherry, Gordon Emmanuel. *Urban Change and Planning: A History of Urban Development in Britain Since 1750*. London: G. T. Foulis & Co., 1972.

Clayton, Eric. *Agrarian Development in Peasant Economies: Lessons from Kenya*. New York: Macmillan, 1964.

Cohen, Robin. *Labour and Politics in Nigeria*. London: Heinemann, 1974.

Collins, Paul, ed. *Administration for Development in Nigeria: Introduction and Readings*. Lagos, Nigeria: African Education Press, 1980.

Constantine, Stephen. *The Making of British Colonial Development Policy, 1914–1940*. London: Frank Cass, 1984.

Cook, Chris and Stevenson, John. *A History of British Elections Since 1689*. Oxon: Routledge, 2014.

Cooper, Frederick. *Africa Since 1940: The Past of the Present*. Cambridge: Cambridge University Press, 2002.

———. *Decolonization and African Society: The Labor Question in French and British Africa*. Cambridge: Cambridge University Press, 1996.

Cooper, Frederick and Ranadall Packard, eds. *International Development and the Social Sciences: Essays on the History and Politics of Knowledge*. Berkeley: University of California Press, 1997.

Cowen, M. P., and R. N. Shenton. *Doctrines of Development*. New York: Routledge, 1996.

Crosby, Travis L. *Joseph Chamberlain: A Most Radical Imperialist*. London: I.B. Tauris, 2011.

Crowder, Michael. *The Story of Nigeria*. London: Faber & Faber, 1962.

Crush, Jonathan, ed. *Power of Development*. Routledge, 1995.

Dale, H. E. *Daniel Hall: Pioneer in Scientific Agriculture*. London: John Murray, 1956.

de Wilde, John C., ed. *Experiences with Agricultural Development in Tropical Africa. 2 vols*. Baltimore: John Hopkins University Press, 1967.

Dean, Edwin. *Plan Implementation in Nigeria: 1962–1966*. Ibadan, Nigeria: Oxford University Press, 1972.

Dibua, Jeremiah I. *Development and Diffusionism: Looking Beyond Neopatrimonialism in Nigeria, 1962–1985*. Palmgrave Macmillan, 2013.

———. *Modernization and the Crisis of Development in Africa: The Nigerian Experience*. Brookfield, VT: Ashgate, 2006.

Drummond, Ian M. *British Economic Policy and Empire, 1919–1939*. London: Routledge, 2015.

Duignan, Peter and L. H. Gann. *The United States and Africa: A History*. Cambridge: Cambridge University Press, 1984.

Eicher, Carl K. and Carl Liedholm, eds. *Growth and Development of the Nigerian Economy*. East Lansing: Michigan State University, 1970.

Ekbladh, David. *Great American Mission: Modernization and the Construction of an American World Order*. Princeton, NJ: Princeton University Press, 2010.

Ekundare, Olufemi R. *An Economic History of Nigeria, 1860–1960*. New York: Africana Publishing Co., 1973.

Eleazu, Uma O. *Nigeria: The First 25 Years*. Ibadan: Heinemann, 1985.

Engerman, David C., Nils Gilman, Mark H. Harefele, and Michael E. Latham (eds.), *Staging Growth: Modernization, Development and the Global Cold War*. Amherst: University of Massachusetts Press, 2003.

Escobar, Arturo. *Encountering Development: The Making and Unmaking of the Third World*. Princeton, NJ: Princeton University Press, 1995.

Ezera, Kalu. *Constitutional Developments in Nigeria: An Analytical Study of Nigeria's Constitution-Making Developments and the Historical and Political Factors that affected Constitutional Change*. Cambridge: Cambridge University Press, 1960.

Falola, Toyin. *Development Planning and Decolonization in Nigeria*. Gainesville, FL: University of Florida Press, 1996.

———. *The History of Nigeria*. Westport: Greenwood Press, 1999.

———. *Culture and Customs of Nigeria*. Westport: Greenwood Press, 2001.

———. *Economic Reforms and Modernization in Nigeria, 1945–1965*. Kent, OH: Kent State University Press, 2004.

Falola, Toyin and Mathew M. Heaton. *A History of Nigeria*. Cambridge: Cambridge University Press, 2008.

Fanon, Frantz. *The Wretched of the Earth*. Translated by Richard Philcox. New York: Grove Press, 2004.

Faulkner, O. T., and J. R. Mackie. *West African Agriculture*. Cambridge: Cambridge University Press, 1933.

Ferguson, James. *The Anti-Politics Machine: "Development," Depoliticization, and Bureaucratic Power in Lesotho*. Minneapolis: University of Minnesota Press, 1994.

———. *Expectations of Modernity: Myths and Meanings of Urban Life on the Zambian Copperbelt*. Berkeley: University of California Press, 1999.

Ferguson, Niall. *Empire: The Rise and Demise of the British World Order and the Lessons for the Global Power*. New York: Basic Books, 2004.

Floud, Roderick; Humphries, Jane and Johsnon Paul, ed. *The Cambridge Economic History of Modern Britain, Volume 2*. Cambridge: Cambridge University Press, 2014.

Forrest, Thomas. *Politics, Policy, and Capitalist Development in Nigeria, 1970–1990*. Boulder, CO: Westview Press, 1992.

Frankel, Jeffrey A. (ed.) *The Regionalization of the World Economy*. Chicago: The University of Chicago Press, 1997.

Freedman, Jim, (ed.) *Transforming Development: Foreign Aid for a Changing World*. Toronto: University of Toronto Press, 2000.

Gailey, Harry A. *The Road to ABA: A Study of British Administrative Policy in Eastern Nigeria*. New York: New York University Press, 1970.

Genova, James Eskridge. *Colonial Ambivalence, Cultural Authenticity, and the Limitations of Mimicry in French-Ruled West Africa, 1914–1956*. New York: Peter Lang, 2004.

Ghai, Dharan, and Samir Radwan, eds. *Agrarian Policies and Rural Poverty in Africa*. Geneva: International Labour Organisation, 1983.

Gilman Nils. *Mandarins of the Future: Modernization Theory in Cold War America*. Baltimore, MD: John Hopkins University Press, 2003.

Gray, Clive S. (ed.) *Inside Independent Nigeria: Diaries of Wolfgang Stolper, 1960–1962*. Burlington, VT: Ashgate Publishing Company, 2003.

Grubbs, Larry. *Secular Missionaries: Americans and African Development in the 1960s*. Amherst: University of Massachusetts Press, 2009.

Gupta, Kulwant Rai. *Economics of Development and Planning History, Principles, Problems and Policies*. New Delhi: Atlantic, 2009.

Hambleton, Robin. *Leading the Inclusive City: Place-based Innovation for a Bounded Planet*. Bristol: Policy Press, 2014.

Havinden, Michael and David Meredith. *Colonialism and Development: Britain and its Tropical Colonies, 1850–1960*. London: Routledge, 1993.

Heffer, Simon. *High Minds: The Victorians and the Birth of Modern Britain*. London: Random House, 2013.

Helleiner, Gerald K. *Peasant Agriculture, Government, and Economic Growth in Nigeria*. Homewood, IL: R.D. Irwin, 1966.

Heyer, Judith; Roberts Pepe and Gavin Williams, eds. *Rural Development in Tropical Africa*. London: MacMillan, 1981.

Hodder, B. W. *Economic Development in the Tropics*. London: Methuen, 1968.

Hodge, Joseph M. *Triumph of the Expert: Agrarian Doctrines of Development and the Legacies of British Colonialism*. Athens, OH: Ohio University Press, 2007.

Hodge, Joseph Morgan. "Historicizing Development: From Intellectual Impasse to New Field of Critical Research." Unpublished. West Virginia University, Morgantown.

Hodge, Joseph M. Hodl, Gerald and Kopf Martina, ed. *Developing Africa: Concepts and Practices in Twentieth Century Colonialism*. Manchester: Manchester University Press, 2014.

Hopkins, Anthony G. *An Economic History of West Africa*. London: Longman, 1973.

Huth, W. P. *Traditional Institutions and Land Tenure as Related to Agricultural Development among the Ibo of Eastern Nigeria*. Madison, WI: Land Tenure Center, 1969.

Hyam, Ronald. *Elgin and Churchill at the Colonial Office, 1905–1908*. London: Macmillan, 1968.

Johnson, Glenn L. "Factor Markets and the Problem of Economic Development." Unpublished paper, 1966.

Kent, John. *British Imperial Strategy and the Origins of the Cold War, 1944–49.* Leicester: Leicester University Press, 1993.

Khan, Yasmin. *The Great Partition: The Making of India and Pakistan.* New Haven: Yale University Press, 2007.

Konadu-Agyemang, Kwadwo and Kwamina Panford, eds. *Africa's Development in the Twenty-First Century.* Burlington, VT: Ashgate Publishing Company, 2006.

Kilby, Peter. *Industrialization in an Open Economy: Nigeria 1945–1966.* Cambridge: Cambridge University Press, 1969.

Knowles, Charlotte Anne, *The Industrial and Commercial Revolutions in Great Britain during the Nineteenth Century.* London: George Routledge & Sons, 1922.

Kothari, Uma, ed. *A Radical History of Development Studies: Individual Institutions and Ideologies.* London: Zed Books, 2005.

Ibezim, Chukwumerije. The New Frontier and Africa, 1961–1963. PhD dissertation, State University of New York at Stony Brook, 1976.

Idachaba, Francis. *Rural Infrastructure in Nigeria.* Ibadan: Ibadan University Press, 1985.

Isaacman, Allen and Barabara Isaacman. *Dams Displacement, and the Delusion of Development: Cahora Bassa and Its Legacies in Mozambique, 1967–2007.* Athens: Ohio University Press, 2013.

Jones, George Howard. *The Earth Goddess. A Study of Native Farming on the West African Coast.* London: Longmans, Green and Co., 1936.

Lagemann, Johannes. *Traditional African Farming Systems in Eastern Nigeria.* Munich: Weltforum, 1977.

Latham, Michael. (ed.) *Staging Growth: Modernization, Development, and the Global Cold War.* Amherst, MA: University of Massachusetts Press, 2003.

———. *The Right Kind of Revolution: Modernization, Development and U.S. Foreign Policy from the Cold War to the Present.* Ithaca: Cornell University Press, 2011.

Leach, Melissa and Mearns, Robin, eds. *The Lie of the Land: Challenging Received Wisdom on the African Environment.* Oxford: James Currey, 1996.

Lee, J.M. and Martin Petter. *The Colonial Office, War and Development Policy: Organization and the Planning of a Metropolitan Initiative, 1939–1945.* London: Maurice Temple Smiths Ltd, 1981.

Lewis, Arthur W. *Reflections on Nigeria's Economic Growth.* Development Center of the Organisation for Economic Co-operative and Development, 1966.

Leys, Colin. *Rise and Fall of Development Theory.* London: James Murray, 1996.

Lyttleton, Edith. *Alfred Lyttleton an Account of His Life.* 1917; repr., London: Forgotten Books, 2013.

Mahoney, Richard D. *JFK: Ordeal in Africa.* New York: Oxford University Press, 1985.

Marsh, Peter T. *Joseph Chamberlain: Entrepreneur in Politics.* New Haven: Yale University Press, 1994.

Masfield, G. B. *A History of the Colonial Agricultural Service.* Oxford: Clarendon Press, 1972.

———. *A Short History of Agriculture in the British Colonies*. Oxford: Clarendon Press, 1950.

Matera, Marc and Bastian, Misty, et al. *The Women's War of 1929: Gender and Violence in Colonial Nigeria*. New York: Palgrave Macmillan, 2012.

Maxon, Robert M. *Going Their Separate Ways: Agrarian Transformation in Kenya, 1930–1950*. London: Associated University Presses, 2003.

McWilliam, Michael. *The Development Business: A History of the Commonwealth Development Corporation*. New York: Palgrave, 2001.

Melson, Robert and Howard Wolpe, eds. *Nigeria: Modernization and the Politics of Communalism*. East Lansing: Michigan State University Press, 1971.

Micale, Mark S., and Dietle, Robert L. *Enlightenment, Passion, Modernity: Historical Essays in European Thought and Culture*. Stanford: Stanford University Press, 2000.

Milner, David. *America's Rasputin: Walt Rostow and the Vietnam War*. New York: Hill and Wang, 2008.

Moon, Suzanne. *Technological and Ethical Idealism. A History of Development in the Netherlands East Indies*. Leiden: CNWS Publications, 2007.

Morgan, D. J. *The Official History of Colonial Development: Developing British Colonial Resources, 1945–51 v.2*. London: Palgrave Macmillan, 1980.

Mous, Dan. *State Power, Agrarian Policies and Peasant Welfare: Politics of Agricultural Marketing and Commodity Boards in Nigeria*. Bloomington: Author House, 2014.

Naoroji, Dadabhai. *Poverty and Un-British Rule in India*. Nabu Press, 2010.

Neill, Deborah. *Networks in Tropical Medicine: Internationalism, Colonialism, and the Rise of a Medical Specialty*, 1890–1930. Stanford: Stanford University Press, 2012.

Ninkovich, Frank. *Modernity and Power: A History of Domino Theory in the Twentieth Century*. Chicago: University of Chicago Press, 1994.

Nnoli, Okwudiba. (ed.) *Path to Nigerian Development*. Westport, CT: L. Hill, 1981.

Norman, David W. *Farming Systems in the Nigerian Savanna: Research and Strategies for Development*. Boulder, CO: Westview Press, 1982.

Nwachukwu, Levi A. and G. N. Uzoigwe. *Troubled Journey: Nigeria Since the Civil War*. Lanham, MD: University Press of America, 2004.

Ochonu, Moses E. *Colonial Meltdown: Northern Nigeria in the Great Depression*. Athens: Ohio University Press.

Obot, Johnson. *Environment and Development in Nigeria*. Port Harcourt, Nigeria: Double Diamond Publications, 2002.

Ojowu, Jeremiah Ode. "Technological Transformation in Nigerian Agriculture: An Analysis of the Nigerian Agricultural Development Policies, including the Role of the Marketing Boards." PhD dissertation, the University of Connecticut, 1980.

Okigbo, P. N .C. *National Development Planning in Nigeria, 1900–1992*. London: J. Currey, 1989.

Onimode, Bade. *Imperialism and Development in Nigeria*. London: Zed Press, 1982.

Osaghae, Eghosa E. *Crippled Giant: Nigeria Since Independence*. Bloomington: Indiana University Press, 1998.

Paden, John N. *Ahmadu Bello, Sardauna of Sokoto: Values and Leadership in Nigeria*. London: Hodder and Stoughton, 1986.

Page, Melvin E. (ed.) *Colonialism: An International Social, Cultural and Political Encyclopedia*. Santa Barbara: ABC-CLIO, 2003.

Parmar, Inderjeet. *Foundations of the American Century: The Ford, Carnegie, & Rockefeller Foundations in the Rise of American Power*. New York: Columbia University Press, 2012.

Paterson, Thomas G. (ed.) *Kennedy's Quest for Victory: American Foreign Policy, 1961–1963*. New York: Oxford University Press, 1989.

Peet, Richard. *Unholy Trinity: The IMF, World Bank and WTO*. New York: Zed Books, 2003.

Pelzer, Peer; Sako, Musterd and Marco Bontje. Inventive City-Regions: Path Dependence and Creative Knowledge Strategies. Burlington: Ashgate, 2012.

Phillips, Anne. *Enigma of Colonialism: British Policy in West Africa*. Bloomington, IN: Indiana University Press, 1989.

Pierce, Steven. *Farmers and the State in Colonial Kano: Land Tenure and the Legal Imagination*. Bloomington: Indiana University Press, 2005.

Richards, Paul. *Indigenous Agricultural Revolution: Ecology and Food Production in West Africa*. London: Hutchinson, 1985.

Rivkin, Arnold. *Africa and the West: Elements of Free-World Policy*. New York: F.A. Praeger, 1962.

———. *The African Presence in World Affairs*. New York: Free Press of Glencoe, 1963.

Rist, Gilbert. *The History of Development: From Western Origins to Global Faith*. New York: Zed Books, 2002.

Rodney, Walter. *How Europe Underdeveloped Africa*. Washington, DC: Howard University Press, 1974.

Rostow, W. W. *The United States in the World Arena: An Essay in Recent History*. New York: Harper & Brothers, 1960.

———. *Eisenhower, Kennedy, and Foreign Aid*. Austin, TX: The University of Texas Press, 1985.

———. *Stages of Economic Growth*. Cambridge: Cambridge University Press, 1990.

Sackley, Nicole. "Passage to Modernity: American Social Scientists, India, and the Pursuit of Development, 1945–1961." PhD dissertation, Princeton University, 2004.

Sada, Pius. *Environmental Issues and Management in Nigerian Development*. Ibadan, Nigeria: Evans Brothers, 1988.

Schraeder, Peter. *United States Foreign Policy Toward Africa: Incrementalism, Crisis and Change*. Cambridge: Cambridge University Press, 1994.

Schuknecht, Rohland. *British Colonial Development Policy after the Second World War: The Case of Sukumaland*. Tanganyika. Berlin: Lit Verlag, 2010.

Scott, James C. *Seeing Like a State: How Certain Schemes to Improve the Human Condition Have Failed*. New Haven: Yale University Press, 1988.

Seaman, L. C. B. *Post-Victorian Britain 1902–1951*. London: Methuen, 1966.

Shenton, Robert. *The Development of Capitalism in Northern Nigeria*. London: James Currey, 1986.

Shephard, Bruce R. *Nigeria, Africa, and the United States: From Kennedy to Reagan*. Bloomington, IN: Indiana University Press, 1991.

Simpson, Bradley. *Economists with Guns: Authoritarian Development and U.S. Indonesian Relations, 1960–1968*. Stanford, CA: Stanford University Press, 2008.

Staples, Amy. *The Birth of Development: How the World Bank, Food and Agriculture Organization and World Health Organization Changed the World, 1945–1965*. Ohio: Kent State University Press, 2006.

Stolper, Wolfgang. *Planning Without Facts: Lessons in Resource Allocation from Nigeria's Development*. Cambridge, MA: Harvard University Press, 1966.

Thompson, Joseph E. *American Policy and African Famine: The Nigeria-Biafra War, 1966–1970*. Westport, CT: Greenwood Press, 1990.

Thurston, Anne. *The Intensification of Smallholder Agriculture in Kenya: The Genesis and Implementation of the Swynnerton Plan*. Oxford Development Records Project, Report 6. Oxford: Rhodes House Library, 1984.

Tiffen, Mary, et al. *More People, Less Erosion: Environmental Recovery in Kenya*. Nairobi: Acts Press, 1994.

Tignor, Robert L. *W. Arthur Lewis and the Birth of Development Eco*nomics. Princeton: Princeton University Press, 2006.

———. *Colonial Transformation of Kenya: The Kamba, Kikuyu, and Maasai from 1900 to 1939*. Princeton: Princeton University Press, 2015.

Tilley, Helen. *Africa as a Living Laboratory: Empire, Development, and the Problem of Scientific Knowledge, 1870–1950*. Chicago: The University of Chicago Press, 2011.

Toyden, S. (ed.) *Constitutionalism and National Development in Nigeria: Proceedings of the 17th Annual Conference of the Nigerian Political Science Association held at the University of Jos, 21–23 November 1990*. Ibadan: Nigerian Political Science Association, 1990.

Ugbong, Innocent, Mbia S. Mbia, and Leonard E. Omang, eds. *An Inter-disciplinary Approach to Issues and Problems of National Development*. Calabar, Nigeria: Index Educational Foundation Publishers, 1999.

Vreeland, James Raymond. *The IMF and Economic Developm*ent. Cambridge: Cambridge University Press, 2003.

Waller, P. J. *Town, City, and Nation: England, 1850–1914*. Oxford: Clarendon Press, 1983.

Watts, Michael. *Silent Violence: Food, Famine, and Peasantry in Northern Nigeria*. Berkeley: University of California Press, 1983.

———. (ed.) *State, Oil, and Agriculture in Nigeria*. Berkeley: University of California Press, 1987.

Westad, Odd Arne. *The Global Cold War: Third World Interventions and the Making of our Times*. Cambridge: Cambridge University Press, 2007.

Zeleza, Paul Tiymabe. *A Modern Economic History of Africa: The Nineteenth Century*. Nairobi: East African Educational Publishers, 1993.

Articles and Chapters

Adams, William M. "Large Scale Irrigation in Northern Nigeria: Performance and Ideology." *Royal Geographical Society* 16, 3(1991): 287–300.

David Anderson and David Throup. "Africans and Agricultural Production in Colonial Kenya: The Myth of the War as the Watershed." *The Journal of African History* 26, 4 (1985).

Austin, Gareth. "African Economic Development and Colonial Legacies." *Revue Internationale de politique de developpement* 1 (2010): 11–32.

Bamba, Abou B. "Triangulating a Modernization Experiment: The United States, France, and the Making of the Kossou Dam in Central Ivory Coast." *Journal of Modern European History* 8, 1 (2010): 66–84.

Bernal, Victoria. "Colonial Moral Economy and the Discipline of Development: The Gezira Scheme and 'Modern' Sudan." *Cultural Anthropology* 12, 4 (1997).

Berry, Sara S. "The Concept of Innovation and the History of Cocoa Farming in Western Nigeria." *The Journal of African History* 15, 1 (1974): 83–95.

Biggs, David. "Breaking from the Colonial Mold: Water Engineering and the Failure of Nation-Building in the Plain of Reeds, Vietnam." *Technology and Culture* 49, 3 (2008): 599–623.

Bonneuil, Christophe. "Development as Experiment: Science and State Building in Late Colonial and Postcolonial Africa, 1930–1970." *Osiris* 15 (2000): 258–281.

Bowman, Andrew. "Mass Production or Production by the Masses? Tractors, Cooperatives, and the Politics of Rural Development in Post-Independence Zambia." *Journal of African History* 52, 2 (2011): 201–221.

Cell, John. "Colonial Rule." In *The Oxfrod History of the British Empire: The Twentieth Century*, Edited by Judith M. Brown and WM. Roger Louis. Oxford: Oxford University Press, 1999.

Cowen, Mike. "Early Years of the Colonial Development Corporation: British State Enterprise Overseas during Late Colonialism." *The Royal African Society*, 83, 330 (1984): 63–75.

Cullather, Nick. "Development? It's History." *Diplomatic History* 24, 4 (2000), 641–653.

———. "Miracles of Modernization: The Green Revolution and the Apotheosis of Technology." *Diplomatic History* 28, 2 (2004): 227–254.

Ehrensaft, Philip. "The Political Economy of Informal Empire in Pre-Colonial Nigeria, 1807–1884." *Canadian Journal of African Studies* 6, 3 (1972): 451–490.

Eicher, Carl K. "The Dynamics of Long-Term Agricultural Development in Nigeria." *Journal of Farm Economics* 49, 5 (December, 1967): 1158–1170.

Eichengreen, Barry. "The British Economy Between the Wars." In *The Cambridge Economic History of Modern Britain, Volume 2*. Cambridge: Cambridge University Press, 2014.

Esselborn, Stefan. "Environment, Memory, and the Groundnut Scheme: Britain's Colonial Agricultural Development Project and Its Global Legacy." *Global Environment* 11 (2013).

Grubbs, Larry. "Bringing 'The Gospel of Modernization' to Nigeria: American Nation Builders and Development Planning in the 1960s." *Peace & Change* 31, 3 (2006): 279–308.

Hume, Nutcombe H. "The Work of the Colonial Development Corporation." *Journal of the Royal Society of Arts* 104, 4984 (1956): 775–791.

Hyden, Goran. "The Reslience of the Peasant Mode of Production: The Case of Tanzania." In *Agricultural Development in Africa: Issues of Public Policy*. Edited by Robert Bates and Michael Lofchie. New York: Praeger, 1980.

Ijere, M. O. "Colonial Policy in Nigerian Agriculture and its Implementation." *Agricultural History* 48, 2 (April, 1974): 298–304.

Iwuagwu, O. "Colonial and Post-Independence Agricultural Policies in Eastern Nigeria, 1946–1980." *Lagos Historical Review* 8 (2008): 64–78.

Lubeck, Paul M. "The Crisis of African Development: Conflicting Interpretations and Resolutions." *Annual Review of Sociology* 18 (1992): 519–540.

Malmsten, Neal R., "British Government Policy Toward Colonial Development, 1919–39." The Journal of Modern History 49, 2 (1977): 1249–1287.

McLoughlin, Peter. "The Sudan's Gezira Scheme: An Economic Profile." *Social and Economic Studies* 12, 2 (June, 1963).

Moon, Suzanne. "The Emergence of Technological Development and the Question of Native Identity in the Netherlands East Indies." *Journal of Southeast Asian Studies* 36 (2005).

Newton, C.S. "The Sterling Crisis of 1947 and the British Response to the Marshall Plan." *The Economic History Review*, 37,3 (1984).

Nwosu, Humphrey N., "Nigeria's Third National Development Plan, 1975–80: Major Problems to Implementation." *Africa Today* 24, 4 (1977): 23–38.

Ojiaku, Mazi Okoro and Gene Ulansky. "Early Nigerian Response to American Education." *Phylon* 33, 4, (1972): 380–388.

Stolper, Wolfgang. "Problems of Development Planning." In *Leading Issues in Economic Development*. Edited by Gerald M. Meier. New York: Oxford University Press, 1976.

———. "Social Factors in Economic Planning with Special Reference to Nigeria," in, Carl K. Eicher and Carl Liedholm, eds. *Growth and Development of the Nigerian Economy*. East Lansing: Michigan State University, 1970.

United Nations. Center for Development Planning, Projections, and Policies. "Implementation of Development Plans: The Experience of Developing Countries in the First Half of the 1970s." *Journal of Development Planning* 12, (1977): 1–69.

Walker, Ezekiel Ayodele. "Structural Change, the Oil Boom and the Cocoa Economy of Southwestern Nigeria, 1973–1980s." The Journal of Modern African Studies 38, 1 (2000): 71–87.

Wallace, Tina. "The Challenge of Food: Nigeria's Approach to Agriculture 1975–80." *Canadian Journal of African Studies* 15, 2 (1981): 239–258.

White, Nicholas J. "Reconstructing Europe through Rejuvenating Empire: the British, French, and Dutch Experiences Compared." *Past and Present* 6 (2011): 211–236.

Wicker, E. R. "The Colonial Development Corporation (1948–54)." *The Review of Economic Studies*, 23, 3 (1956): 213–228.

Young, Alden. "Accounting for Decolonization: The Origins of the Sudanese Economy, 1945–1964." PhD dissertation, Princeton University, 2013.

Index

Adams, Theodore Samuel, 95
Advisory Committee on Economic Development and Social welfare, 30, 32
African agriculture, 69, 71, 75, 81, 83, 89, 116–17
African authorities, 71–78, 115, 138
African farmers, xxv, 15, 72, 74–76, 9, 82, 84–85, 90, 99, 107, 109, 114, 135, 137, 150, 155
African farming systems, 69, 79, 81
African housing, 34
African labor, xxv, 39, 93, 101
African leaders, 63, 77, 98, 151, 157
African staff, 37, 39, 48, 73, 88, 95, 107–8, 114
Africanization, 159
agrarian bias, xxiii–xxiv, 62, 69–71, 73, 75, 77, 79, 81, 83, 85, 87, 89, 91, 93, 95, 97, 99, 101, 103–5, 107, 109, 111, 113, 115, 117, 119, 160
agrarian system, 70
agricultural bias, xix, 69
agricultural development, xix, xxiii, xxv–xxvi, 51, 62, 69–70, 72, 74–75, 79, 85, 87–88, 105, 109–12, 114–16, 121–23, 125–27, 129, 131, 133–37, 139, 141–43,145–47, 149, 151–53, 155, 158
agricultural extension, 43, 51, 75, 149
agricultural methods, 76
agricultural policy, xii, xxiv, 64, 70–71, 73–74, 85, 89, 91, 105,107, 114, 121
agricultural produce, 100
agricultural production, xi, xv–xvi, xxiii, 52, 70–71, 85–87, 89, 117, 131, 133, 144
agriculture department, xix, xxiii, 71, 73–78, 84, 86, 88–97, 99, 106, 108, 111–12, 114–15, 118–19, 130–31, 149, 151–52
agriculture system, 74
Althusser, Louis, 159
Amalgamation, 72, 98
Amery, L. S., xxii, 16, 18
Arthur Richards, xix, 32, 101–2
Arusha Declaration, 157
Attlee, Clement, 123
Azikiwe, Nnamdi, 46

Baldwin, Stanley, 16, 18
Balfour, Lord, 12
Bambara nuts, 147
Beach, Michael Hicks, 10
Berlin Conference, 159

Birmingham, 2–9, 21
Birmingham Political Union, 3, 21
Bornu Province, 59
botanist, 109
British colonial administration, xii
British government, xii, 1, 22–23, 28, 54, 93, 123, 128
Bush-fallow rotations, 80

Caine, Sidney, 25
capital markets, 34
cashew, 79
cassava, 81, 105
cattle, 59, 89–90, 110, 119, 141
central administration, 30
Central Bank of Nigeria, 158
central development Board, 44–46, 52
Chamberlain, Joseph, xiv, xviii, xxii, xxvi–3, 5, 7, 9, 11–13, 15–17, 19–23, 29, 34, 42, 150
Chancellor of the Exchequer, 8, 10, 16, 18, 38
chartered companies, 1
Chief Commissioner, 33, 36, 45–46, 72, 95, 101–4
Chief Conservator of Forests, 32
Chinese labor, 12
Christian Socialists, 28
Churchill, Winston, 12, 16, 18, 23, 43
civil war, 159
civilizing mission, 62, 150
Clauson, Gerard, 30
Clifford, Hugh, 72, 100–1, 118
cocoa, xi–xiii, xv–xvi, 69, 75, 91, 95, 110
Cold War, xxii, xxvi, 152
colonial administration, xii, 1, 30, 74, 121
colonial agricultural policy, xii
colonial development, xiv, xvi, xviii–xix, xxii–xxiii, 1, 3, 5, 7, 9–11, 13, 15, 17–23, 25, 28–30, 34, 41–43, 47, 53, 58, 63–65, 67, 70, 94, 117, 121, 123,127, 130, 138, 140, 142–44, 152–53, 155, 160
Colonial Development & Welfare Acts, xvi
Colonial Development Act, xviii–xix, 18–19, 23, 29
Colonial Development Corporation, 123, 138, 152
Colonial Development Fund, 19, 30, 94
Colonial Economic Advisory Committee, 30
colonial occupation, xiv, xvi–xvii, xix–xxii, 20, 25–26, 31, 34, 56, 61, 63, 69–70, 91, 94, 100–2, 114–15, 121–22, 140, 145, 150–51
colonial office, xviii–xix, xxiv, 8, 11–12, 22–23, 25, 30, 35, 55, 65, 143, 160
colonial officers, 70
colonial people, xiv, xvi, xxii, 10, 14, 17, 20, 25–28, 34, 42, 53, 61, 75, 83, 123, 150
colonial power, xiii, xvi–xvii, 116
colonial rule, xi–xii, xvi, xxiii–xxiv, 14, 27–28, 32, 37, 41, 45–46, 53, 72, 82, 94, 115, 130, 150, 157–58, 160
colonial scientists, 83
colonial service, 59, 63, 73, 113
colonial state, xiii, xv–xvi, xix, xxiii, xxv, 17, 23, 26–27, 30–32, 35, 39–41, 43–44, 46, 51–54, 62–64, 69–72, 74–76, 78, 84, 92–95, 100, 102, 104, 106–8, 112–14, 130, 132, 136–38, 145, 150–51, 159
Colonial Stock Act, 10
colonialism, xiii, xxv–xxvi, 14, 22, 32, 37, 39, 62, 66, 72, 94, 115, 118, 137, 150, 152, 154–55, 159
color line, xxiii, 39
Commissioner of Labor, 32
communism, xxii
Conference of Directors of Agriculture, 97

conflict, xvii, xix, xxiii, 4, 70–71, 73, 76, 94–95, 98, 102–4, 113–14, 118, 150
conservatives, 5–6, 8, 16, 22, 124
constitution, 63, 101, 119, 157
constructive exploitation, xviii, 150
constructive imperialism, xxii, 1–3, 5, 7, 9, 11, 13–15, 17, 19–21, 23
Copperbelt strike, 27, 64
corn, 81, 125, 129, 134–35, 144, 146
corruption, xvii, xx
cotton, xi–xii, 81–82, 88, 93, 136, 144
crown colony, 13

dam, 13, 43, 136
decolonization, xvi, xxv, 23, 26, 41, 53, 61, 64, 67
decolonization movement, xvi, 26, 41, 61
demonstration farms, 78–79, 106
dependency, xvii, 51–52, 62, 107
depression, xii–xvi, xix, xxv, 2, 8, 15, 25, 27–28, 31, 42, 69, 121, 160
development commission, 35–36, 38
development department, 33, 49–50, 126
development officers, 35–36, 39–41, 50, 58, 66
development plan, xvi–xxi, xxiii, xxvi, 20, 25, 30–31, 39, 41, 43, 47–52, 54, 58, 61–62, 65–66, 70, 101, 104–5, 113–14, 121, 141, 160
development planning, xvi–xvii, xx–xxi, xxiv, xxvi, 23, 30–32, 44, 46–47, 55–57, 61, 64, 67, 136, 160
development proposals, 31, 33, 35, 37, 52, 64–65, 104
Development Secretary, 38, 44, 46, 48–49, 56–57, 101, 104
developmental state, 25
Director of Agriculture, xxiii, 32, 64, 71, 73, 75, 78, 87, 97, 109, 111–13, 134, 142, 155
Director of Education, 32
Director of Food production, 97–99
Director of Public Works, 32, 46, 65
Director of Veterinary Services, 32
diseases, xii, xv, 11, 60, 84
Disraeli, Benjamin, 10
District Officer, 29, 31, 72, 108, 130, 152
Divisional Development Committees, 31
Dixon, George, 3, 7
doctrine of development, xiii, 13–14
dual mandate, xii–xiii, xxv

Earl of Crewe, 13
East Africa Groundnut scheme, 114, 122–23, 127, 132, 145
Eastern region, 45
economic depression, xii, xiv, 8, 15, 27, 42
economic development, 10–11, 28–30, 32, 34–35, 42–43, 117, 123, 151, 155, 160
economic policy, 23, 30, 34, 63
education, ix, 3–8, 11, 21, 32, 35, 39–41, 53, 63, 73, 93, 116, 159
Education Reform Act, 5
Edward VII, King 12
Egypt, 122
electricity, ix, 34, 43
emir, 72, 75, 77–78, 115, 148
Empire Marketing Board, 16
engineer, 53, 55, 59, 109, 131, 143, 155
entomologists, 109
Enugu, 102
environments, 71, 83–84, 116–17, 130–31
erosion, 81–83, 110–11, 116, 130, 141
European colonialism, 62
experimental farms, 73, 90, 108
experimentation, xxiv, 59–60, 84–85, 90, 110, 114, 121–22, 127, 130, 132–34, 144–45, 150
experts, xx, xxiv, 25, 30, 54, 57–58, 63, 77, 84, 102, 109, 117, 122, 129–32, 135, 140, 155, 160

exploitation, xv–xvi, xviii, xxii, 13–14, 26–28, 34–35, 46, 53, 61, 86, 94, 121–22, 150
export, xi–xii, xv, xx, 16–17, 69, 87–88, 104, 135, 145
export crops, xv, 135
exports, xi, xv, 15–17, 43, 91, 105, 124

Fabian Society, 28
failure of development, xvii, xx, xxiiindex
Fair Deal, xxi
fallow, 79–80, 82, 126, 128, 135
farm schools, 78, 110–11
farmers, xii–xiii, xv–xvi, xxiii, xxv, 15, 17, 47, 52, 60, 70, 72, 74–76, 78–85, 90–91, 94, 99, 105–7, 109–10, 114–15, 125–27, 129, 131–32, 135, 137, 144, 147–50, 155
farming, xii–xiii, xxiii, 20, 69–70, 73–83, 85, 89–90, 105–7, 109, 111, 114, 116–117, 119, 125, 136, 147
farming methods, 76, 79
fascism, xxii, 16
Fascist Party, 16
Faulkner, O. T., 73, 116
Fenton, Roy-Pentelow, 158
FIDES, 121
field trials, xxiii–xxiv, 70–71, 106, 114, 127, 144–45
flax, 93
food production, 69, 87, 91, 96–99, 105, 116, 123
foodstuffs, 91, 96, 123
forestry, 29, 34, 48–49, 51, 55, 59–60, 66–67, 86, 88, 98, 101, 109
foundations, xv, xxi, xxvi, 91
France, xiv, xxi, 63, 121
French development policy, xxii

Gambia Egg scheme, 114
Gater, George, 50, 65
geneticist, 109
Gezira Scheme, 132, 136, 149, 152–54
Ghadambaliya, 125
Ghana, xii–xiii, xvi, 65, 86, 124
Gladstone, William Ewart, 4, 7
Glanville, R. R., 92
Goldie, George Taubman, 1
Gosplan, 160
Governor of Nigeria, xix, 14, 29, 32, 57, 86, 140, 155
Great Depression, xii–xvi, xix, xxv, 2, 15, 25, 27–28, 42, 69, 121, 160
green manuring, 89–90, 114
Green Revolution, xvi, xxvi, 154
Gresswell, Dick, 142
Grey, Albert, 2
Grogan, E. S., 82, 116
groundnuts, xi–xii, 88, 124–25, 129, 134–35, 144, 147, 155

Hall, George Henry, 57
Hitler, Adolf, 28
home rule, 8
horticulturist, 109
Hoskyns-Abrahall, T., 30
House of Commons, 4, 13, 16, 22–23, 155
human side of development, xix
hut tax, 13
Huxley, Elspeth, 133, 154

Ibadan, xii, xxvi, 73, 90, 102, 107–8
IMF, xx, xxiv, 69
Imperial Economic Committee, 16
imperial estates, 6, 15, 20, 42
imports, xi, xv, 17, 91, 104, 122
independence, xx, 46, 63, 72, 98, 103, 144, 157–59
Independent Labour Party, 28
India, 8, 42, 66, 80, 84, 86, 88, 122, 155
Industrial Revolution, xi, 2
infrastructure, ix, xiv, xvi, xviii, xxii, xxv, 18–19, 42, 61, 121
intercropping, 80–82
international experts, xx, xxiv, 160
international organizations, 69

Ireland, 8
irrigation, 32, 53, 59, 62, 105, 109, 111, 127, 136
irrigation systems, 59

Jones, Arthur Creech, 28, 57, 64, 123
Julius Nyerere, 157

Kaduna, 19, 102, 147, 154
Kainji Dam, 43
Kano, 95, 115
Kenya Land Commission, 82
Keynesian economic model, xv
Kingsley, Mary, 13

labor unions, 53
labour Government, xxiv, 16, 19, 57, 114, 122
lagos, 30–32, 35, 45–46, 101–2, 108, 112, 118, 148, 154, 159
land degradation, 83
land tenure system, xii, 70, 77, 146
legislative council, 32, 45, 48–49, 52–53, 55–56, 58–60, 62, 157
Lever Brothers, 99
Lewin, C. J., 83
Lewis, Arthur, 64
Liberal Party, 7–8, 12, 14, 22
Liberal Unionist Association, 8
liberalism, xxii
liberals, 5, 7, 13
livestock, 32, 59, 117
Lloyd, George Ambrose, 28
loans, xviii, 10, 17–19, 29, 35, 37, 47, 54, 58, 63, 124, 157
local administration, 39, 54–55, 71, 75–76, 78, 111, 115
local press, 26, 37, 52, 58
locally produced knowledge, xxi, 71, 81, 114, 135, 148
Lugard, Frederick, 14, 72, 74
Lyttleton, Alfred, 12, 22
Lyttleton Constitution, 157

Macauley, Herbert, 46
MacDonald, Malcolm 25, 65
Machakos district, 83
Mackie, xix, xxiii–xxiv, 64, 71–79, 81, 84–101, 103–20, 125, 130–31, 150–51
Macpherson, John, 140
Macpherson Constitution, 157
Mai-Bornu, Aliyu, 158
manure, 89–90, 111
market, xi, xiii, xv–xvi, xxv, 9, 11, 16, 27, 34, 124, 134
marketing boards, xv
mechanization, 110, 122, 127, 133, 135, 148, 151
mechanized agriculture, 132
mechanized farming, 70, 81, 125
medicine, 11, 22
Mercer, O. E., 128
metropole, xv–xviii, xxi, xxv, 14, 18, 25–26, 30, 37, 50, 64, 122, 157, 160
metropolitan, xvi, xviii–xix, 1, 10–11, 14–15, 17, 20, 25–26, 37–38, 52, 121, 145, 150, 160
metropolitan government, 1, 11, 17, 37, 52, 145
military, 9, 15, 73, 86–89, 93, 100
Milner, Lord, 18
mixed farming, 73, 85, 89–90, 111, 114, 117, 119
modernization, xvii, xx–xxii, xxv–xxvi, 151, 154
modernization theorists, xvii
Mokwa scheme, 121–22, 125–29, 139, 143, 149, 151–52
moor plantation, 73, 110
multiyear planning, 160
Mussolini, Benito, 16
mycologist, 109

National Council of Nigeria and the Cameroons, 46, 53
National Education League, 4, 7, 21
National Liberal Federation, 7
Nationalist Movements, 37, 54

native administration, 76–78, 115
native lines, 13, 70, 74
Nazi Party, 16
Nazism, 16
Ndayako, 127, 146–47
Niger Agriculture Development Scheme, xvii, xx, 114
Niger Delta Protectorate, xi
Nigerian Administration, xxiii, 36, 39, 41, 143
Nigerian Civil War, 159
Nigerian colonial state, 30, 32, 35, 40, 53, 62, 70–72, 112
Nigerian development plan, xvi, 39, 47–48, 66, 101, 105
Nigerianization, 158–59
Nigerian soldiers, 42
The Nigerian Worker, 53
Noel Hall, 35, 65
Northern Nigeria, xiv, xxv, 45, 85, 87, 89, 115, 142, 144, 155
Northern region, 45–46, 59, 89, 101, 111, 134–35, 138, 140, 146, 155
Northern Rhodesia, 27, 74, 83–84

Obudu, ix, xiv
oil boom, 104–5
oil seeds, 88
oil seed mission, 124
oliver Stanley, xix, 33, 42, 57
Overseas Food Corporation, 123, 152
Overseas Resources Development Act, 123, 152

palm oil, xi, xxiv
Pannini, 127
Parkinson, D. J., 66
Parliament, xvi, xviii, 7, 10, 19, 21, 25, 28–29, 32–33, 43, 51, 63, 123
peasant agriculture, 52, 74, 100
peasant cultivation, 74
peasant farmers, xv, 75, 81, 83
peasant production, xiii, 74, 76, 81
peasants, xxv, 74–76, 81, 132
Pedler, Frederick, 65
planning process, xvii–xx, xxiii, 25–26, 55, 151
plantation agriculture, xii–xiii, 100
plow, 90, 125, 127, 148
political control, xi, 157
political officers, 76–77
Portuguese, 121, 152
postcolonial development, xx, 136
Postwar Economic crisis, xiv, 15, 52
potatoes, 95
poultry, 59, 105, 109, 111, 122
precolonial, xi–xii
production, xi–xvi, xix, xxiii–xxv, 6, 15, 17, 19, 26–27, 31–32, 34, 52, 62, 69–71, 73–79, 81–83, 85–89, 91–93, 95–101, 105, 114, 116–18, 122–25, 127–28, 130–33, 136, 144, 155
proletariat, xiii
Provincial Commissioners, 103
Provincial Development Committees, 30, 39, 44, 46
public infrastructure, ix, xvi, xviii, xxii, 121

race, 22–23, 28, 39, 41
racial ideology, 41, 62
Rackhouse, M. V., 134, 155
Radicals Program, 7
recurrent expenditure, 29, 49, 140, 142
regionalism, 72, 101
regionalization, 23, 72, 101–102, 140
research, xii, xv–xvi, xviii, xxii–xxiii, 11, 15–17, 19–20, 29, 34, 42, 60, 63, 70–71, 73, 79, 84–85, 90, 105–6, 109–12, 114, 116–17, 127, 135, 145, 150, 155
research center, xii, xv–xvi
Resident Minister, 33, 35, 65
residents, 14, 29–30, 71, 76, 103, 144, 146

revenues, xiv, xvi, xxiii, 17–18, 26–27, 47, 51–52, 54, 58, 62, 70, 92, 105, 122, 134, 145
Rhodes, 1–2, 10, 14, 115
Richards, Arthur, xix, 32–33, 35–39, 44–46, 48–50, 54–55, 57–61, 65–67, 101–3, 113, 116–17, 120, 150, 157
Richards Constitution, 157
rinderpest, 89
riots, 27
Royal Niger Company, 1
Royal West Africa Frontier Force, 41

Salisbury, 8–10
Samaru, 107, 111
schemes, xxi, 5–6, 26, 29–30, 32–33, 35–39, 47–51, 55–62, 67, 69, 77, 93–94, 97–98, 103–6, 109–11, 114, 122–24, 126–27, 130–34, 136, 139–40, 149–53, 155
science and technology, 11, 15, 123
scientific bureaucracy, 131
scientific research, xvi, xviii, xxii, 17
Second Colonial Occupation, xiv, xvi–xvii, xix–xxii, 20, 34, 56, 61, 69–70, 91, 94, 100–2, 114–15, 121–22, 140, 145, 150–51
Secretary of State, xvii, xxiii, 18, 28, 56–58, 65, 92, 139, 153
Secretary to the Government, 32
Sheffield Reform Association, 7
shifting cultivations, 80
Sierra Leone, 13, 79, 116, 118
Sisal, 93
slavery, xi, 12
Smith, F.E.V., 33–35, 37–40, 48–52, 54–56, 59, 65–67, 84, 154
Smith, John, 84
social conditions, 28, 34, 42
social experiment, xxiv, 114, 129–32, 145
social scientists, xvii, xxi, 151
social welfare, 28, 30, 32, 34, 61, 121, 160
soldiers, 14, 32, 41–42, 63, 100, 111
South Africa, 1–2, 12, 22
South Africa Company, 1–2
South of the Sahara, 47, 69, 151
Soviet Government, 160
statutory commission, 38
Stephen, Campbell, 28, 64
Sterling Crisis, xxiv, 114, 122, 152
Stockdale, Frank, 66
stock farm, 108, 110–11
stock market crash, xvi, 27
Sudan Plantation Company, 126
Suez Canal, 10
sugar cane, 88, 95
Superintendent of Agriculture, 73
swollen shoot, xii
systemic racism, xxiii, 41

Tanganyika, 79, 116, 123, 144, 157
Tanganyika African National Union, 157
taxation, xv–xvi, 15, 18, 27, 34, 62
technical departments, xix, 71–72, 75–77, 79, 99, 102–4, 114, 150
telecommunications, 34
Tempany, Harold, 50
Temples, Charles, 14
Ten Year Plan of Development and Welfare, 58, 60
ten-year development plan, xxi, 20, 25, 30
Thomas, James Henry, 19
Tobacco Scheme at Kasungu, 122
totalitarian ideologies, 16
Toure, Sekou, 159
Trade Union Congress of Nigeria, 53
training farm, 125
Transvaal, 2, 13
treasury, xviii, xxii–xxiii, 10, 18–20, 29, 34, 38, 49–50, 56, 60, 64–66, 124, 142–43, 150, 160
Truman, Harry, xxi

tropical diseases, xv, 11, 60
tropical medicine, 11, 22
trusteeship, 1, 28
trypanosomiasis, 110

Ujamaa, 158, 160
unemployment, xiii, xviii, xxii, 16, 18–20
United Africa Company, xii
United States, ix, 15, 122

veterinary department, 97
Victoria Nile, 13

war, xiv–xvii, xix, xxi–xxii, xxiv–xxvi, 3, 14–16, 22–23, 25–27, 31–33, 39–42, 53, 63–64, 70–71, 73, 85–89, 91–96, 100–1, 107, 114, 117, 121–22, 136, 152, 159
wartime production, 31, 85
welfare, xvi, xviii–xix, xxiii, 13, 20, 25–30, 32, 34–35, 42, 47, 58,60–61, 67, 87, 108, 118, 121, 126, 143–44, 160
West Africa, xi–xiii, xvi, xxiv–xxv, 23, 41, 64–65, 80, 82, 92, 116–17, 124, 128, 146, 152
West African Pilot, 53
Western region, 45
Whig, 7–8
Williams, J. B., 55, 67
women, 27, 53, 64, 107, 109, 114
women's war, 27, 53, 64
World War I, 15, 23, 136
World War II, xiv–xvi, xix, xxi, xxv, 25, 31–32, 41, 63, 70–71, 85–86, 91, 121

yam, 80–81, 105

Zimbabwe, 2

About the Author

Bekeh Utietiang Ukelina is assistant professor of African history at the State University of New York, Cortland. His research examines ideologies and practices of development in Africa, south of the Sahara. He is the founder and director of the digital project, developmentschemes.com, a crowdsource project that collects, visualizes and shares stories on the long and short term impact of development schemes in Africa. More of his scholarship and work is at www.bekeh.com.

www.ingramcontent.com/pod-product-compliance
Ingram Content Group UK Ltd.
Pitfield, Milton Keynes, MK11 3LW, UK
UKHW041630031026
15587UKWH00001B/197

9 781498 52924